The Early Trope Repertory of
Saint Martial de Limoges

Number Two in the Princeton Studies in Music

the early trope repertory of saint martial de limoges

By Paul Evans

Princeton University Press
Princeton, New Jersey
1970

Publication of this book has been aided by
the Louis A. Robb Fund of Princeton University Press
and the Elsie and Walter W. Naumburg Fund in the
Department of Music, Princeton University.

Printed in the United States of America
by Princeton University Press

To Sally

PREFACE

The trope represents one of the most significant musical developments of the early Middle Ages. Along with other types of additions to and interpolations within the official chant of the Western church, it provided one of the main creative outlets for church composers in the centuries immediately following the Carolingian standardization of the church's liturgy. Nevertheless, there are still many gaps in our knowledge of the origins and early development of this form, and the attempts to define the trope and to trace its history have frequently led to disagreement and confusion.

Much of the trouble results, I believe, from a lack of familiarity with the sources themselves—with the tropers and with the texts and music that these manuscripts contain. My aim, therefore, has been to make available in transcription the basic trope repertory of one of the most important centers of troping activity, the abbey of St. Martial de Limoges in southern France, as this repertory developed in the tenth and early eleventh centuries.

For this purpose, I have chosen to transcribe the Proper tropes and a selection of Ordinary tropes from one of the most important of the St. Martial manuscripts, Paris, Bibliothèque Nationale, fonds latin 1121. This is the earliest *fully* transcribable St. Martial troper, dating from early in the eleventh century. I have also compared these transcriptions with the other extant St. Martial tropers, especially with those dating from the tenth century. In this way it has been possible to obtain a comprehensive view of the trope in southern France in the early stages of its development, and on this basis to take a fresh look at the text and music of the tropes and at some of the problems that still obscure the history of this important musical form.

The conclusions reached in this study are based primarily on St. Martial sources, but they are not limited entirely to them. Tenth- and eleventh-century tropers from other areas have also been consulted, and their evidence is presented whenever pertinent.

I am indebted above all to the Bibliothèque Nationale in Paris for the opportunity to study the St. Martial tropers and related manuscripts at first hand, and I am particularly grateful to the director and staff of the Cabinet des Manuscrits for their continual helpfulness and interest. Other libraries and institutions made manuscripts available to me: the Bibliothèque de l'Arsenal in Paris, the Bibliotheque Municipale in Cambrai, the Basilica of Ste. Anne in Apt, the British Museum in London, and the Bodleian Library in Oxford. To these institutions and to their librarians I should also like to express my appreciation.

In addition, I am indebted to the Most Reverend Rembert Weakland, O.S.B., for his valuable help; to Mlle. Solange Corbin, whose constant interest, enthusiasm, and assistance greatly facilitated my work in Paris; and above all to Professor Oliver Strunk, whose wisdom, judgment, and insight helped to guide this work from its inception. Finally, I should like to thank Linda Peterson of Princeton University Press for her expert and sympathetic guidance in preparing this book for publication.

CONTENTS

The Early Trope Repertory of
Saint Martial de Limoges

CHAPTER I

THE MEANING OF TROPE

One of the central problems in the history of troping is that of terminology. "Qu'est-ce qu'un Trope?" Thus Léon Gautier began his pioneer study of the trope in 1886,[1] and although numerous answers have been advanced, the question still remains a critical one. In fact, the very attempt at definition has helped in large measure to obscure the essential nature of the trope.[2]

Too many modern definitions have been partial in their approach. Thus, the literary historian, although not unaware of the musical aspects of the trope, has tended to define the form solely in terms of the function of its text. For Gautier, a trope was the "interpolation of a liturgical text" or the insertion of a new, unofficial text into the official text of the liturgy.[3] Clemens Blume, while finding the word "interpolation" too restrictive, retained Gautier's literary bias when he extended the definition to include the embellishment of a

---

[1] Léon Gautier, *Histoire de la Poésie Liturgique au Moyen Age: Les Tropes,* Paris, 1886.

[2] For earlier definitions of the word "trope," see Gautier, *Histoire,* pp. 53ff., and C. Blume and H. M. Bannister, *Analecta Hymnica Medii Aevi,* Vol. 47, *Tropi Graduales...,* Leipzig, 1905, pp. 6ff. For important recent works on trope terminology, see especially Jacques Handschin, "Trope, Sequence, and Conductus," *New Oxford History of Music,* Vol. 2, Oxford, 1954, pp. 128ff.; the various studies of Heinrich Husmann mentioned throughout this book; Bruno Stäblein, "Die Unterlegung von Texten unter Melismen...," *Report of the Eighth Congress of the International Musicological Society, New York 1961,* Vol. I, pp. 12-29, and "Tropus," *Die Musik in Geschichte und Gegenwart,* Vol. XIII, Kassel, 1966, cols. 797-826; and Richard Crocker, "The Troping Hypothesis," *Musical Quarterly,* LII (1966), 183-203.

[3] Gautier, *Histoire,* p. 1: a trope is "l'interpolation d'un texte liturgique...l'intercalation d'un texte nouveau et sans autorité dans un texte authentique et officiel."

liturgical text by means of introductions, insertions, and terminal additions.[4]

The music historian, on the other hand, has sometimes gone too far in attempting to redress the balance and has made unwarranted claims for musical supremacy in the tropes. Thus Handschin, for example, objected to Gautier's definition because "the trope is a musical phenomenon: it is, in fact, a melodic interpolation, which supplied the framework for a literary or poetic interpolation."[5]

Furthermore, most modern definitions of the trope, whether made by literary or music historians, tend to expand the meaning of a precise and specific medieval term, "tropus," into a comprehensive, generic term encompassing various unrelated forms which would never have been called "tropes" in the early Middle Ages. This unfortunate tendency is seen, for example, in the statement of Handschin's that "the sequence is a subdivision of the trope: it is the trope connected with the Alleluia of the Mass.... Since the sequence became particularly prominent, the term 'trope,' which properly includes sequence, is also used, in a more restricted sense, to indicate any kind of trope which is not a sequence. So far the terminology is not in dispute."[6] Despite the qualification "not in dispute," this position seems untenable. No extant medieval troper *ever* identifies the sequence as a kind of trope. This is a modern assumption based on the misapplication of the precise medieval terminology.

---

4 *Analecta Hymnica,* Vol. 47, p. 7: "Tropus ist die Interpolation oder die durch Interpolation, d.h. durch Einleitungen, Einschaltungen und Zusätze bewirkte Ausschmückung eines liturgischen Textes." Such definitions have not always been limited to literary historians. Thus, for example, the *Harvard Dictionary of Music* defines the trope as follows (p. 768): "In the Roman liturgy of the 9th to the 13th century a textual addition to the authorized texts as they were set down by St. Gregory (c. 600)."

5 Handschin, "Trope, Sequence, and Conductus," p. 128.

6 *Ibid.*

The reason for this confusion is easily found. If one isolates a single aspect of the historical trope as its essential quality—namely, its interpolation in an official liturgical chant—and makes this the basis of a definition, the term "trope" can then be applied to other forms of interpolation, even when they lack certain specific characteristics of the trope and are never so named in the Middle Ages. The speciousness of this simplification can readily be seen, and the damage it does in any attempt to arrive at an understanding of the trope as it was conceived by its medieval creators is obvious. To reach such an understanding we must avoid modern formulations of this sort and look at those compositions which are specifically identified as tropes in the earliest tropers.

The manuscripts of the tenth and early eleventh centuries are strikingly consistent in their use of the term "tropus." The pieces thus labeled fall into two basic groups: additions to the antiphonal Proper chants of the Mass—including the Offertories in this category—and additions to the chants of the Ordinary.

The first of these groups is by far the larger. It includes additions, either as introductions or as line-by-line interpolations, to the Introit antiphon, the Offertory, and the Communion of the major church feasts. In addition, the Introit psalm verses and doxology and the Offertory verses may be troped. One other type of trope may be included here, although strictly speaking it is connected with an addition to the Mass rather than with an official Mass chant. It is the trope "ad sequentiam"—a short preface trope which introduces the singing of the melismatic sequence after the Alleluia verse. The use of this type of trope was apparently not widespread, and examples of it are rare.[7]

The texts of all these Proper tropes refer to specific feasts. They relate the texts of the Mass chants which they embellish to their particular feast, and they are thus intended for use only on that day. The music as well as the text are newly composed additions to the official liturgical chant.

---

[7] See my discussion of the "sequence trope" in "The Tropi ad Sequentiam," *Studies in Music History: Essays for Oliver Strunk,* Princeton, 1968, pp. 73-82.

The tropes of the Ordinary of the Mass form a much smaller
group, although they were destined to outlive the more important
tropes to the Proper. The primary categories in this group are additions to the Gloria, the Sanctus and Benedictus, and the
Agnus Dei. There are, in addition, a few minor types of Ordinary tropes, examples of which are extremely rare. These include
the so-called tropes "ad rogandum Episcopum," or short introductory tropes in which the bishop was invited to intone the Gloria,
and tropes to the Kyrie and the Ite missa est.[8]

These pieces, like the Proper tropes, consist of newly composed
music, but their texts do not necessarily refer to a specific feast.
In fact, the majority of the texts, like those of the chants they embellish, are general in nature and thus can be used interchangeably
for any feast desired.

The above division into tropes of the Proper and tropes of the
Ordinary is not arbitrary.[9] The majority of tropers implicitly recognize it. The main series of tropes in the average troper consists
of the tropes to the Proper chants of the Mass, arranged in the order of the church calendar and, under each feast, in the order of
their occurrence in the Mass. The Ordinary tropes, on the other
hand, like the Ordinary chants themselves, are kept in a separate
series, arranged by category, at the end of the main series of
Proper tropes.

The Proper tropes form a far more extensive and important
group than those to the Ordinary in the first period of troping, in
the tenth and early eleventh centuries. Of the Proper tropes themselves, the Introit tropes were the most extensively cultivated.

---

[8] Those pieces which are frequently called Kyrie "tropes" in modern
reference works are in reality Kyrie prosulae. See below, p. 10.
For a discussion of the St. Martial Gloria tropes, see Klaus Rönnau, *Die
Tropen zum Gloria in excelsis Deo,* Wiesbaden, 1967.

[9] However, to call these divisions Lesser and Greater Tropes respectively, as has been done by Gautier, *Histoire,* p. 75, and by W. H. Frere,
The Winchester Troper, London, 1894, p. x, is not only historically unwarranted but actually misleading, for it fails to reflect their relative
importance in the earliest period of troping.

Thus, for example, Paris 1240,[10] a St. Martial troper from the beginning of the tenth century and the earliest full troper extant, contains the following number of items in each category:

> *Proper:* 80 tropes
> > Introit: 49 tropes
> > Offertory: 21 tropes
> > Communion: 5 tropes
> > Ad sequentiam: 5 tropes
>
> *Ordinary:* 20 tropes
> > Gloria in excelsis: 13 tropes
> > Sanctus: 3 tropes
> > Agnus Dei: 3 tropes
> > Ad rogandum Episcopum: 1 trope

Thus, four-fifths of the manuscript's one hundred tropes are for the Proper of the Mass, and almost one-half of the total is made up of Introit tropes.

Another troper, Paris 1121, from the beginning of the eleventh century, represents the fully developed, classical form of the St. Martial troper. Its contents are as follows:

> *Proper:* 207 tropes
> > Introit: 160 tropes
> > Offertory: 25 tropes
> > Communion: 18 tropes
> > Ad sequentiam: 4 tropes
>
> *Ordinary:*[11] 37 tropes
> > Gloria in excelsis: 24 tropes
> > Sanctus: 7 tropes
> > Agnus Dei: 6 tropes
> > Ad rogandum Episcopum: none.

---

[10] Throughout this study, manuscripts from the Bibliothèque Nationale in Paris will be identified simply as "Paris" followed by the shelf number. Thus, the above reference should be understood to read: Paris, Bibliothèque Nationale, fonds latin MS 1240. A MS from the series of "nouvelles acquisitions" will be listed simply as Paris n.a. 1871, and so forth.

Once again, the same general proportions are maintained. Over four-fifths of the total (85 percent) are Proper tropes, and the number of Introit tropes has increased to nearly two-thirds of the entire contents.

These tropes are the only ones that are specifically identified as such in the early manuscripts. What are their common characteristics, and what are the essential elements which distinguish them from the various other types of unofficial chant that were current in the tenth and eleventh centuries and are often preserved in the tropers themselves?

In the first place, the texts of the tropes, as we have noted, are additions to the official text of the liturgical chants that they embellish. These trope texts may be in poetry or in prose, they may be newly composed or drawn from the Bible, they may be general or related to the feast of the day, but in all cases they comment upon and amplify the official liturgical text.[12]

These additions occur in two forms. First, they may be preface tropes which introduce the official text. The following example is a trope to the Epiphany Offertory *Reges Tharsis* (Paris 1121, f. 10):

> *Trope:* Regi Xpisto iam terris manifestato, quem adorant
>   hodie Magi, psallite omnes cum propheta dicentes:
>
> *Offertory:* Reges Tharsis et insule munera offerent; reges
>   Arabum et Saba dona adducent: et adorabunt eum
>   omnes reges terre, omnes gentes servient ei. (Ps. 71)

Historically, this is probably the original form of troping.[13] Certain categories of tropes are invariably found in the form of

---

[11] Paris 1121 lacks the Sanctus and Agnus tropes. The figures given here are from the very closely related manuscript Paris 1119. There is also a gap in the series of Proper tropes at the feast of St. Andrew, and if we included the Andrew tropes from Paris 1119, it would increase the above figure for Introit tropes to 163.

[12] See Chapter IV, below, for a detailed discussion of the trope texts.

[13] See Heinrich Husmann, "Sinn und Wesen der Tropen," *Archiv für Musikwissenschaft,* XVI (1959), 147, and below, p. 21.

prefaces, including the tropes "ad sequentiam" and "ad rogandum Episcopum." The tropes to the Introit psalm verses and doxology are usually introductory, as indeed are the great majority of Offertory and Communion tropes.

The second form of troping consists of line-by-line interpolations, in which a trope introduces each phrase of the official chant. The following example is for the Introit *Etenim sederunt* of the feast of St. Stephen (Paris 1121, f. 5):

Trope: Hodie Stephanus martyr celos ascendit, quem propheta dudum intuens eius voce dicebat:
Introit: Etenim sederunt principes et adversum me loquebantur.

Trope: Insurrexerunt contra me Iudeorum populi inique,
Introit: Et iniqui persecuti sunt me.

Trope: Invidiose lapidibus oppresserunt me;
Introit: Adiuva me Dominus Deus meus.

Trope: Suscipe meum in pace spiritum,
Introit: Quia servus tuus exercebatur in tuis iustificationibus. (Ps. 118)

In only one case, that of the Sanctus tropes, is this general order of interpolation not followed. Here, the liturgical Preface itself serves as the introduction to the chant, and there is thus no place for an introductory trope. Instead, the tropes must follow the three statements of the word "Sanctus." We can see this process clearly in the following Sanctus trope from Paris 1119 (f. 247v-248)—the official text is italicized here:

End of Preface: ... *sine fine dicentes:*
Sanctus Deus pater ingenitus,
Sanctus Filius eius unigenitus,
Sanctus Spiritus paraclitus ab utroque procedens, *Dominus Deus sabaoth* .. etc.

It should be noted that the Sanctus as a whole ends with the official text and not with a line of trope.

The second distinctive characteristic of the trope is its music, and it is this factor, perhaps more than any other, that is of decisive importance in differentiating the trope from other types of additions to the liturgy. Not only is the music of the trope newly composed, but it and the text are simultaneously conceived. In other words, a trope is not constructed by adding words to a preexisting melody, whether the latter is part of the chant, as in the case of the prosulae discussed below, or is itself an addition, as in the prosa or "sequence," as it is more commonly called today.[14] On the contrary, it is a true musical composition in which

---

[14] The almost general acceptance today of the word "sequence" is most unfortunate. "Sequentia" is found in what must have been its original sense in all of the French and English tropers and in some of the Italian. In these manuscripts, the term is used to refer to the extended melismatic addition which follows the Alleluia of the Mass. When this melody is supplied with a text, the term used for the text is "prosa," that is, the "prose" text added to a preexistent melody. French usage recognized the essentially literary origin of the form by retaining the term "prose" for the completed composition, even when the text ceased to be prosaic, as in the case of the poetic "proses" of Adam de Saint-Victor. In Germany, however, the solution was different, and the musical term "sequentia" was applied to the finished composition. It should be noted, however, that this development was relatively late, since Notker himself refers to his compositions only as "hymni." On this question, see Heinrich Husmann, "Sequenz und Prosa," *Annales Musicologiques*, II (1954), 61-91, and Richard Crocker, "The Repertory of Proses at Saint Martial de Limoges in the 10th Century," *Journal of the American Musicological Society*, XI (1958), 149-164.

The German usage is inconvenient, since the term "sequence" must be constantly qualified as either a "melismatic" sequence or a sequence "with text." Nor is it at all necessary to follow it, since we possess in the French terminology a precise and equally authentic usage. The French terminology will be used throughout this study, and should be understood as follows:

> prosa = "sequence" in its current sense of melody with text.
> sequentia = the extended melisma added after the Alleluia of the Mass. It is equivalent to the nonmedieval term "sequela," used, for example, by Dom Anselm Hughes in *Anglo-French Sequelae*, London, 1934.
> prosula = a piece created by adding a text to a preexistent melisma in Alleluia and Offertory verses, the Kyrie, the Gloria trope line *Regnum tuum solidum*, etc.

new words are set to music, and the whole serves to embellish the liturgical chant. The stylistic ramifications of this compositional process are far-reaching. In order to demonstrate more clearly the musical distinctiveness of the trope, we may consider for a moment those other types of additions to the liturgy which have so frequently been mislabeled "trope": the prosa and the prosula.

Both the prosa and the prosula are basically literary in their conception. The prosa is created by adding a text to the preexistent melismatic sequentia which follows the Alleluia. The less familiar prosula makes use of the same additive process, but here the scope is smaller, and the source of the original melisma is varied. The distinctive characteristics of these compositions can perhaps be seen most clearly in the prosula.

In the tropers, the term "prosula" refers to the following types of additions: [15]

1. Texts added to the melismas of responsorial chants of the Mass, especially the melismas of Alleluia and Offertory verses, but also on occasion those of Graduals and Tracts. Example 1[16] gives the Alleluia *Mirabilis Dominus* with its two prosulae, *Psallat unus* for the Alleluia and *Mirabilis atque* for the verse. In order to show clearly the relationship between the two forms, the official chant is given in the first line with the prosulae immediately beneath. Example 2 is the prosula *Invocavi te altissime* sung to the

---

[15] It should be noted that Paris 1118, alone among the St. Martial tropers, uses the term "tropus" indiscriminately for both tropes and prosulae as here defined. This confusion may have resulted from the inclusion of a certain number of prosulae along with the Ordinary chants which they accompany in the main sequence of Proper tropes —a very unusual practice in Aquitainian manuscripts.

[16] This and the following examples will be found in the section of transcriptions, on pp. 263ff.

final melisma "invocavi te" of the Offertory verse *Respice in me* for the Offertory *Ad te Domine.* [17]

2. The so-called Kyrie "tropes," in which texts are added to the melismas of the Kyrie. [18] Example 3 is the prosula *Tibi Xpiste supplices,* presented as it occurs in Paris 1119, with each line of the prosula followed by the melismatic Kyrie line.

3. Textual additions to the Osanna melisma of the Sanctus. Example 4 is the prosula *Osanna dulcis est,* set to the second Osanna melisma of a Sanctus melody no longer to be found in modern chant books. The melismatic version is given below the prosula. [19]

4. Texts added to the melisma of the Gloria trope line "Regnum tuum solidum...." Example 5 gives first the trope line as found in the Gloria trope *Laus honor Xpiste* in Paris 1084, f. 115v. This is followed by the Regnum prosula *Per te Xpiste,* transcribed from Paris 1119, f. 134. [20]

5. Textual additions to the melisma "Fabrice mundi" of the Christmas Respond *Descendit.* This form, however, was of relatively limited significance at St. Martial. [21]

---

[17] The Offertory verse itself may be found in Paris 903, ff. lv-2, reproduced in facsimile as Vol. XIII of the *Paléographie Musicale,* Tournai, 1925. It is also found with some variants in *Offertoriale sive Versus Offertoriorum,* ed. C. Ott, Paris, 1935, p. 6.

[18] Not to be confused with the true Kyrie tropes mentioned on p. 4.

[19] See J. Smits van Waesberghe, "Die Imitation der Sequenztechnik in den Hosanna-Prosulen," in *Festschrift Karl Gustav Fellerer,* Regensburg, 1962, pp. 485-490.

[20] See the discussion of the Regnum prosula by Klaus Rönnau, "Regnum tuum solidum," *Festschrift Bruno Stäblein,* Kassel, 1967, pp. 195-205.

[21] Among the St. Martial manuscripts, collections of *Fabrice* prosulae are found only in Paris 1118, ff. 117-119; Paris 1084, ff. 7-9; and the proser Paris 1338, ff. 85v-86v—that is, in precisely those manuscripts that do not originate at St. Martial itself. This type of prosula is also found at St. Gall, Nevers, etc. See Gautier, *Histoire,* p. 166, note 1, sec. xvii.

Certain distinctive characteristics stand out clearly in a study of these examples. In the first place, the prosulae are always composed of a text added to a preexistent melisma, whether the latter is a melisma of the official chant or is itself an addition, as in the Regnum prosulae. The prosulae of the Proper chants of the Mass, as, for example, the Offertory verse prosula *Invocavi te* (Example 2), offer striking evidence of this principle, since here the priority of the version without added text can readily be determined in the countless official chant books of the period. But there can be little doubt that the principle is also at work in the other prosulae as well. Not only is the general style of all the prosulae identical, whatever the source of their original melismas, but there is also strong notational evidence in support of this assumption.

Thus, for example, the Kyrie prosula *Tibi Xpiste supplices* (Example 3), as it is preserved in Paris 1120, makes use of a curious and rare notational practice which might be termed a "split oriscus." That is to say, at each place in the Kyrie melisma where the normal Aquitainian oriscus is used (- ♏ = ♫ at the unison), the prosula melody in its syllabic setting represents the first of these unison notes with a normal punctum on the first syllable and the second with an isolated oriscus sign on the second syllable. This isolated oriscus is used, for example, on the syllable "-ces" of "supplices" and on the "dig-" of "digneris" in the first line. In other words, a neumatic sign, which is meaningful only as a component element of a larger group, is here made to function as a simple punctum. This can only mean that the prosula writer, in setting his text, was preserving the notational pattern of a preexistent melisma, even though this pattern was no longer pertinent to his own work. [22] Thus, it is difficult

---

[22] Cf. Ferretti's discussion of the oriscus in the introduction to *Paléographie Musicale,* XIII, 177ff., where he notes the existence of the "oriscus syllabique" but does not cite this use of it. It is interesting to note that the oriscus used in Paris 1120 is the typical French rather than Aquitainian form (⋈). Although the French oriscus is not unknown in the earlier Aquitainian notation, its appearance here in this late-tenth-century troper strongly suggests that the Kyrie prosula in question, and perhaps even the form itself, came to St. Martial from

to accept the suggestion[23] that these Kyrie interpolations were originally tropes whose text and music were composed together and that the melismatic Kyries of the modern chant books represent troped Kyries later stripped of their texts. Even though the Kyrie melodies and the prosula texts added to them were doubtless composed at about the same time, the typical additive process of the prosula was strictly followed. In the few true Kyrie tropes that do exist, the melody of the trope is distinct from that of the Kyrie it embellishes.[24]

The second characteristic of these prosulae is that their texts, like those of the early prosae, are in prose; hence their name "prosula," the diminutive of "prosa."[25] This is the inevitable outgrowth of the process of adding texts to an existing melody, since the free melodic construction of the melisma makes the addition of a metrical text impossible.

Practically the only poetic device which occurs in the prosulae is the occasional use of assonance on the vowel sound of the original melisma.[26] We may note, for example, the assonance on the final *a* of "Osanna" in *Osanna dulcis est* (Example 4) and on the *e* of "te" in *Invocavi te altissime* (Example 2). This insistence by the prosula writer on the vowel sound of the origi-

---

the north at a comparatively late date. This possibility is strengthened when we recall that no Kyrie prosulae are found in the original section of the earliest St. Martial troper, Paris 1240.

[23] See, for example, W. Apel, *Gregorian Chant,* Bloomington, 1958, p. 432.

[24] Parallel to the use of the oriscus discussed above is the "split pes" on "plebs" (l.4) in the version of this Kyrie prosula contained in Paris 1120. But cf. *Paléographie Musicale,* XIII, p. 166 of Introduction.

[25] Compare the alternate name "verba" found, for example, in the Novalesa troper at Oxford (Douce 222). This, too, implies the notion of adding "words" to an existing melody.

[26] There is occasionally an attempt to introduce rudimentary rhyme and even rhythm when the musical scheme allows, but this obviously happens very irregularly. Cf., for example, "suscipe cum agmina/angelorum cantica" in Example 4.

nal melisma in his own text argues strongly in itself for the priority of the melody.

Another example, more complicated than simple assonance but again striving for the preservation of the sounds of the original melisma, is found in the opening of the Alleluia prosula *Psallat unus spiritus* (Example 1). Here both vowels and consonants are retained to duplicate the sounds of "Alleluia":

Al-le-lu- - - - - - -ia
Psal-lat u-nus spiritus et u-na

The relation of the prosula text to the text that it embellishes is necessarily determined by the location of the melisma in the original chant. Normally, the prosula text either follows the original text, as in the Offertory verse, Alleluia, and Osanna prosulae, or is interpolated within it, as in the Regnum and Alleluia verse prosulae. Since a melisma does not precede a chant, prosulae are rarely found functioning, like the tropes, as introductory texts. It is true that the Kyrie prosulae, which set to words the entire melody of the Kyrie, precede the melismatic repetition of the Kyrie. But they could just as easily follow the melismatic version, as is indeed the case with the similar Alleluia prosulae.

The third striking characteristic of the prosulae is their musical style. This style is almost exclusively syllabic, one syllable of new text being supplied for each note of the original melisma. Except for a rare use of a group of two or three notes on a given syllable of the prosula text, as, for example, on "cunctipotens" in the first line of the Kyrie prosula *Tibi Xpiste supplices* (Example 3), on "*cru*-ce" in the second line of the Regnum prosula *Per te Xpiste* (Example 5), and so forth, the only use of neumatic writing occurs where part of the text of the original chant is incorporated into the prosula with its original setting, as, for example, at "Dominus noster" in the Alleluia verse prosula *Mirabilis atque laudabilis* (Example 1), or where a new text is supplied for a section of the text of the original chant, as, for example, "Tibi Xpiste" for "Kyrie" (Example 3) and "Psallat" for "*Alle*-luia" (Example 1).

This strictly maintained syllabic style should not suggest that the creators of the prosulae were simply following a mechanical process of composition by counting up the number of notes in the melisma and arbitrarily writing a text with the requisite number of syllables. The care with which the assonance was placed at the end of melodic phrases or neumatic groups and the skillful incorporation of the original text into the prosula text clearly demonstrate a high degree of literary and musical sensitivity on the part of the creator. The fact remains, however, that the appropriate musical style for the prosulae was considered to be syllabic, and this style is consistently maintained throughout the prosula repertory.

Precisely those characteristics of the prosula which have been outlined above are to be found again in the early prosae. The prosae are composed of texts added to a preexistent melody, in this case the melismatic sequentia following the Alleluia. Their texts are in prose and frequently make use of assonance on the final *a* of "Alleluia." They are not introductory pieces, but function as an extended coda to the Alleluia. Their musical style is strictly syllabic. Even the double versicle construction of the prosa occurs in a limited way in the Regnum prosulae.

This identity of concept is clearly seen in the occasional use in the tropers of the term "prosa" for both prosae and prosulae, notably in the oldest extant troper, Paris 1240, where a collection of the two types of pieces is labeled "Congregatio Prosarum" (f. 43v). Thus, the term "prosula" can be understood simply as a "small prosa," that is, a piece of smaller dimensions than the prosa proper. This relationship is evident when we compare an early prosa with an Alleluia prosula like *Psallat unus spiritus* (Example 1), which might almost be a prosa in miniature.[27]

---

[27] Note, however, that despite the similarity in technique, the Alleluia prosula is distinguished from the prosa by its position before the Alleluia verse rather than after, and by being based on the official Alleluia melisma rather than on the added sequentia.

If we keep these characteristics of the prosa and prosula firm-
ly in mind, we cannot fail to recognize the essential qualities of
the genuine, historic trope.

Admittedly, both the trope on the one hand and the prosa
and prosula on the other represent aspects of the same general
practice of embellishing the liturgy with unofficial additions and
interpolations, a practice which flourished from the ninth century
on. Admittedly, too, both forms, although following different
compositional procedures, result in the addition to the official
liturgical text of a newly composed text amplifying and com-
menting upon it—a fact which has on occasion blinded literary
historians to the basic musical distinctions between the trope
and the prosula.

But beyond these general similarities, the two forms differ
strikingly in their essential character. Thus, while the prosa and
prosula are created by adding a text to an existing melisma, the
trope is a true musical composition, adding both text and music
to the official chant. As a result, the prosa and prosula are almost invariably in prose, while the text of the trope, although
it may be in prose, can be, and frequently is, in verse. Furthermore, we often find that many different prosula or prosa texts
are adapted to a single melisma, whereas a given trope text and
its melody form a unique combination. Finally, the invariable
syllabic style of the prosa and prosula is not found in the tropes,
which are frequently neumatic in style and even, on occasion,
melismatic, reflecting the style of the chants that they embellish.

CHAPTER II

THE HISTORICAL POSITION OF THE TROPE

The trope as we have described it belongs to a definitely cir-cumscribed period of music history. Contrary to the impression given by a work like Gautier's, which considers various derived forms as if they were tropes, thereby extending the history of the trope well into the polyphonic period of Gothic music, the trope in its classical form had a relatively short life, from the ninth century to the middle of the eleventh century, although it flourished at a number of centers throughout western Europe during that period.

Gautier's division of the history of liturgical interpolation into two periods is, however, a useful one, if we recognize the truly distinctive characteristics of these periods.[1] Thus, Gautier's emphasis on the predominance of rhyme in the second period, that is, in the twelfth and thirteenth centuries, is a valid stylistic observation. But the essential distinction, it seems to me, is purely formal. In a word, the first period of troping is charac-terized by the overwhelming preponderance of tropes to the Proper of the Mass, whereas after the middle of the eleventh century, that is, in Gautier's second period, these Proper tropes almost completely disappear, and even the tropes to the Ordinary are reduced to a relatively insignificant number. To put it in another way, the second period of "troping," if we may call it that, is characterized by the almost complete absence of tropes in the original, classical form described in the previous chapter. Instead, we find a host of related forms, such as the Benedicamus Domino "tropes," connected primarily with the Office rather than the Mass, and deriving stylistically from the syllabic manner of the prosula. Although the syllabic style remains, the composi-tional process ceases to be additive, and we now have a prepon-derance of texts in verse.

---

[1] Gautier, *Histoire*, pp. 147ff.

These forms are not without considerable interest, particularly
in their relationship to the rise of Latin and vernacular poetry
and to such musical forms of the polyphonic period as the conductus. But they have already moved far from the original concept of troping, which is our primary concern here.

In dealing with the question of the origins of troping, we are
faced at the outset with a difficulty common to the study of
all medieval chant, namely, that the manuscripts which preserve
this repertory come at a date well after the period of its creation
and early development. Thus, the earliest troper that we possess,
the St. Martial troper Paris 1240, dating from the early decades
of the tenth century, already contains a full repertory of tropes
for the major church feasts, and the pieces have already achieved
the form which will be standard for all subsequent French tropers.
We can only assume that a considerable amount of troping activity
must have preceded this manuscript. But beyond this our docu-
mentary evidence will not allow us to go, and any more precise
answer to the question of the origin of troping must be based
largely on conjecture.

A few hints, however, may suggest a possible setting and occasion for the creation of this new musical form. The occurrence
of trope texts in classical hexameters in even the oldest tropers
suggests a possible connection with the circle of poets at the
Carolingian court, an impression which is perhaps strengthened
by the appearance in Paris 1240 of the Palm Sunday processional
hymn *Gloria laus et honor* written by one of the greatest of these
Carolingian poets, Theodulf of Orleans (ca. 760-821).[2]

Another possibility concerns the work of St. Benedict of
Aniane (ca. 750-821). The ceremonial innovations and developments at his monastery near Montpellier in the south of France

---

[2] For the work of Theodulf and the other Carolingian court poets, see
F. J. E. Raby, *A History of Christian-Latin Poetry,* 2nd edn., Oxford,
1953, pp. 154ff.

provide a frame in which the tropes can easily be fitted.[3] For example, the newly introduced daily processions to all the altars of the monastery church would have required additional processional music, at least on the high feast days.[4] And in general, St. Benedict's emphasis on increasing the liturgical prayer of his community might have given an impetus to the sort of extension of liturgical music that we find in the process of troping. After the death of Charlemagne, Louis the Pious built for Benedict the abbey of Inde, later Cornelimünster, in the Rhineland. This abbey was, as Dom David Knowles says, "to serve as a model for the whole of the Empire."[5] From here, the new practices could easily spread throughout the West. The Council of Aachen of 817 was indeed called to regulate monastic custom throughout the Empire. The ceremonial elaboration of the liturgy in the monasteries of Europe at the beginning of the ninth century, then, may have given ample occasion for the introduction of troping.

From the absence of a precise reference to the trope in the works of Amalarius of Metz (ca. 780-850), we can infer that troping, if it did exist in his time, was still not widely known. Perhaps it remained a monastic practice which was not yet generally recognized. Although an *argumentum ex silentio* is always dangerous, the suggestion carries some weight when we recall that Amalarius' liturgical references are unusally explicit and

[3] See especially the *Vita* by his disciple Ardo in *Patrologia Latina*, Vol. CIII, col. 379. For the historical position of Benedict, see A. Fliche and V. Martin, *Histoire de l'Église*, Vol. 6, pp. 259ff., and bibliography, p. 255, note 1. Also Edmund Bishop, *Liturgica Historica*, Oxford, 1918, pp. 212ff.

[4] The vast majority of early tropes accompany a liturgical action, and their function in extending the music for that action is obvious. Thus, for example, the Introit tropes serve as processional music before the Mass on great feasts. It is also interesting to note, in this connection, that many of the St. Martial tropers also contain collections of processional antiphons.

[5] David Knowles, *The Monastic Order in England*, Cambridge, 1950, p. 26.

that he does, in fact, refer to the sequentia and other types of melodic liturgical interpolations.[6]

By the end of the ninth century, however, the practice of troping must have been established, and there exist a few early trope texts which can be attributed to known authors and which could date from the ninth century. These include the introductory Introit tropes attributed by Ekkehard IV[7] to Tuotilo of St. Gall (d. after 912) and the Gloria trope *Quem vere pia laus* by Hucbald of St. Amand (d. 930).[8] But here we already approach the beginning of the written tradition of the tropers themselves.

The manner in which troping originated and developed can to a certain extent be inferred from the manuscript sources that still survive. Wholly untenable, it seems to me, is the frequently advanced theory that the tropes developed through a process of supplying texts for melismatic additions already made to the chants of the Mass—a process thus analogous to that by which the prosa was created.[9] Instead, the trope apparently arose as an

---

[6] One passage in Amalarius' *Liber Officialis* has sometimes been interpreted as referring to Kyrie tropes or prosulae. In describing the Mass, he says: "Ac ideo dicant cantores: 'Kyrie eleison, Domine Pater, miserere; Christe eleison, miserere, qui nos redemisti sanguine tuo'; et iterum: 'Kyrie eleison, Domine Spiritus Sancte, miserere' " (*Amalarii Episcopi Opera Liturgica Omnia,* Vol. II, *Liber Officialis,* ed. J. M. Hanssens, Vatican City, 1948, pp. 283-284). It seems unlikely to me that the words "Domine Pater, miserere," etc., refer to a specific prosula text. No such Kyrie prosula exists, and it is even doubtful that Kyrie prosulae can be considered among the earliest examples of the prosula form, since they are lacking in the original parts of Paris 1240. It seems far more probable, and in keeping with the general tenor of Amalarius' work, that these texts are simply exegetical amplifications.

[7] On Tuotilo, see Wolfram von den Steinen, *Notker der Dichter,* Berne, 1948, I, 524. Also Raby, *A History of Christian-Latin Poetry,* pp. 220-221.

[8] See Rembert Weakland, "Hucbald as Musician and Theorist," *Musical Quarterly,* XLII (1956), 69.

[9] I have discussed this question in "Some Reflections on the Origin of the Trope," *Journal of the American Musicological Society,* XIV (1961), 119-130.

independent musical composition which functioned as an introduction or preface to various actions or chants of the Mass, much
as the liturgical Preface functions as an introduction to the Sanctus and the Canon of the Mass.[10]

Thus, for example, the preface trope to the Introit serves as
an introduction to the Mass itself: "Hodie est, Fratres, Omnium
Sanctorum festivitas...."[11] In the same way, preface tropes are
used to introduce the action of the Offertory and the Communion. The tropes "ad rogandum Episcopum," as we have seen,
served as an invitation to the bishop to intone the Gloria: "Sa-
cerdos Dei excelsi, veni ante sanctum et sacrum altare, et in
laude regis regum vocem tuam emitte, supplices te rogamus et
petimus. Dic, Dompne: *Gloria in excelsis Deo.*"[12] In addition,
tropes were sometimes used to introduce the singing of the
sequentia.

In time, the preface trope was expanded by a process of adding
internal tropes to each phrase of the chant, and this type of trope
with its line-by-line interpolation of a given chant became standard during the tenth century. That this was the actual line of
development, that preface tropes did actually precede the tropes
composed of several lines, is suggested by several pieces of indi-
rect evidence in the trope repertory itself.

On the basis of a study of Christmas Introit tropes in various
national traditions, Husmann notes the variability of the internal
trope lines and concludes that, in general, the internal tropes and
the preface tropes are independent of each other and apparently
arose in different periods, with the preface tropes as the original
part of the repertory.[13]

---

[10] See, on this point, Heinrich Husmann, "Sinn und Wesen der Tropen,"
pp. 135ff. According to Husmann, the trope originated as an invitation to
perform a given liturgical chant (p. 137), and he maintains that introductions
actually form the original layer of the trope repertory (p. 147).

[11] Introit trope for the feast of All Saints, Paris 1121, f. 40v.

[12] Paris 1118, f. 19v. Cf. Husmann, "Sinn und Wesen der Tropen," p. 137.

[13] *Ibid.,* pp. 146-147.

Moreover, I find that, within a single tradition, there is a pro-
portional increase in the number of full tropes as opposed to preface tropes in the course of the tenth century. Thus, a manuscript
like Paris 1240 contains a far higher percentage of introductory
tropes than any subsequent troper from St. Martial.[14]

But perhaps the most convincing evidence is found in the St.
Martial troper Paris 1084, which dates from the tenth century.
This manuscript is complex, consisting of a basic original series
of tropes which was augmented during the tenth or early eleventh
centuries by two additional, although separate, series.[15] Besides
the straightforward adding of new items to the basic repertory,
one also sees here an interesting process in which additional lines
were supplied for what were originally preface tropes, thus bringing these tropes into line with later practice.

This is done simply by giving a cue for the original line, which
occurs in the main troper, and then supplying the new lines in
full. Thus, for example, on f. 75v occurs the following Introit
preface trope for the feast of St. John the Baptist:

> Iste puer magnus propheta vocatus ab utero matris, nam dicit
> ipse: [INTROIT] *De ventre matris meae vocavit me Dominus*
> etc.

On f. 45v, however, in one of the additional series of tropes,
the piece is found in this form:

> Iste puer. *De ventre.* [i.e., cue only]
> Ieremie more quondam vatis venerandi. *Sub tegumento* etc.
> Parcere pacificis et debellare superbos. *Posuit me* etc.[16]

---

[14] The existence of full tropes in Paris 1240 indicates that this process
was obviously under way before the tenth century.

[15] Jacques Chailley, *L'École Musicale de Saint-Martial de Limoges jusqu'à
la Fin du XIe Siècle,* Paris, 1960, p. 85, suggests a date in the second quar-
ter of the eleventh century for the additional series. But this seems to be
too late on the basis of notational similarities with Paris 1120.

[16] In line 2 the MS has "condam" instead of "quondam," and in line 3
"Carcere" instead of "Parcere," the latter being an error of the rubricator.
Cf. Paris 1121, f. 25v. Note also the echo of Virgil in line 3 (*Aeneid* VI,
853). The Introit is taken from Isaiah 49, while the second trope line refers
to the parallel passage in Jeremiah 1:5. We thus have an interesting combination of classical and Biblical scholarship here!

In other words, the original introductory trope has been expanded by the addition of two hexameter trope lines to a full three-line trope, and it is in this form that the trope is found in such later St. Martial manuscripts as Paris 909 and Paris 1121. There are many similar examples in Paris 1084.

The process of extension primarily affected tropes to the Introit and to the Gloria, the two categories chiefly cultivated during the tenth century.[17] In other early categories, such as the Offertory and Communion tropes, where the increase of repertory was relatively slight, the pieces remain predominantly preface tropes.

In the course of the tenth and early eleventh centuries, then, the art of troping experienced its greatest development, and creative activity was manifested in two directions: 1. by the amplification of already existing tropes through the addition of internal trope lines; and 2. by the addition of tropes completely new to the repertory. In the latter case, the increase of repertory took place not so much by the supplying of tropes for more and more feasts, but rather by the augmenting of the number of pieces available for the feasts which were already troped. Throughout the period of troping, the calendar of major feasts for which tropes were supplied remained relatively stable.

During the eleventh century, a decline in the popularity of troping set in. The tropes to the Proper of the Mass, the most important section of the repertory in the early period, disappear almost completely from Western manuscripts by the end of the century, and I know of only one French manuscript from the twelfth century which contains Proper tropes: the Nevers troper, Paris n.a. 1235. Some Ordinary tropes were carried over into later manuscripts, but the amount of new composition seems to have been relatively small. By the twelfth century new forms had arisen which, with the prosa, were to dominate in the field of sacred monophonic composition.

We have tried to indicate why and when the tropes appeared. It remains to say a word about the place where the idea of troping

---

[17] See above, pp. 4-6.

may have originated and the possible course of its diffusion throughout western Europe. Again, only tentative answers can be suggested. A thorough study and comparison of all the extant tropers
will be required before anything approaching a definitive answer
can be advanced, and even then the complete lack of trope manuscripts from such important centers as Jumièges, Fleury, and St.
Martin of Tours may preclude a truly satisfactory answer.

Two distinct repertories of tropes exist: 1. the Germanic or
East Frankish, represented in particular by the tropers of St. Gall;
and 2. the Anglo-French or West Frankish, found, for example,
in the tropers of St. Martial de Limoges. Although these two
repertories have few specific pieces in common, they both contain
the same basic categories of tropes, and in both the same feasts
are troped. It is therefore difficult to suppose that troping grew
up independently in the two areas, particularly in view of Notker's
story of the monk of Jumièges at St. Gall.[18]

A common point of origin might logically be sought in northeastern France and the Rhineland, that is, in the heartland of the
Carolingian realm. Certainly, Metz was a great center of musical
and liturgical activity in the eighth and ninth centuries, and St.
Benedict's monastery near Aachen would serve as an obvious
point of diffusion for the new liturgical embellishments, whether
he found the idea of troping already existing in northeastern
France or brought it with him from his first monastery at Aniane
near Montpellier in the south.[19]

---

[18] See especially Husmann, "Die St. Galler Sequenztradition bei Notker und
Ekkehard," *Acta Musicologica,* XXVI (1954), 6ff.

[19] See above, pp. 18-19. There is, in fact, some slight evidence that troping
may have originated in the south. The earliest Aquitainian troper, Paris 1240,
contains certain peculiarities which distinguish it from the later St. Martial
manuscripts and relate it more closely to the northern tropers. It is quite
probable that the standard St. Martial repertory, as found in the tropers
from the end of the tenth and the beginning of the eleventh centuries, was
reintroduced from the north, perhaps from St. Martin of Tours. See my
article "Northern French Elements in an Early Aquitainian Troper," *Festschrift Heinrich Husmann,* Munich, 1969.

There is some evidence to support the supposition that troping first developed in northeastern France and the Rhineland, although admittedly this evidence is more suggestive than conclusive. In the first place, one of the earliest indications of troping activity is to be found in what is possibly a ninth-century manuscript from Toul, near Metz, in northeastern France (Munich, Bayerische Staatsbibliothek, clm. 14843).[20] In the second place, tropers from the Rhineland — such as the Mainz troper (British Museum Additional MS 19768, from around 960) and the troper from Prüm, near Trier (Paris 9448, dating from around 990)—show an unusual combination of items from both the French and Germanic repertories. However, these Rhenish manuscripts, although they are among the early extant tropers, still originated well after the probable date of the origins of troping, and it is thus possible that they represent a later synthesis of the two fully developed repertories rather than the early germinal repertory from which the others developed. As far as northeastern France is concerned, no full tropers whatsoever survive from the Messine notational area, and we are thus lacking direct evidence from what may well be the crucial area for the origins of the trope.[21]

Troping was also known in Italy, but the evidence of the Italian tropers suggests that the practice was not indigenous. The trope apparently came to Italy both from France and the Germanic regions. Thus, for example, the tropers from Nonantola, in northeastern Italy, show the strong influence of the St. Gall

---

[20] See Handschin, "Trope, Sequence, and Conductus," p. 153, and *Analecta Hymnica,* Vol. 53, p. xiv. Heinrich Husmann, however, questions this early date in *Tropen- und Sequenzenhandschriften,* Répertoire International des Sources Musicales, Vol. B V 1, Munich, 1964, p. 79.

[21] The precise role of the "monk of Jumièges" in the diffusion of the trope is problematic. Notker makes no direct reference to tropes, but this is not necessarily conclusive, since Notker's primary concern was the prosa. But even if the Jumieges MS did contain tropes, it is hard to imagine why troping would have to be introduced into St. Gall from as far afield as Jumièges. Perhaps the process was already known by Notker's time. Certainly his teacher knew of the existence of the prosa.

tropers,[22] while a troper from Novalesa, near the French border, contains a repertory which is predominantly French.[23] An assessment of the precise influence of the two repertories and their diffusion throughout Italy must await a detailed study of the Italian tropers.[24]

It may be helpful at this point to draw a tentative outline of the history of the trope on the basis of the preceding discussion. Tropes first appeared, perhaps, in the course of the ninth century, beginning as newly composed introductions to various categories of the official chant. These introductory tropes were then extended by adding line-by-line interpolations to the entire chant. The place of origin may well have been northeastern France or the Rhineland, and from here the form spread both to the west and to the east, receiving in the two areas a related but independent development which is reflected in the distinctive repertories of the Anglo-French and the Swiss-German tropers. The practice of troping was then introduced into Italy from each of these areas independently.

The earliest categories of tropes appear to be those to the Introit, the Offertory, and the Communion in the Proper of the Mass and to the Gloria in the Ordinary. The first and last of these were especially cultivated in the course of the tenth century, as were also, to a lesser degree, the tropes of the Sanctus and Agnus. Two other categories of limited importance also appear in the tenth century: the tropes "ante sequentiam," which occur as marginal additions in the early tenth-century troper Paris 1240 but which apparently achieved only limited popularity, and the tropes to the Ite missa est, which only occur in a few manuscripts.

The life of the early trope was intense but brief. The high point of the development seems to lie in the tenth century, when

---

[22] See, for example, Rome, Casanat. 1741, facsimile ed. by G. Vecchi, in *Monumenta lyrica medii aevi*, Ser. I, Vol. I, Modena, 1955.

[23] Oxford, Bodleian Library, Douce 222.

[24] See Günther Weiss, "Zur Rolle Italiens im frühen Tropenschaffen," *Festschrift Bruno Stäblein*, Kassel, 1967, pp. 287-292.

a burst of creative activity toward the end of the century considerably augmented the existing trope repertory. Numerically, the most important category in this development was that of the Introit trope. A decline began to set in during the eleventh century, and the tropes to the Proper of the Mass, which had been most important in the earlier period, disappear almost completely from Western manuscripts after the middle of the century. Only the Ordinary tropes continued to exist into the later period, and even here the amount of new composition seems to have been small. By the twelfth century new forms had arisen, especially in connection with the Office chants, and these, with the prosa, became the primary categories of composition in the so-called second period of troping.

CHAPTER III

THE TROPERS

The tropers of St. Martial de Limoges have been the object of
intensive study.[1] Their importance for the history of early medieval music, literature, and art is undeniable, for they provide an
almost unrivaled picture of the artistic activity of a single important medieval monastic center from the tenth to the twelfth
centuries. They have served as an important source for the study
of the Latin planctus and the origins of vernacular poetry, the
development of medieval Latin verse and the liturgical drama,
the music of the sequentia and the rise of polyphony, the history

[1] The standard history of St. Martial de Limoges is still the work by
Charles de Lasteyrie, *L'Abbaye de Saint-Martial de Limoges,* Paris, 1901.
The chronicles of the monastery have been edited by H. Duplès-Agier,
Chroniques de Saint-Martial de Limoges, Paris, 1874. An up-to-date summary of the abbey's history can be found in the excellent catalogue of the
exposition of St. Martial MSS at Limoges in 1950, *L'Art Roman à Saint-
Martial de Limoges,* Limoges, 1950, pp. 11-24. For a general study of the
musical activity at St. Martial, see Jacques Chailley, *L'École Musicale de
Saint-Martial de Limoges jusqu'à la Fin du XIe Siècle,* noting especially the
bibliography, pp. 385-418. The St. Martial tropers as a group are discussed
with varying degrees of thoroughness in the following works: Gautier,
Histoire, pp. 69ff.; Léopold Delisle, *Les Manuscrits de Saint-Martial de
Limoges,* Limoges, 1895, and *Cabinet des Manuscrits de la Bibliothèque
Impériale,* Vol. I, Paris, 1868, pp. 388-397; *Analecta Hymnica,* introductions to Vols. 7 and 47; *Catalogue Général des Manuscrits Latins de la
Bibliothèque Nationale de Paris,* Paris, 1939ff., where each MS is discussed
under its shelf number; Chailley, *op.cit.,* pp. 73-118, and the summary of
this discussion in Chailley, "Les anciens tropaires et séquentiaires de l'École
de Saint-Martial de Limoges (Xe-XIe S.)," *Études Grégoriennes,* II (1957),
163-188; Richard Crocker, *The Repertoire of Proses at Saint-Martial de
Limoges (Tenth and Eleventh Centuries),* Yale dissertation (unpublished),
1957; Heinrich Husmann, *Tropen- und Sequenzenhandschriften;* Günther
Weiss, "Zum Problem der Gruppierung südfranzösischer Tropare," *Archiv
für Musikwissenschaft,* XXI (1964), 163-171; and David G. Hughes, "Further Notes on the Grouping of the Aquitanian Tropers," *Journal of the
American Musicological Society,* XIX (1966), 3-12. Special studies of individual MSS or specific aspects of the St. Martial repertory will be mentioned
where pertinent in the following discussion.

of Romanesque art and the development of medieval manuscript illumination.

For the purposes of the present study, which is concerned with the music of the early St. Martial trope repertory, it is possible to select from this rich and variegated corpus nine manuscripts which are of primary importance for the history of the trope in the tenth and early eleventh centuries. The basis of selection has been twofold. Since the dominant element in the trope repertory up to the middle of the eleventh-century was the trope to the Proper of the Mass, I have chosen only those manuscripts whose primary constituent element is the Proper trope. Thus, early prosers, like the one contained in Paris 1138 and 1338, have been omitted, as well as those later eleventh-century manuscripts, like Paris 1132 to 1137, which contain only tropes to the Ordinary. In addition, I have chosen only those tropers which we know were in the library of St. Martial in the Middle Ages, whatever their ultimate place of origin.[2] Thus, Aquitainian tropers, like Paris 779 and Paris n.a. 1871, although they are related to the St. Martial manuscripts, have been omitted from primary consideration,[3] while a troper like Paris 903, although it was drawn up for the abbey of St. Yrieix, has been included, since it passed into the St. Martial library in the course of the Middle Ages. This criterion may appear arbitrary, but it does guarantee a degree of geographical unity without demanding an a priori solution to the vexing question of provenance.

The following are the nine tropers thus selected, with possible date and place of origin:

1. Tropers which may have been drawn up originally for use at the monastery of St. Martial itself or for some other establishment in the immediate area of Limoges: Paris 1240—between 933 and 936; for St. Martial.

---

[2] On the library of St. Martial and its acquisition by the Royal Library in the eighteenth century, see the works by Delisle cited above on p. 29, note 1.

[3] It should be noted that Chailley, at least, considers Paris 779 a St. Martial troper. See Chailley, *L'École Musicale,* p. 102.

Paris 1120—late tenth or early eleventh century; for
   St. Martial?
Paris 1121—early eleventh century; for St. Martial.
Paris 909—eleventh century.
Paris 1119—eleventh century.

2. Tropers which show distinctive variants in their trope
    repertory and which quite probably originated outside
    the immediate sphere of influence of St. Martial, although
    finding their way into the St. Martial library at some point
    in the Middle Ages:

Paris 1084—tenth century?
Paris 1118—between 988 and 996.
Paris 887—eleventh century.
Paris 903—eleventh century; for St. Yrieix (while basi-
   cally a Gradual, this manuscript also contains a com-
   plete series of tropes at the end).

Of these nine manuscripts, Paris 1121 has been chosen as the
basis for transcription, since, among the tropers originating at
St. Martial itself and containing the fully developed St. Martial
trope repertory, it is the earliest one which can be transcribed
with a degree of assurance.

Format of the Tropers

It is possible to learn a good deal about troping from a consideration of the external makeup and the contents of the tropers themselves. For one thing, the page dimensions of a troper are usually
small. Paris 1120, the smallest of the St. Martial tropers, measures
a mere 230 by 105 millimeters (approximately 9 by 4 inches), and
the narrowness of the page strikingly resembles the dimensions of
the medieval cantatoria, the chant books for soloists.[4] Paris 1121

---

[4] St. Gall 359 and the eighth-century "Gradual" of Monza furnish good
examples of the cantatorium. Small size is not limited to tropers from St.
Martial. One can cite the tiny portions of the tenth-century Autun troper,
Paris Arsenal 1169, or the small square format of certain German tropers
such as the tenth-century Mainz troper in the British Museum, Add MS
19768.

is one of the largest St. Martial tropers, yet it measures only 265 by
170 millimeters (approximately 10½ by 6½ inches), and even these
larger dimensions contrast sharply with those of a regular
Aquitainian choirbook of the period.[5]

The discrepancy between the size of a regular choirbook and
that of a troper, as well as the contents of the latter, suggests that
the troper was intended for a solo singer. The large dimensions of
a Gradual would allow a medieval choir of six or eight men, gath-
ered around the choir stand, to read it without difficulty. The
small-sized troper could have been used conveniently by only one
or two singers, especially since the scribes did not compensate for
the small page by decreasing the number of lines per page or by
using proportionally larger neumes.

Another striking external characteristic of the tropers is their
utilitarian makeup. With rare exceptions, the manuscripts are not
elaborately illuminated. Among the St. Martial manuscripts, only
Paris 1121 is consistently decorated with figured initials of some
degree of elaborateness. The famous paintings of musicians in the
tonarium of Paris 1118 are almost the only illuminations in that
manuscript.[6] For the rest, Paris 1120, Paris 1119, and Paris 1084
have a few illuminated initials, but these are sporadic, quite simple,
and in a limited range of colors. The four remaining manuscripts
are without notable illumination.[7]

In some cases, a more elaborate decoration may have been intended. In Paris 1119 and Paris 909, for example, the text scribe
has left space for large initials at the beginning of certain feasts,
but no illuminator has filled them in. Instead, the rubricator, in

---

5 Paris 903 is a typical example of the Aquitainian choirbook. This manuscript from St. Yrieix, while containing tropes, is essentially a Gradual. It
measures 405 x 315 mm. (approximately 16 x 12 in.). The Gradual of Albi,
Paris 776, has similar dimensions (405 x 207 mm.).

6 In the troper itself, Christmas and Easter are marked with figured initials, while smaller ones are used for St. Stephen and the Assumption of
the B.V.M.

7 This generalization is, on the whole, valid for all tropers, whatever their
place of origin. There are, however, a few exceptional tropers with very
elaborate decoration, such as British Museum Caligula A XIV (from Hereford?),
Paris Arsenal 1169 (the Autun troper), and so forth.

completing the text of the manuscript, has supplied a simple capital and filled in the remaining space with horizontal lines.

The rubrics themselves are not particularly decorative. In many
cases, red is the only colored ink used for these and for the small
capitals at the beginning of individual trope lines.[8] Often the rubricator omits the capitals altogether, and sometimes the headings for
the feasts as well.

The accuracy with which the text is copied varies considerably,
as does the care and thoroughness with which corrections are made.
The neume scribe makes many of the corrections to the text in the
course of adding the musical notation. He supplies missing words
and syllables and alters the word spacing when it hinders the proper
distribution of his neumes.

The musical notation, on the other hand, is usually very accurate,
and corrections are rare. Occasionally the neume scribe makes a
false start at the beginning of a line, placing his neumes too high or
too low for proper vertical spacing, but he corrects the error immediately.

All these factors point to the functional nature of the tropers.
They were not generally considered as precious treasures which
must be carefully drawn up and lavishly adorned, but as utilitarian
books for definite, practical use. The musical notation was of primary importance for this, and it is even possible that the trope
singer himself was entrusted with supplying the neumes.[9]

The practical purpose of the tropers also helps to account for
the existence of many manuscripts in which certain pieces occur

---

[8] Contrast with this Oxford Bodleian 775 (a troper from Winchester),
which, although without illumination, uses a great variety of colors for the
simple capitals.

[9] There is no evidence at this period (i.e., before the eleventh century) of
scribes especially qualified as music copyists, and it seems far more likely
that, at least for the earlier tropers, a member of the choir — and probably
the trope singer himself — notated the book for his own use. See Solange
Corbin, *La Notation Musicale Neumatique — Les Quatre Provinces Lyonnaises,* University of Paris thesis (unpublished), 1957, pp. 607ff., and E.
Lesne, *Histoire de la Propriété Ecclésiastique en France,* Vol. IV, *Les
Livres; "Scriptoria" et Bibliothèques, du commencement du VIIIe à la
fin du XIe Siècle,* Lille, 1938.

without notation. The lack of neumes disturbed Gautier, who
thought they had been "forgotten" by a careless scribe.[10] However, since the troper was intended for practical use, there was no
need to supply neumes for all the texts, but only for those that the
trope singer was actually going to use.

Apparently the procedure for drawing up a troper was as follows:
the text scribe based his manuscript on an exemplar which, for one
reason or another, might not agree in every detail with current or
local practice, and this exemplar was faithfully copied. The neume
scribe—that is, perhaps, the trope singer—then provided the melodies for those pieces which were to be used at the Mass throughout
the year, and he might even reverse the order of some of the tropes
where local practice demanded.[11]

Of the nine St. Martial tropers under consideration, only four
are more or less consistently notated throughout: Paris 1121,
the main troper of Paris 1084, Paris 887, and Paris 903.[12] The
remaining manuscripts contain a considerable number of trope
texts without notation.

If additional tropes were to be used or new pieces added to a
troper, the additions could be made either marginally at their proper place in the series of tropes or on the blank folios at the end of
a section. The latter method of addition suggests another external
characteristic of these manuscripts. A troper is heterogeneous and
sectional in its makeup, frequently with Proper and Ordinary tropes
in separate series, and often with such additional elements as prosae,
sequentiae, prosulae, processional antiphons, and certain liturgical
chants, each contained in separate sections. Such a collection was
rarely set up as an unalterable unity, and even where a single scribe
is responsible for large stretches of a manuscript, care is taken to

10 Gautier, *Histoire,* p. 103.

11 See especially the marginal notes in Paris 1118, where certain pieces
are qualified with the remark "non est bonum," and where the order of
Introit tropes and Introit Psalm verses for certain feasts is altered by marginal cues.

12 Paris 1121 is already something of a special case due to the more than
usual elaborateness of its decoration. Paris 903 is also exceptional in that it
is basically a Gradual which contains a troper as an integral part.

begin each new component on the first folio of a new quire. In this way, additions could be made to each section, or new sections could be added, without disturbing the basic order within each group. The original structure of even an extremely complex manuscript like Paris 1084 can thus be determined with some degree of certainty, although precise points of juncture are often obscured by subsequent erasures and additions.[13]

This point is worth stressing for two reasons. On the one hand, it is precisely the heterogeneous nature of the manuscripts and the ease with which additions could be and were made to them which account for many of the real difficulties and the resulting controversies in determining the provenance and the date of origin of a manuscript as a whole. On the other hand, the individual sections of a manuscript are apt, for the same reasons, to retain unaltered the basic unity of their original repertory, with additions usually occurring on blank folios at the end of sections or on additional quires. This is a valuable asset in studying that specific part of the manuscript which contains the tropes themselves.[14]

Contents of the Tropers

The varied contents of the St. Martial tropers give some indication of the functions these manuscripts were expected to fulfill. Bishop Frere's definition of a troper serves as a useful point of

---

[13] Trope manuscripts with unified contents are rare. Those that do exist fall into two main types: 1. those manuscripts where a troper forms a supplementary part of a Gradual, and where continuity is preserved, regardless of sections, throughout the manuscript as a whole (e.g., Paris 903); and 2. those manuscripts which contain *only* a troper and where, if other elements such as prosae and antiphons are included, these additional elements are found in their place within the main series of tropes (e.g., Paris 779; this manuscript is, however, incomplete at both beginning and end, and thus may not form an exception to the general principle).

[14] Among the St. Martial tropers, there is one example of a far more drastic method of addition or, more properly, substitution. In Paris 909, two whole quires of the original manuscript have been removed from the main trope series and have been replaced by substitute quires containing a new trope repertory for certain feasts. See below, p. 44.

departure: "All new developments in musical composition, failing to gain admission into the privileged circle of the recognized Gregorian service-books, were thrown together so as to form an independent music-collection supplemental to the official books; and that is exactly what a troper is."[15]

This definition is basically precise. The dominant elements in a troper are certainly the so-called extra-liturgical forms of trope, prosula, prosa, sequentia, and processional antiphon. But there is an important and significant exception to this generalization. A troper frequently contains certain categories of liturgical compositions, especially various chants intended for soloists, such as Alleluia verses, Tracts, and Offertory verses.

The table on page 37 indicates the component elements of each of the nine St. Martial tropers. It will be seen from this table that "pure" tropers as such are rare. Only Paris 1118 and Paris 1119 are completely without Proper Mass chants, although even these manuscripts contain untroped items from the Kyriale.

Two important omissions in the contents of the tropers should, however, be noted. None of the manuscripts contains either Graduals or hymns. The latter omission is perhaps not surprising, since hymns are primarily Office chants, while the troper almost exclusively contains pieces for the Mass. Hymns were normally collected in separate manuscripts or hymnals.

The absence of Graduals, however, raises an interesting question, since the Gradual is the only solo Mass chant that is not included in these early St. Martial tropers. In attempting to account for this absence, we find that Bishop Frere's definition can lead to confusion. By emphasizing the division between liturgical and extraliturgical elements, it tends to obscure what is apparently the essential principle in determining the contents of a troper, namely, that they were for the use of a specific singer.

The majority of the pieces are for soloists. The tropes themselves, as we have already suggested, were probably sung by a

---

15 Frere, *The Winchester Troper,* p. vi.

Contents of the St. Martial Tropers

	1240	1120	1121	909	1119	1084	1118	887	903
Proper tropes	X	X	X	X	X	X	X	X	X
Ordinary tropes:									
Gloria	X	X	X	X	X	X	*	X	X
Sanctus	*	X		X	X	X	*	X	X
Agnus	*	X		X	X	X	*	X	X
Kyrie prosulae		X			X	X	*	X	X
Regnum prosulae		X	X	X	X	(X)		X	
Other prosulae (Alleluia, Offertory, etc.)	X					X	X		G
Processional Antiphons		X	X	X					X
Tonarium	X		X	X		X	X		
Prosae	X	X	X		X	X	X	X	X
Sequentiae			X	X		X	X	X	
Proper Mass Chants — Alleluias with their verses			X	X		X			G
Proper Mass Chants — Tracts			X	X					G
Proper Mass Chants — Offertory verses		X	X	X					G
Proper Mass Chants — Holy Week chants	X	X	X+	X+				(X+)	G
Proper Mass Chants — In Letania Maiore	X	X+	X+					(X+)	G
Laudes Regiae	X						X		
Varia:									
Gregorius presul	X	X							
Ants. de 3 Pueris		X	X						
Ants. Nat. BMV		X							
Invitatories			X						
Lamentatio Hier.			X						
Gospel Ants.			X						

* = Ordinary tropes contained in the main series of Proper tropes and not in a separate section.

X+ = Pieces found among the processional antiphons or elsewhere, but not in the main trope series.

G= Pieces contained in the Gradual (Paris 903 only).

( ) = An addition to the primary manuscript.

solo singer.[16]   The prosae, too, were apparently intended for
solo performance, with the choir or another soloist repeating
the melismatic sequentiae.[17]   The Mass elements contained in
a troper are likewise all solo chants: Tracts and Alleluias, Offertory verses, the solo sections of the Holy Week services, and so
forth. Only the Graduals are missing.

A possible explanation for this omission is suggested by the
early *Ordines Romani,* which indicate that the Gradual and the
following Alleluia or Tract were performed by different singers
at the ambo. The Ordo of St. Amand (ninth century) states
that, after the lection, a singer "accipit cantorium et psallit in
ambone et dicit responsorium; similiter et *alius* Alleluia."[18]
This second singer, the singer of the Alleluia or Tract, may well
have been the "tropista" at St. Martial, since in this way it would
be possible to account for the occurrence of Alleluias and Tracts
and the absence of Graduals in the tropers.

Such a conclusion must, of course, be tentative, since there are
no documents from this period which indicate the precise musical
duties of individual singers in the medieval choir. But the evidence
does suggest that the tropers were above all practical, utilitarian
manuscripts, drawn up for the convenience of a specific singer or
singers, even if the precise division of musical labors might vary
somewhat from place to place. The distinction between liturgical
and extra-liturgical, between official chant and nonofficial embellishment, which Bishop Frere emphasized in his definition, obviously carries far more weight with us today than it did for the
musicians of the tenth century. After all, not only do official

16 See above, p. 32. I use the term "solo singer" in the singular for
convenience, but it is quite possible and even probable that two soloists
shared this role. The rubrics of the Rogation Litany, for example, refer
specifically to "duo cantores."

17 Cf. on this question Husmann, "Alleluia, Vers und Sequenzen," *Annales
Musicologiques,* IV (1956), 19, where he contends that the prosa was originally soloistic, while the sequentia was its choral repetition.

18 L. Duchesne, *Christian Worship,* 5th edn., London, 1919, p. 458. Italics
mine. On this question, see J. Froger, *Les Chants de la Messe aux VIIIe et
IXe Siècles,* Paris, 1950, p. 17.

chants occur in tropers, but also certain unofficial pieces, notably the prosulae, are quite common in Aquitainian Graduals.[19]

One other point should be considered before leaving this discussion of the solo nature of the contents of a troper. It has been suggested, notably by Gautier,[20] that a choir may have possessed several tropers which could be distributed among the singers for a choral performance of the tropes. Certainly, the large number of tropers preserved at St. Martial might give rise to such a belief. However, the idea goes against what we know about medieval performance; a medieval choir would be far more likely to perform choral chants from a single large choirbook like the Gradual. Furthermore, the large number of tropers at St. Martial, as at St. Gall, should perhaps be attributed to the zeal of the monastery's librarian in collecting manuscripts rather than to any desire for choral performance. In fact, it is probable that no more than one or two manuscripts were in use at any single time at St. Martial, at least in the early period of troping, and this idea is supported by the relatively limited number of surviving tropers from other centers of troping, with the exception of St. Gall.[21]

The organization of the tropes within their own section of the manuscript is the same in almost all of the St. Martial tropers. The principle is this: the tropes for the Proper of the Mass are presented in one section, arranged according to the calendar order of the feasts and, within each feast, according to their order of performance during the Mass, namely, Introit tropes, sequentia tropes, Offertory tropes, and Communion tropes. This principal section is followed by separate sections containing the tropes for each of the Ordinary chants, namely, Kyrie tropes or prosulae, Gloria tropes, Sanctus tropes, and Agnus tropes.

In only one case, that of Paris 1118, are tropes for the Proper and Ordinary combined in one series. The basic order is still that

---

[19] For example, Alleluia and Offertory prosulae are contained in the regular Mass formularies of the St. Yrieix Gradual (Paris 903), the Albi Gradual (Paris 776), and so forth.

[20] Gautier, *Histoire,* p. 98.

[21] For example, two from Winchester (tenth century and eleventh century), two from Nevers (eleventh century and twelfth century), and so forth.

of the church calendar, but within each feast both Proper and Ordinary tropes are arranged according to their place of performance in the Mass.[22]

Problems of Determining Provenance and Date

An extremely difficult problem faces anyone who attempts to determine the precise date and provenance of a given troper. This is primarily because a troper, by its very nature, precludes a consistent application of the well-established and reliable criteria used in finding the age and place of origin of other medieval liturgical manuscripts. Some specific examples will make this clear.

One of the surest ways of determining the provenance of a Gradual or Antiphoner is by means of its calendar of feasts, whether this calendar is explicitly indicated in a separate part of the manuscript or is only suggested by the Mass formularies which the manuscript contains. By means of the local saints included in a calendar, and especially any indication of a patron saint, by suggestion of peculiar local liturgical practices, by the appearance or absence of datable feasts, and so forth, one can frequently arrive at a very precise notion of the provenance, and sometimes even the approximate date, of the manuscript in question.

In a troper, however, the evidence of the calendar is of variable usefulness, since such a manuscript supplies tropes only for the most important feasts of the church year. One of these major solemnities will, of course, be the patronal festival, and this will be helpful when the name of the patron is distinctive enough to permit a precise localization. This is indeed the case, for example, with St. Yrieix in Paris 903 and with St. Cyr in the Nevers tropers

---

22 This method of arrangement in a single series is unusual among Aquitainian tropers. It is found again only in Paris 779 and Apt 17, where even the prosae have been brought into their place in the main series. This type of organization probably reflects an influence from the northeast, since it is found in tropers from Autun (Paris Arsenal 1169) and Nevers (Paris 9449 and Paris n.a. 1235) and, further afield, from Prüm (Paris 9448), Echternach (Paris 10510), and Mainz (London B.M. Add. 19768). The normal sectional organization of the St. Martial tropes is, on the other hand, typical of the northwest, being found in tropers from Paris (Paris 13252) and Arras (Cambrai 75) and in the Anglo-Saxon tropers.

Paris 9449 and Paris n.a. 1235. However, if an establishment stands under the vocable of, say, St. Peter or St. Stephen, that is, saints who would normally have a troped Mass anyway, there will be nothing in the contents of the troper to indicate this patronal function. Likewise, the appearance of tropes for St. Martial in itself gives little indication of precise provenance, since the cult of the Saint was widespread in Aquitaine and elsewhere.

Furthermore, very few tropers contain a separate full calendar as part of their contents. Paris 1240 is one of the few exceptions to this generalization.

All this does not mean that the calendar indications in a troper are useless. On the contrary, much valuable information may be gained from the list of troped feasts, and the provenance of some tropers has been determined in precisely this way. But it must be stressed that such information is limited at best, and one cannot assume that it will solve the problem of provenance in any particular case.[23]

Another important method for determining the provenance of a liturgical manuscript is to consider the variable Gradual elements that it contains. Thus, for example, the specific series of Alleluia verses for the Sundays after Pentecost were successfully used for this purpose by Leroquais in his studies of the liturgical manuscripts of France. But this method, too, is of limited usefulness as far as the tropers are concerned, since there is little consistency in the specific types of Mass chants contained in any given manuscript, and thus direct comparisons are often impossible. In addition, certain Proper chants, such as the Offertory verses or the Tracts, which might conceivably serve as a basis for determining provenance, have not received the detailed study necessary for establishing their value in this respect.

A further difficulty in determining the date and provenance of tropers is the fact that only a limited number of them survive. The

---

[23] A good cautionary example is the eleventh-century Anglo-Saxon troper London B.M. Caligula A XIV, which has wandered from London to Canterbury to Gloucester to Hereford in its search for a place of origin. And this is not an isolated case.

total number of tropers from all periods is something over two hundred, as compared to the thousands of extant liturgical manuscripts.[24] Of first-period tropers from France and England—the early West Frankish group—which most directly concern us here, there are only about twenty, of which no more than half a dozen can be localized or dated with complete accuracy. Furthermore, the geographical distribution of these manuscripts, with the exception of the Aquitainian group, is a random one. Thus, as we have noted before, we lack tropers from such important centers as Jumièges, St. Martin of Tours, Fleury, and St. Denis. With this limited number of sources, no comprehensive group of known manuscripts can be set up as a basis of comparison for identifying the unknown.

What general criteria are available, then, for studying the provenance and date of the tropers? Theoretically, we might expect that the most useful information would be furnished by the musical notation. Unfortunately for the study of the St. Martial tropers, however, we have no detailed and exhaustive study of Aquitainian notation comparable to the important work of Mlle. Solange Corbin on French neumatic notation, in which all known manuscripts containing that notation have been analyzed and classified.[25] Obviously, such a study of Aquitainian notation could not profitably be made on the basis of the tropers alone, since any reliable identification of the notation of individual scriptoria and of important local peculiarities would require a wide knowledge of the purely liturgical Aquitainian manuscripts.[26]

---

[24] For an inventory of the tropers, see Husmann, *Tropen- und Sequenzenhandschriften,* although it should be noted that he omits from consideration those tropers which form part of a Gradual, such as Paris 903, Paris n.a. 1235, and so forth. Therefore, the list of manuscripts given by Blume and Bannister in the introduction to Vol. 47 of the *Analecta Hymnica* still remains a useful guide.

[25] Corbin, *La Notation Musicale Neumatique.*

[26] For example, Dom Ferretti's study of Aquitainian notation in the Introduction to Vol. XIII of the *Paléographie Musicale,* despite its obvious interest, is of limited general value in this respect since it is based primarily on a single manuscript, Paris 903. Dom Suñol's brief account of Aquitainian notation in *Introduction à la Paléographie Musicale Grégorienne,* pp. 260-281, is interesting primarily for the plates that accompany it.

Nevertheless, certain notational peculiarities within the limited group of the tropers can be very useful in determining relationships among the manuscripts, even if more precise indications of provenance and date must await a comprehensive study of Aquitainian notation. Thus, for example, we learn that the main troper of Paris 1084 (ff. 53v-123) is closely related to Paris 1118 by its notation and may, indeed, come from the very same scriptorium. On the other hand, the notation of the additional series of tropes occurring in Paris 1084 on ff. 38v-51 differs strikingly from the notation of the main troper and, in fact, very closely resembles that of Paris 1120, one of the manuscripts from the St. Martial group of tropers.

Another important criterion for determining the relationships among the Aquitainian tropers is furnished by certain peculiarities of the trope repertory contained in the individual manuscripts. By comparing the contents of the manuscripts, it is possible to establish two clear-cut families of tropers as indicated in the list of St. Martial manuscripts presented earlier.[27] Thus, for example, all the manuscripts of the first group, except Paris 1240[28]—that is, Paris 1120, 1121, 909, and 1119—contain the Easter Introit trope *Factus homo de matre.* However, the manuscripts of the second group—that is, Paris 1084 (main troper), 1118, 887, and 903— all lack this particular Introit trope. Interestingly enough, it is found in the additional series of tropes in Paris 1084, mentioned above, which, as we have seen, is already related to the first group of tropers by its notation. Another example, from the same feast, is the Agnus trope *Pro cunctis deductus,* which occurs in Paris 1120, 1121, 909, 1119, and in the additional series of Paris 1084, but which is absent in the main troper of Paris 1084 and in Paris 1118, 887, and 903.

This significant difference in repertory is also supported to a certain extent by slight but consistent melodic variants between the two groups of manuscripts.

---

[27] Pp. 30-31.

[28] Paris 1240 contains far fewer tropes than the other manuscripts and for this reason cannot always be conveniently compared with them.

In addition to these general criteria for studying the interrelationship of the manuscripts, there are a number of specific historical
references which are helpful in determining dates and origins of certain of the manuscripts. Thus, for example, Paris 1240 and Paris
1118 contain liturgical acclamations—the *Laudes Regiae*—which
mention specific, datable historical personages, such as kings, popes,
bishops, and abbots, and thus allow a localization of the specific
manuscripts.[29]

The whole question of the apostleship of St. Martial, which was
such a burning issue at Limoges in the 1020's and which was finally
resolved in favor of the apostolic claims of the Saint at the Council
of Limoges in 1031, can also be helpful in studying certain of the
St. Martial tropers.[30] The most concrete liturgical result of the
ultimate acceptance of St. Martial within the ranks of the apostles
was the substitution of the Mass *Probavit* for the Confessor's Mass
Statuit ei. Thus, in Paris 1120 and Paris 1121, the original Statuit
cues for the tropes of St. Martial have been erased and replaced by
Probavit cues, and we can assume that the tropers in question were
drawn up before the apostleship controversy and were altered for
use during or after it. The same is probably also true of Paris 909,
where the section of the manuscript containing the St. Martial
tropes has been replaced by a new quire in which the Probavit cues
are used. On the other hand, Paris 1119, which has the Probavit
cues *in manu prima,* must have originated after the dispute.

However, the apostleship question does not allow us to be more
specific than this about the dates of the tropers. For one thing,

---

29 For a general study of the *Laudes Regiae,* see Kantorowicz, *Laudes
Regiae,* Berkeley, 1958, with an appendix on the music of the *Laudes* by
Manfred Bukofzer, pp. 188ff.

30 For the history of the controversy, see the works cited above, p. 29,
note 1. For material on Adémar de Chabannes, the monk who played such
a decisive role in the debate, see L. Delisle, *Notice sur les manuscrits
originaux d'Adémar de Chabannes,* Paris, 1896; *Chronique d'Adémar de
Chabannes,* ed. J. Chavanon, Paris, 1897; and Paul Hooreman, "Saint-Martial
de Limoges au Temps de l'Abbé Odolric (1025-1040)," *Revue Belge de
Musicologie,* III (1949), 5-36. The proceedings of the Council of Limoges
may be found in Mansi, *Sacrorum Conciliorum Nova et Amplissima Collectio,*
Vol. 19.

the apostleship was an important issue for a good many years at
the beginning of the eleventh century, and there is no reason to
assume that the changes in the tropers awaited the definitive deci-
sion of the Council of Limoges in 1031. For another thing, a certain
number of tropers retain the Statuit cues regardless of their date of
origin. Thus, the earliest troper Paris 1240 still indicates Statuit for
the St. Martial tropes, presumably because the manuscript had ceased
to be used by the time of the apostleship controversy. Similarly, the
manuscripts of the second group of tropers—Paris 1084, 1118, 887,
and 903—all retain the Statuit cues unaltered, although the last two
must certainly date from the eleventh century. One can only assume
from this that the urge to recognize St. Martial's apostleship in the
cues of a troper—and in the Apostle's Mass, for that matter—was
a very local affair, limited perhaps to the Saint's own abbey and its
environs. We know that Paris 903, the St. Yrieix Gradual, does not
come from Limoges, and this is probably also true of the other three
manuscripts of the group. By the time these manuscripts entered the
St. Martial library, the Proper trope sections had apparently ceased
to be used, and there was no further need to alter the trope cues. At
any rate, it is clear that the evidence of the St. Martial trope cues is
of limited applicability.

The Nine St. Martial Tropers

In discussing the specific St. Martial manuscripts which serve as
the basis for this study, we may limit ourselves to those sections of
the manuscripts which contain tropes in the strict sense of the term,
since it is these pieces that are our primary concern. As a conse-
quence, many of the problems involving the manuscripts as a whole
need not concern us. A discussion of the full contents of the tropers
can be found in Chailley's studies of the St. Martial school.[31]

One of the most important aspects of Chailley's bibliographical
study of the St. Martial manuscripts, it seems to me, was his renewed
emphasis on the disparate origins of the tropers. One can disagree

---

[31] Chailley, L'École musicale, pp. 73-118, and "Les anciens tropaires,"
in Études Grégoriennes, II, 163-188. See also Husmann, Tropen- und
Sequenzenhandschriften, passim.

quite rightly with some of his specific attributions and with some of
the details of his manuscript description, but this in no way detracts
from the central fact, namely, that many of the so-called St. Martial
tropers originated outside the abbey of St. Martial, and even on occasion outside the immediate area of Limoges.

This difference of origin is underlined by basic differences of repertory and by definite notational relationships. Thus, we find that
those manuscripts coming from St. Martial itself, although each has
its own individual characteristics, still represent a more or less distinctive, unified whole as compared with those other Aquitainian tropers
which only later found their way into the St. Martial library.

We shall turn first to the manuscripts of the St. Martial group.

Paris 1240

Paris 1240 is the oldest St. Martial troper, and, indeed, the oldest
full troper still extant from any of the medieval centers of troping.
There seems to me no reason to reject the generally accepted date
of 933-936, based on the acclamations on f. 65.[32] The calendar,
which begins on f. 10v, lists Easter as March 27, and this suggests
the year 908, although the arguments for the later date still seem
more compelling.[33] That the manuscript originated at St. Martial
also seems well established by the calendar, the acclamations, and
the appearance of St. Martial as the only local saint in the principal section of the troper.

Nevertheless, Paris 1240 is in many ways distinct from the other
manuscripts of the St. Martial group. For example, it contains far
fewer tropes than the other tropers, and there are peculiarities of

---

[32] See the important study of the manuscript by H. M. Bannister, "The
Earliest French Troper and its Date," *Journal of Theological Studies,* II
(1901), 420-429. This is Chailley's MS B, which he discusses in *L'École
musicale,* pp. 78-80, and in "Les anciens tropaires," pp. 165-166. See also
Husmann, *Tropen- und Sequenzenhandschriften,* pp. 137-139; and my
"Northern French Elements."

[33] See Chailley, "Les anciens tropaires," p. 165. I disagree, however, with
the specific way in which Chailley divides the MS, at least as far as the trope
section is concerned, although admittedly the organization of this manuscript
is very complex.

repertory and distinct melodic variants which set it off from the others. However, the family resemblance is still there, and the manuscript's peculiarities can be attributed to its early date, originating as it does before the St. Martial repertory had been fully developed and established.

Paris 1240 is a relatively small manuscript, measuring 230 by 160 millimeters. The main trope section contains a single series of Proper tropes, beginning on f. 18v, and a group of Gloria tropes, beginning on f. 38. The tropes are notated with fair consistency through Pentecost, but after that notation becomes rare. There are numerous additions, and various hands are involved in the musical notation. Surprisingly enough, certain pieces are supplied with French rather than Aquitainian neumes.

Paris 1120

Paris 1120 is the smallest of the St. Martial tropers, measuring 230 by 105 millimeters. Its format resembles that of a cantatorium. The manuscript dates from the early eleventh century or even perhaps, in terms of its notation, from the end of the tenth century. It probably originated in St. Martial,[34] and it is one of the tropers in which the Statuit cues have been altered to Probavit.

The notation, although showing some effort at heightening, is on the whole too imprecise for transcription, and there is no custos. The opening part of the trope section is missing, and the manuscript begins on f. 1 in the middle of the Epiphany trope *Eia Sion gaude*. The Proper tropes are followed by a group of Kyrie prosulae—so labeled in the manuscript—beginning on f. 67 and by Ordinary tropes running from f. 74 to f. 102.

Paris 1120 has a far more extensive repertory than the other tropers of this group, but in general only those tropes of Paris 1120 which also appear in Paris 1121 have notation, while the text of the others has been left without neumes. In fact, the

---

[34] It is assigned to St. Martin of Limoges in Vol. 47 of the *Analecta Hymnica*, but the evidence for this is insufficient, I think.

evidence suggests that Paris 1120 served as the direct model for Paris 1121.[35]

Paris 1121

Paris 1121, then, has a somewhat smaller repertory than Paris 1120, but it is carefully notated throughout. The neumes are heightened with considerable accuracy, and the custos is regularly used. The manuscript nevertheless dates from early in the eleventh century, and it originated at St. Martial itself. For these reasons, it has been chosen for transcription in this book and serves as the basis of our detailed study of the tropes of St. Martial.

The Proper tropes begin on f. 2 and the Ordinary tropes on f. 42. Unfortunately, there are some gaps in the manuscript. The Proper tropes break off after the first few words of the first trope for St. Andrew, and there are no Sanctus or Agnus tropes whatsoever. However, the probable contents of these sections are indicated by the closely related manuscripts Paris 909 and Paris 1119.

The manuscript is of moderate size, measuring 265 by 170 millimeters. On the whole, it is more closely unified than many of the St. Martial tropers and has been drawn up with considerable care and with more elaborate decoration than usual. As with Paris 1120, the Statuit cues for St. Martial have been replaced by Probavit.

Paris 909

Paris 909 is an eleventh-century manuscript, and in size it is quite close to Paris 1121, measuring 265 by 160 millimeters. Although the precise place of its origin is uncertain, its repertory relates it closely to the St. Martial group.[36] It contains many of the tropes

---

35 The Introit trope for Easter Tuesday, *Expurgans populos,* furnishes a good example of the relationship. In Paris 1120, the letters "e" and "x" of the first word are combined in the ornamental capital, the text itself beginning "-purgans." In Paris 1121, the text scribe mechanically put down the "-purgans," but the rubricator failed to notice the small "x" on the capital "E" in Paris 1120, and thus supplied only the capital "E," making the word read "Epurgans" in Paris 1121.

36 See Chailley, *L'École musicale,* p. 90. Chailley suggests a possible origin at St. Martin of Limoges, although Husmann, *Tropen- und Sequenzenhandschriften,* p. 118, still attributes the MS to St. Martial itself.

of Paris 1120 which do not occur in Paris 1121, but as in Paris 1120 these are without notation.

The Proper tropes begin on f. 9, and the Ordinary tropes on f. 86, continuing to f. 109. The Statuit cues for the St. Martial tropes have not simply been erased; rather, the whole quire in which those tropes were contained has been removed and replaced by a new one (ff. 41-48). Not only are the new Probavit cues supplied in the added quire, but there are also a number of Martial tropes included which are not to be found in the other manuscripts. Other quires have also been added elsewhere in the manuscript, the section from f. 59 to f. 85 being an addition to the original troper.[37]

Paris 1119

Paris 1119 is another eleventh-century troper whose precise origin is not known, but which was drawn up under the influence of St. Martial.[38] Its trope repertory is very closely related to that of Paris 909 and the other manuscripts of this group. Proper tropes begin on f. 4, Kyrie prosulae on f. 84, and Gloria tropes on f. 90. Sanctus and Agnus tropes are found on ff. 244-251. Alone among these manuscripts, Paris 1119 contains the Probavit cues for the tropes of St. Martial in the original hand, and the rubric for the feast reads "In Festivitate S. Marcialis Apostoli" (f. 54v).

The provenance of the remaining four manuscripts is far from certain. We do know that they entered the library of St. Martial at some point in the Middle Ages and that they have certain peculiarities of repertory which distinguish them from the preceding group of tropers, which originated at St. Martial itself or in the immediate area of Limoges. But except for the Gradual from St. Yrieix—Paris 903—it is difficult to localize them with any precision. What we can say is that they represent that larger group

---

[37] For a discussion of this manuscript and the possible contribution of Adémar de Chabannes—especially the *versus* on f. 202—see Hooreman, *op.cit.*

[38] See Chailley, *L'École musicale*, pp. 101-102. The troper is assigned to St. Augustine of Limoges in Vol. 47 of the *Analecta Hymnica.* Husmann, *Tropen- und Sequenzenhandschriften,* p. 126, suggests "another Limoges church," perhaps St. Pierre.

of Aquitainian tropers within which the St. Martial tropers discussed above form a self-contained subgroup. Thus, the following
manuscripts have definite affinities with those other Aquitainian
tropers which, as far as we know, had no connection whatever
with the abbey of St. Martial at Limoges, including such manuscripts as the eleventh-century Moissac troper, Paris n.a. 1871,
and the eleventh-century troper in the library of the Basilica of
Ste. Anne in Apt.[39]

Paris 1084

The troper of Paris 1084 is extremely complex in structure. The
main troper (ff. 53v-123) contains a full set of Proper and Ordinary
tropes. It is supplemented by two additional series of tropes, one
of which (ff. 123-152), the earlier in date, brings the repertory of
the troper more or less into line with that of Paris 1118. The other
series of additional tropes (ff. 38v-51) takes into account both the
main troper and this added series and, as we have noted above,[40]
brings the total repertory of Paris 1084 into agreement with that
of the manuscripts of the St. Martial group.

    Paris 1084 is probably the oldest troper of the non-St. Martial
group, dating from the tenth century.[41] The notation of the main
troper is closely related to that of Paris 1118, but although some
care is given to heightening the neumes, the lack of custodes makes
transcription highly problematic. The catalogue of the Bibliothèque
Nationale assigns the manuscript to St. Géraud d'Aurillac, but this

---

[39] On the Moissac troper, see H. M. Bannister, "Un Tropaire-prosier de
Moissac," *Revue d'Histoire et de Littérature Religieuses,* VIII (1903), 554-
581. On the Apt manuscript, see Abbé J. Sautel, *Catalogue descriptif et
illustré des manuscrits liturgiques de l'Église d'Apt,* Carpentras, 1921, pp. 48ff.

[40] P. 43.

[41] Chailley, *L'École musicale,* p. 85, perhaps puts his chronology too late,
considering the relationship of the manuscript with the other St. Martial
tropers. Incidentally, Chailley's unidentified "Dux Macor" (p. 84) results of
course from a scribal error for "dux Magorum" or "the leader of the Magi."
The normal abbreviation for "magorum"—magoꝛ—is miscopied as "macor"
in Paris 1084. The correct text of this Epiphany trope can be found, among
other places, in Paris 1121, f. 9v.

ascription is perhaps valid only for the series of added tropes on ff. 123-152.[42] At any rate, the main part of the manuscript originated outside of the direct influence of St. Martial.

Paris 1084 is relatively small, the pages measuring only 240 by 140 millimeters.

Paris 1118

Paris 1118 can be dated between 988 and 996 on the basis of the Laudes Regiae beginning on f. 38v.[43] Thus, this troper, and Paris 1240 in the first group, are the only ones that can be dated with precision. The provenance of the manuscript, however, is not quite so clear. Its trope repertory certainly excludes it from the St. Martial group, and Chailley argues for a more southern origin, perhaps in the region of Auch.[44] But a more precise localization is perhaps not possible.

The notation of the troper, similar to that of Paris 1084, is heightened with some consistency, but in general its impreciseness and the lack of a custos make transcription problematic although certainly possible.[45]

The repertory of tropes in Paris 1118 (ff. 1-103v) is large, containing many items not found in the other tropers. It is thus an important source for the study of the non-St. Martial group. Unfortunately, a certain number of the pieces lack neumes.

Proper and Ordinary tropes are combined in one series, the Ordinary tropes thus being assigned a specific place in the cycle of feasts. In addition, the manuscript gives cues for the non-troped Proper chants, so that it is possible to reconstruct the Mass formularies in use. Tropes are supplied for certain feasts which are not troped in

---

[42] Husmann, *Tropen- und Sequenzenhandschriften*, p. 120, however, would also attribute the whole MS to Aurillac, along with Paris 887 and Paris n.a. 1871.

[43] See Dreves' introduction to Vol. 7 of the *Analecta Hymnica*.

[44] Chailley, *L'École musicale*, pp. 94-96. See also Husmann, *Tropen- und Sequenzenhandschriften*, pp. 124-126.

[45] Manuscripts like Paris 1118 can of course be used perfectly well for transcription whenever adequate controls are available.

any other manuscript in either of the two groups, while some other troped feasts in Paris 1118 are found again only in Paris 887.

The manuscript measures 245 by 150 millimeters. It is well known for the paintings of minstrels found in the tonarium on ff. 104-114v.

Paris 887

Very little can be said regarding the date and origin of Paris 887. It is certainly an eleventh-century manuscript, and Blume and Chailley both attribute it to St. Martin of Limoges.[46] However, Husmann assigns it to Aurillac, and the peculiarities of its trope repertory would seem to put it outside the direct influence of the later St. Martial manuscripts.

Paris 887 is, indeed, a curious manuscript. On the whole, it stands very close to the non-St. Martial Aquitainian tropers such as Paris 1118. But there are also some interesting similarities with the oldest St. Martial troper, Paris 1240. Thus, for example, Paris 887 alone of the later manuscripts contains Paris 1240's strikingly different version of the melody of the Epiphany Introit trope *Adveniente Xpisto*.[47] At the same time, however, there are many other important variants in Paris 1240 which are not found in Paris 887, and sometimes the version of Paris 887 is nearer to Paris 1121 than to any of the other manuscripts. This suggests something of the extreme complexity of the relationships between Paris 887 and the other manuscripts under consideration. It suggests, too, that although Paris 887 and Paris 1240 are not directly related, they both drew on a common tradition of troping which is not represented in the other tropers of either group.

Nonetheless, the strongest affinities of Paris 887 in both repertory and notation are with the non-St. Martial group, and we shall consider it here as an example of that group, leaving these complicated interrelationships for a later study.

---

[46] See Introduction to Vol. 47 of *Analecta Hymnica*, and Chailley, "Les anciens tropaires," p. 180.

[47] This version is found again, interestingly enough, in certain northern French tropers—for example, in the Nevers troper Paris 9449.

Proper tropes are found on ff. 8-46. Ordinary tropes and prosulae are on ff. 47-86. There are numerous corrections in the text, and apparently the manuscript as a whole was carelessly drawn up. The neumes have a very distinctive upward slant.

Paris 903

Paris 903 is perhaps the most familiar of all the St. Martial manuscripts, since the first part of it—the Gradual—has been published in facsimile as Volume XIII of the *Paléographie Musicale*. It is an eleventh-century manuscript in a large format, measuring 405 by 315 millimeters, and it was drawn up for the monastery of St. Yrieix, which, although not far from Limoges, was actually a dependency of St. Martin of Tours.[48]

The manuscript is a unified whole, and the troper consequently is in the main scribal hand. Tropes to the Proper are found on ff. 147v-163, and Ordinary tropes on ff. 163-179v. The trope repertory is relatively restricted, the practice being to limit the number of Introit tropes to three for all but the most important feasts. Nonetheless, it is possible to see the close relationship between this repertory and that of the other manuscripts of the non-St. Martial group.

The notation of Paris 903 is extremely clear and accurate, as a glance at Volume XIII of the *Paléographie Musicale* will indicate, and it alone of the nine manuscripts under consideration makes use of a dry-point line for orienting the neumes.

---

[48] See the discussion of the manuscript by Dom Gabriel Tissot in the Introduction to *Paléographie Musicale*, XIII, 9-53.

CHAPTER IV

THE TEXTS OF THE TROPES

The texts of the tropes have been to a large extent the domain of the literary historians. As valuable as their work has been, it is obvious that their literary interests will condition their approach to the subject, and that this will often lead to a distorted picture of the trope. Thus, for example, the magnificent collection of trope texts presented by Blume and Bannister in Volumes 47 and 49 of the *Analecta Hymnica* does not give us a true cross section of existing tropes, since it has been expressly limited to poetic texts. Although the editors have interpreted "poetic" in the broadest possible way,[1] important trope texts — many of these among the earliest — have had to be omitted because they are in prose. Furthermore, the trope texts in *Analecta Hymnica* have not always escaped editorial emendation, when such changes have fitted a predetermined poetical scheme more conveniently. But the tropers furnish neumes for these suppressed syllables, and we must assume that they were sung, despite the demands of metrical propriety.

Another difficulty for the literary historian arises from the quality of the texts. Admittedly, the literary quality of the tropes is not always of the highest order. The embarrassment of the critic can be seen in the work of Gautier, who is relieved to find that the texts are at least theologically orthodox, whatever their lack of literary merit.[2] Yet such an approach fails to emphasize the importance and originality of the form as far as its music is concerned. This was not the last time in history that an undistinguished text served the purposes of musical creation. It should thus not be out

---

[1] See especially the introduction of *Analecta Hymnica*, Vol. 49, Leipzig, 1906, for a discussion of this point by Blume.

[2] Gautier, *Histoire*, p. 7: "Si le style en est peu relevé, les doctrines en sont hautes."

of place to consider once again the texts of the tropes, their function and form, and their relationship to their musical setting.

The primary function of the trope texts is didactic and devotional. In the Mass formularies of the Gradual, the texts of the Proper chants have been drawn predominantly from Biblical passages which have some relevance to the central idea of the specific feast.[3] Since many chant texts are drawn from the Psalter—the Old Testament "hymnbook" of the church—they can only present a general commentary on the specifically Christian events represented in the church calendar.

Thus, for the Introit of the feast of St. Stephen, to comment upon Stephen's trial before the high religious court of the Sanhedrin and his subsequent martyrdom by stoning, an appropriate passage is chosen from Psalm 118, *Beati immaculati:*[4]

> Princes sat, and spoke against me: and the wicked persecuted me: help me, O Lord my God, for thy servant was exercised in thy justifications. [Introit *Etenim sederunt*]

Starting from this general commentary on a given feast, the writer of the trope text proceeds to relate it explicitly to the specific theme of the feast.

Drawing our illustration once again from the feast of St. Stephen, we may cite as an example the Introit trope *Hodie Stephanus martyr* (Paris 1121, f. 5). The text of the Introit is italicized:

---

3 Of the Proper chants which are troped in Paris 1121, only the Introit *Gaudeamus omnes* for All Saints and for the Assumption and the Nativity of Our Lady, and the Offertory *Protege Domine* and the Communion *Crux Ihesu* for the Exaltation of the Holy Cross use texts which are not of Biblical origin. The sources of the remaining chant texts are as follows: from the Liturgical Psalter (that is, the Psalms and Canticles)—23; from the Old Testament, including the Apocrypha—10; from the New Testament —20.

4 Psalms will be cited throughout this study according to the numbering of the Vulgate.

Today Stephen the martyr went up into heaven; of him the prophet once said, lifting up his voice: *"Princes sat, and spoke against me,* the Jewish people rose up against me wickedly, *and the wicked persecuted me;* full of hate, they crushed me with stones: *help me, O Lord my God,* take up my soul in peace, *for thy servant was exercised in thy justifications."*

The "prophet" referred to is, of course, the psalmist David. Following an introduction which identifies the source of the text and announces the feast of the day, the words of the psalmist are amplified and turned into a direct speech of the protomartyr himself.

The New Testament furnishes an equally large number of the chant texts which have been embellished with tropes. Although among the Mass chants as a whole the Psalter is the primary source of texts, this frequent occurrence of New Testament texts in connection with the tropes need not surprise us. Tropes were written only for the major feasts of the Christian year, and it is for precisely these feasts, many of which commemorate the major events in the life of Christ and the early church, that New Testament texts would be most appropriate. The relationship of a trope to one of these New Testament chant texts will, of course, differ somewhat from that of a trope used with a general Psalter text, since the connection between the chant and its feast is already explicit.

For example, the Introit *Nunc scio* for the feast of St. Peter gives Peter's speech after the angel rescues him from Herod's prison (Acts 12:11):

Now I know in very deed that the Lord hath sent his Angel, and hath delivered me out of the hand of Herod and from all the expectation of the people of the Jews.

The trope *Divina beatus Petrus* gives the Biblical setting for this utterance and provides a devotional amplification (Paris 1121, f. 27):

Blessed Peter, delivered by divine mercy, coming to himself, said: *"Now I know in very deed that the Lord hath sent his Angel* and the light of his justice, by which he hath enlightened me, and led me out of the prison, *and delivered me out of the hand,* my Saviour, out of the hand of the cruel plunderer *Herod and from all the expectation* which had surrounded me in the wicked council *of the people of the Jews."*

Thus, the two trope texts just cited, although they embellish different types of chant text, arrive at much the same finished form. Both present a speech of the saint whose feast it is. In the case of Stephen, however, the speech is based on a psalm text, whereas Peter's speech is merely an amplification of his own words in the Biblical narrative.

This oratorical or narrative type of text is very common among the early tropes, and it will be seen that the dramatic elements which characterize such pieces as the *Quem queritis* and the later liturgical drama are already inherent here in an undeveloped form.[5] An even more striking example is the Epiphany trope *Ecclesiae sponsus* to the Introit *Ecce advenit* (Paris 1121, f. 9). A dramatic setting is given, and then the speech of the Magi proceeds to combine passages from the Gospel narrative (Matthew 2:1-2) with the Old Testament text of the Introit (Malachi 3):

Bridegroom of the Church, light of the Gentiles, consecrator of baptism, redeemer of the world! *Behold he comes,* Jesus, whom the Kings of the Gentiles seek in Jerusalem with mystical gifts, saying: "Where is he who is born *ruler and Lord?* We saw his star in the East, and we knew that the King of Kings was born, *and a kingdom is in his hand,* to whom alone is owed honor, glory, praise, and jubilation, *and power and dominion."*

In addition to these narrative texts, there are many trope texts more purely didactic in content. Thus, another Epiphany Introit

---

[5] This dramatic element can also be found in the official chant itself. Cf., for example, the Christmas Respond *Quem vidistis pastores dicite* (*Liber Responsorialis,* p. 58), etc.

trope, *Haec est praeclara dies* (Paris 1121, f. 8v), takes as its subject the three "miracles" which are traditionally associated with
the feast of the Epiphany and which were suggested in the opening epithets of the preceding trope: the adoration of the Magi
("light of the Gentiles"), the baptism of Jesus ("consecrator of
baptism"), and the marriage feast at Cana ("bridegroom of the
Church"). In this way, the significance of the day is made clear
to the faithful:

> This is the glorious day, made sacred by three miracles, on
> which we sing with the Prophet, saying: *Behold he comes,* he
> to whom the Magi today offer gifts, and, as King over all, they
> adore him who is everywhere *ruler and Lord.* Baptized by John
> in the Jordan, the Son is made manifest by the voice of the
> Father, whose honor *and kingdom is in his hand, and power.*
> Today he changed water into fine-tasting draughts by means of
> his power *and dominion.*

Another example of a didactic trope text is *Quia naturam nostrae
humanitatis,* for the feast of the Assumption of St. Mary (Paris 1121,
f. 35). Relating the events of the Assumption to the text of the
Introit *Gaudeamus omnes,* the trope becomes a popular commentary
on the doctrine of the incarnation:

> Because he united the substance of our humanity with the sub-
> stance of his divinity, *let us all rejoice in the Lord,* in whom the
> blessed Apostle instructed us to rejoice, *celebrating a festival day
> in honor of the Virgin Mary,* who today ascended into heaven,
> having defeated the prince of death; *for whose Assumption the
> Angels rejoice,* admiring that she bore God and man, *and give
> praise to the Son of God.*

Other trope texts are more purely devotional in their content,
presenting neither a specific narrative nor a doctrinal commentary.
Thus, the Introit trope *Mortificando sua propter te* for the feast of
SS. Philip and James (Paris 1121, f. 17) is a general meditation on
martyrdom, with no specific reference to the saints of the day.
The Introit is *Exclamaverunt ad te,* with text from 2 Esdras 9:27:

Having mortified their bodies for thee, the Saints *cried to thee, O Lord, in the time of their tribulation,* their enemies having struck them down, and the prince of the world having conquered; *and thou heardest them from heaven,* so that, sweetly resounding, they may sing to thee forever: *Alleluia, alleluia.*

Whatever the particular emphasis of the trope texts, however, their function is the same. They relate the text of the chant to the specific celebration of the day. Thus, even the trope for SS. Philip and James just quoted, although its content is quite general, specifically connects the text from 2 Esdras with the idea of Christian martyrdom.

In technique, too, these trope texts are similar to each other. Two distinct types of trope line are apparent in the preceding examples: 1. introductory tropes; and 2. intermediate or interpolated tropes.[6] The function of the introductory trope is seen most clearly in such examples as *Hodie Stephanus martyr, Divina beatus Petrus,* and *Haec est praeclara,* where the feast of the day and the source of the chant text are precisely indicated.[7] But even in an example like *Mortificando sua propter* the introductory nature of the first trope line is clear, since it supplies the subject ("Sancti") of the verb ("exclamaverunt") of the Introit.

It is probable that these introductory tropes represent the earliest form of troping and, as we have already suggested, that the idea of further embellishment by interpolation was introduced only later.[8] All the examples cited so far have been fully devel-

---

[6] The manuscripts consistently use the word "tropus" for each of the individual lines of a trope. Thus, in keeping with medieval usage, it would be more accurate to speak of an "Introit with tropes," each line being considered as a trope, rather than to say "a four-line Introit trope," as in current usage.

[7] See Stäblein, "Zum Verständnis des 'klassischen' Tropus," *Acta Musicologica,* XXXV (1963), 89, where he speaks of certain tropes resembling "rubrics set to music." However, I doubt that the tropes were quite as unselfconscious as Stäblein suggests, particularly when one considers the large number of tropes in classic hexameters.

[8] See above, pp. 20ff.

oped tropes with three or four trope lines functioning as introduction and as interpolation. But many tropes consist solely of a simple introduction. A few examples will make this introductory function clear.

The following trope, *Ecce dies adest,* introduces the Introit *Nunc scio* for the feast of St. Peter:[9]

> Behold, this is the day which is greatly exalted with the feast of the prince of the Apostles, on which, delivered from his prison by an Angel, coming to himself he said: *"Now I know in very deed that the Lord has sent his Angel. . . ."*

The trope *O dux Magorum* introduces the singing of the sequentia on the feast of the Epiphany (Paris 1121, f. 9v):

> O leader of the Magi! Praise, glory, and eternal joy be unto thee! Also let us all say indeed: *Alleluia.*

The trope *Sic ait en Xpistus* introduces the Communion *Mitte manum* for the first Sunday after Easter (Paris 1121, f. 17):

> Behold, Christ speaks thus, when Thomas doubts his wounds: *"Put in thy hand, and know the place of the nails. . . ."*

The most extended form of the introductory trope is found, of course, in such developed prefaces as the famous *Quem queritis in sepulchro* for the Easter Introit *Resurrexi.* The version here given is from Paris 1121, f. 11v:

> "Whom seek ye in the sepulchre, O Christians?"
> "Jesus of Nazareth, who was crucified, O heavenly ones."
> "He is not here, he has arisen, as he foretold. Go and announce that he has arisen."
> Alleluia.
> The Angel abiding at the sepulchre announces that Christ has arisen.
> Behold, that is fulfilled which he [said] of old by the Prophet, speaking thus to his Father:
> *"I arose and am still with thee. . . ."*

---

[9] The text is given here according to Paris 1118, f. 73. Paris 1121 has already expanded this to a three-line trope.

Many of these introductory tropes were later expanded. The trope *Ecce dies adest,* quoted above, occurs in tenth-century manuscripts as an introductory trope, but in Paris 1121, dating from the beginning of the eleventh century, internal tropes have been added, thus making a full three-line trope. Although the original introduction is in prose, the additional lines are hexameters. The full Latin text as found in Paris 1121, f. 26v, follows:

Ecce dies adest apostolorum principis festivitate valde sublimis,
qua ab angelo ereptus de carcere, ad se reversus, dixit: *"Nunc*
scio vere quia misit Dominus Angelum suum;

"Non tulit en Xpistus memet sub carcere tentum,
  "Et eripuit me de manu Herodis, et de omni exspectatione

"Infandi simul ac solvit formidine cuncta
  "Plebis Iudaeorum."

A similar example, the Introit trope *Iste puer magnus,* has already been cited in Chapter II.[10]

These, and numerous other examples, suggest two points about the amplification of the tropes. In the first place, the process of extending individual tropes was well under way in the tenth century. In the second place, the original medium of expression for the tropes was prose, and not classical poetic meters such as hexameters, despite the large bulk of hexameter texts in the finished trope repertory. Both of these statements require further discussion.

We have seen that the process of transforming introductory tropes into full tropes by the addition of intermediate lines existed in the tenth century. Can the evidence be pushed back any further than that? Paris 1240, from the beginning of the tenth century, is the earliest full troper we possess, and therefore direct comparisons cannot be made with other sources in order to find earlier forms of the tropes contained in it. Nevertheless, various pieces in this troper

---

10 See above, pp. 22-23. Sometimes one finds tropes in which an introductory hexameter is followed by prose interpolations, but they are scarce. See, for example, the Pentecost Offertory trope *Pangite iam,* Paris 1121, f. 24.

suggest that the process of amplification had indeed taken place in certain cases before the manuscript was compiled.

Thus, the Epiphany Introit trope *Descendens ab aetherei* combines a prose introduction with one internal trope in prose and two more in hexameters (Paris 1240, f. 21):

Descendens ab aetherei stellato sui solio regni, *Ecce advenit,*
Ut sedeat[11] domo David patris sui, *Dominator Dominus,*

Omnes ut populos societ sibi foedere firmo,
  Et regnum in manu eius,

Quod dabit ipse suis illicque erit hic et in ẹvum,
  Et potestas, et imperium.

Since the line "Ut sedeat" exists, in a varied form, as an introductory trope itself in Paris 1084, Paris 1118, Paris 1120, and other tropers, and as the first line of a two-line trope in Paris 1121, where the second line is an hexameter, it is quite possible that it is out of place in *Descendens ab aetherei* in Paris 1240. No subsequent version of the piece gives the line. If this were so, the picture of a prose introduction to which were added two hexameter interpolations would be even clearer.

Another example of what may have been an expanded introductory trope in Paris 1240 is the Introit trope *Hodie mundo festivus* (Paris 1240, f. 38). Here the opening and closing lines are in prose, the middle lines being hexameters:

Hodie mundo festivus illuxit dies Omnium Sanctorum, hodie martirum turba tripudiat in cẹlis, et nos in terris *Gaudeamus omnes in Domino,*

Consonet hore simul nostrorum flos meritorum,
  Diem festum celebrantes sub honore Sanctorum Omnium,

Aeterni socii fulgoris germinis alti,[12]
  De quorum solemnitate gaudent Angeli,

In qua hodie Omnium Sanctorum condignis laudibus veneramur,
Et collaudant filium Dei.

---

[11] MS reads "sedead."
[12] MS reads "altim."

The subsequent history of these lines is once again pertinent, since it clearly shows the interchangeability of internal trope lines and suggests once again the priority of the prose introduction. In almost all of the St. Martial tropers, lines 2 through 4 follow the introductory trope line *Eia plebs devota,* itself an hexameter. The introductory trope *Hodie mundo festiva* ("dies" now being treated as feminine) stands alone in Paris 1084, Paris 1118, Paris 903, and so forth, whereas it is completed with two different hexameter lines in the later manuscripts of the St. Martial group, Paris 1120, Paris 1121, the additional series of Paris 1084, and so forth.

Admittedly, the evidence presented by such examples is not conclusive, but it certainly suggests that the process of extending original introductory tropes by the addition of internal trope lines stretches well back before the date of Paris 1240 into the ninth century. This process could equally well have affected those tropes in Paris 1240 which are completely in prose or completely in hexameters, but evidence of this is now hidden from us.

These examples also support the second observation that we made above, concerning the priority of prose texts to poetic texts in the origin of troping. Admittedly, Paris 1240 contains a large number of hexameter trope lines, and no doubt a certain number of hexameter tropes were written from the first under the influence of the Carolingian poets. But it is equally true that the hexameter and other poetic forms became more prominent as the history of the trope unfolded.

Thus, those feasts which must have been among the first to be embellished with tropes often show a preponderance of prose texts. For example, in Paris 1240 all four of the Christmas tropes are in prose, and even in Paris 1121 six of the seven tropes for this feast have prose texts. Similarly, those feasts which are not troped in Paris 1240 and which must thus have been subjected to troping at a later date are frequently supplied almost exclusively with metrical tropes. Thus, for example, all the tropes in Paris 1121 for Tuesday and Wednesday in Easter week have hexameter texts. The tropes for the feast of St. Augustine are in hexameters and elegiac distichs, the latter form never occurring in Paris 1240.

The interpolated or internal trope lines vary considerably in style and form. They may be fairly extended, self-sufficient texts which "introduce" the various phrases of a chant. This is true, for example, of many of the tropes with hexameter texts. Or they may simply consist of a few words, carefully interpolated into the chant text and extending and enriching its meaning. Thus, the Purification trope *Adest alma virgo* (Paris 1121, f. 11) consists of five lines, if "line" is not too large a term for these simple verbal additions:

Here is the dear Virgin Mary, here is the Word made flesh, adoring whom all *we have received thy mercy, O God,* the eternal light, Christ the Lord, *in the midst of thy temple,* in the arms of St. Simeon; *according to thy name, O God, so also is thy praise,* glory, salvation, and honor *unto the ends of the earth;* in the fullness of grace, *thy right hand is full of justice.*

Whatever the form, the writers have exercised considerable ingenuity in incorporating their additions smoothly into the text of the chant. Their purpose, once again, is to amplify and to give a specific reference to the chant. Thus, in the example just cited, the internal trope lines clearly relate the Introit text from Psalm 47 to the Purification of St. Mary and Simeon's recognition of Christ as a "light" to the Gentiles.

Prose may well have been the original medium of the trope texts, but the classical quantitative measures soon played an important role and came to occupy a dominant position in the trope repertory. As we have seen, hexameter texts are already to be found in the earliest troper, Paris 1240, and by the time of Paris 1121, at the beginning of the eleventh century, well over half the tropes use hexameters entirely or in part.

We have already considered the texts in which prose and hexameters are mixed and have pointed to their possible significance in demonstrating the priority of the prose texts. But the vast majority of the poetic tropes consist entirely of hexameters. In these pieces, each phrase of the chant is usually introduced by a single hexameter line. In some cases, however, two hexameter lines may be used as an introduction, with the remaining lines being either single or double. Introductory tropes, too, often consist of hexameters. In all of these cases, a connective word or phrase may be added to the hexameter text in order to make a smooth juncture with the succeeding chant line. The following Introit trope for Pentecost, *Mystica paracliti virtutum* (Paris 1121, f. 23v), illustrates a number of these points:

> Mystica paracliti virtutum flamma choruscans,
> Ecce diem decorat celebrem, cui psallite laudes,
> Eia:
> > *Spiritus Domini,*
>
> Almi certe patris verbi quoque spiritus idem,
> > *Replevit orbem terrarum, alleluia,*
>
> Distribuens linguas Xpisti iunioribus omnes,
> > *Et hoc quod continet omnia,*
>
> Infera digniter et supera facta cuncta perhornans,
> > *Scientiam habet vocis;*
>
> Angelicis modulis promamus voce canora:
> > *Alleluia, alleluia, alleluia.*

This example also illustrates another fact about the hexameter trope texts. The hexameter is no longer a vital and living form for these anonymous monastic poets. The hexameter texts frequently represent a sterile and mechanical exercise in classical Latin versification, one which does not always avoid the schoolboy's errors. Thus, in the fourth interpolation of the preceding example, the quantities of the fourth foot do not constitute a dactyl, and the line can be scanned only by arbitrarily altering the syllable lengths:

$$\overset{\prime\,\cup\cup}{\text{Infera}} \mid \overset{\prime\,\cup\cup}{\text{digniter}} \mid \overset{\prime}{\text{et}} \| \overset{\cup\cup}{\text{supe}} \mid \overset{\cup}{\text{ra}} \overset{\prime\,\cup}{\text{facta}} \mid \overset{\prime}{\text{cuncta}} \overset{\cup}{\text{per}} \mid \overset{\prime\,\bar{}}{\text{hornans.}}$$

By far the majority of metrical trope texts consist of dactylic hexameters, but one other classical measure is occasionally found. This is the elegiac distich. The following example of this form is an Introit trope for the feast of St. Augustine (Paris 1121, f. 35v):

Sanctus Agustinum mundo quia rite beavit
  Spiritus eximium constituendo patrem,
    Statuit ei Dominum testamentum pacis,

Doctrine radiis perlustrans abdita mentis
  Cum dedit hunc orbis parmologum docili,
    Et principem fecit eum,

Turificando preces cedens redolere perhennes
  Vota Deum primo solvat et altithrono,
    Ut sit illi sacerdotii dignitas,

Nunc memorare tuae presul super aethera turme
  Quo valeat summo cantica fere Deo,
    In aeternum.

Leonine verses as such, that is, metrical lines with dissyllabic rhymes before the caesura and at the end of the line, do not occur in the St. Martial trope repertory. They apparently begin to appear in medieval poetry only during the eleventh century. However, we occasionally find an anticipation of them in the use of monosyllabic rhyme, as, for example, in the final distich and elsewhere in the preceding example:

Nunc memorare tuae presul super aethera turmae
  Quo valeat summo cantica fere Deo. . . .

Rhyme and assonance sometimes occur in connection with prose trope texts. The following is a Christmas Introit trope (Paris 1121, f. 3v):

Ad aeternae salutis gaudia
et nos salvandi gratia,
  Puer natus est nobis, et filius datus est nobis,
Rex lumen de lumine regnat in iustitia,
  Cuius imperium super humerum eius,
Qui caelestia
simul et terrestria
fundavit patris sapientia,
  Et vocabitur nomen eius:
Altissimi filius et
  Magni consilii Angelus.

Since this recurrence of terminal sounds is underlined musically, it is quite unlikely that the effect was accidental.

Assonance is found in the following prose introduction to the Easter sequentia (Paris 1121, f. 13v):

Xpistus surrexit ex mortu<u>is</u>,
mort<u>is</u> confract<u>is</u> vincul<u>is</u>;
gaudentes Angeli
vocem in alt<u>issimis</u>
proclamant, dicentes:
   Alleluia.

Rhyme, even of this primitive sort, is quite exceptional in the St. Martial repertory. But accentual verse is even rarer. This is all the more striking when we recall the frequent use of accentual texts at St. Gall.[13] Among the few examples in Paris 1121 is the following opening of an Introit trope for St. John the Evangelist in trochaic rhythm, and even here, the subsequent lines are in prose (Paris 1121, f. 6v):

Ecce iam Iohannis adest,
   veneranda gloria,
Cui Xpistus ampliora
   dona credens mistica,
     In medio Ecclesiae aperuit os eius. . . .

The primary literary influence on the trope writer was, of course, the Latin Bible. In addition to subject matter and vocabulary, the writer on occasion took whole sections of the Biblical text and adapted them to his purposes. We have already cited the Epiphany trope *Ecclesiae sponsus,* in which the account of the Magi given by St. Matthew is presented literally in the trope text.[14]

An even more striking example is the Introit trope *Ecce omnes redempti* for the first Sunday after Easter (Paris 1121, f. 16v). The Introit text, *Quasi modo geniti,* is drawn from 1 Peter 2 and

---

[13] See, for example, R. Weakland, "The Beginnings of Troping," *Musical Quarterly,* XLIV (1958), 485.

[14] See above, p. 58.

refers to the newly baptized, who are the special object of the Mass of this day. The following are the pertinent passages from the first Epistle of St. Peter (2:1ff.):

> Deponentes igitur omnem malitiam . . . sicut modo geniti infantes, rationabile, sine dolo lac concupiscite, ut in eo crescatis in salutem, si tamen gustastis quoniam dulcis est Dominus. Ad quem accedentes lapidum vivum. . . . Vos autem genus electum, regale sacerdotium, gens sancta, populus acquisitionis. . . .

The trope is constructed in the following way (note that the Introit is italicized, and direct quotations from the Epistle are enclosed in quotation marks):

> Ecce omnes redempti, "genus electum, regale sacerdotium, gens sancta, populus adquisitionis, deponentes omnem malitiam. *Quasi modo geniti infantes,"* alleluia, "si gustastis quoniam dulcis est Dominus, *rationabile sine dolo,* ut in eo crescatis in salutem, *lac concupiscite,"* alleluia. "Accedentes ad lapidem vivum," canite omnes: *Alleluia, alleluia.*

It will be seen that except for the opening "Ecce omnes redempti," the Alleluias, and the words "canite omnes," the whole text is derived from the Biblical passage. It is ironic to see the selectivity of the compiler of the chant text reversed by the ingenious exercises of the trope writer in extending the Biblical quotation.

Although the influence of the Vulgate is dominant, the other reading of the monkish poets — even including the pagan classics— has also left its mark. Thus, for example, the full version of the Introit trope *Iste puer magnus* for St. John the Baptist[15] contains the following hexameter line: "Parcere pacificis et debellare superbos." It has been adapted, with a slight Christian modification, from the following line of Virgil (*Aeneid* VI, 853): "Parcere subiectis et debellare superbos."

Let us summarize briefly. The function of a trope text is to introduce a liturgical text. In addition, the trope text may be ex-

---

[15] See above, p. 22.

tended to include interpolations within the liturgical text which
provide a didactic or devotional commentary on that text. In all
cases, the trope makes explicit the relationship between the Biblical
text of the chant and the events or doctrines commemorated by the
Mass formulary of a given feast day. Trope texts may be in the form
of either prose or poetry. Among the verse forms used, the quantitative dactylic hexameter predominates. Other quantitative verse
forms, such as the elegiac distich, as well as accentual verse, rhyme,
and assonance occur infrequently. The literary background of the
trope writer is typical of that of the learned monk of his age. Thus,
the Vulgate stands as the primary source of language and content,
but echoes of the pagan Latin classics are not lacking.

   Before turning to a consideration of the music itself, it might be
pertinent to say a word here about the relationship of these trope
texts to their musical setting. Although the great majority of poetic
trope texts are written in quantitative verse, that is, with the length
of syllable as the determining factor, the musical settings ignore
vowel quantity and rely only on the stress accent of each word as
the basic principle of text declamation. In addition, text elision
is ignored in the musical settings. There is thus no distinction in
style between settings of poetic and of prose texts. In this, the
trope is like the official chant, whose rare metrical texts are set
without regard for quantity.

   The Introit trope *Confligunt proceres Ihesus* for the feast of
St. Stephen (f. 6) is the one piece in Paris 1121 which makes anything like a systematized attempt to set a metrical text according
to quantity. The principle apparently involved is that of setting
the long syllable of a dactylic foot to three note-values and the
two short syllables to one and two note-values respectively, in
what might be considered an imagined 6/8 time:

Confli |gunt proce | res. . . .

But the example is unique, and even in this trope the principle is
applied so casually that the result may well be accidental.

There is perhaps one conclusion that we may draw from this apparent failure to distinguish between poetic and prose texts in the musical setting. It is unlikely that the functions of poet and composer were generally exercised by the same man, since the two were working according to completely different principles. The poet composed his hexameter trope texts according to quantity, while the trope singer handled all texts alike, whether poetry or prose, considering only the stress accent of the words in his musical settings.

CHAPTER V

THE MUSICAL STRUCTURE OF THE TROPES

In turning to the musical analysis of the tropes, it is important to emphasize that the music of the tropes represents a continuation of the central musical tradition of Gregorian chant composition. The tropes are written in the predominantly neumatic style characteristic of the antiphonal Mass chants that they embellish. Modal formulas are frequently used as the basis of melodic construction. Text declamation follows the principles of the chant itself. Insofar as innovations may be found, they primarily concern the overall formal construction of the pieces. In particular, the length and uniformity of the hexameter trope lines give a conciseness of phrase to the melodies, and frequently there is a sense of symmetrical organization controlling the relationship between the individual trope lines within the framework of the chant.

It is important to note in this connection that the individual trope lines are to a large extent brief, independent, self-sufficient musical compositions. It is perhaps simplest to think of them as small solo pieces introducing and interspersed within a choral Mass chant. Although in general the musical style harmonizes with that of the chant, and although the attempt is often made to adjust the opening and close of the trope line to the surrounding chant, the individual lines are usually musically complete within themselves and end with a true cadence.

It should also be pointed out at the outset that we are dealing with a body of music that was composed over a relatively long period of time. Thus, a complete uniformity of musical style can hardly be expected. The later a trope was composed, the further it will be from the composition of Gregorian chant as a living tradition, and the more likely it is to show traces of a developed, independent musical style. Paris 1240, which dates, as we have seen, from around 930, gives us our earliest control for determining the date of individual St. Martial tropes, but unfortunately even here we have no way to chart the considerable development which must have preceded this troper.

Let us now consider some of these points in more detail. Examples will be cited from Paris 1121 by their numbers in the transcription of the manuscript found on pages 127-251.

Melodic Style

The predominant melodic style of the tropes is neumatic. That is to say, the syllables of the text are generally set to composite neumes or groups of notes, rather than to single neumes (as in the prosae and prosulae) or to extended melismas (as in the elaborate responsorial chants of the Mass and Office). This is, of course, not altogether surprising, since the neumatic style is characteristic of precisely that Mass chant which was, in the early period, the principal object of troping, namely, the Introit antiphon.

The neumatic style of the tropes is not always as consistently maintained as that of the Introits, and we may thus find in a given trope both syllabic passages and elaborate melismas which would not be found in a typical Introit. In addition, there is a wider diversity throughout the trope repertory as a whole, as compared to the Introits, with examples ranging from the simple to the quite elaborate. This diversity may, incidentally, reflect a chronological stylistic development. Nonetheless, the basic melodic style of the tropes still closely resembles that of the Introits, and it is in relation to the latter that we may best study it. Furthermore, it is precisely this neumatic style which characterizes all the tropes, whether for the Introit itself or for such elaborate chants as the Offertory or some examples of the Agnus Dei.

As an illustration of the relationship between the style of the tropes and that of the Introit, we may look at the three Introit tropes for St. Stephen which occur in Paris 1240 as well as in Paris 1121. They are, with their numbers in the transcription of Paris 1121: *Hodie Stephanus martyr* (#11), *Salus martyrum* (#13), and *Clamat hians caelis* (#14). These tropes and their Introit *Etenim sederunt* show a marked similarity of melodic style. Thus, for example, the melodic writing of the Introit, in which equal prominence is given to single notes on the one hand and to groups of two, three, and four notes on the other, and in which the longest neumes contain only five or six notes, compares quite closely to that of the tropes *Hodie Stephanus martyr* and *Salus martyrum.* Only the trope *Clamat hians* is somewhat more ornate than its Introit, containing melismas of eleven and twelve notes and a relatively small percentage of single neumes.

These Stephen tropes are more or less typical examples of the trope-Introit neumatic style. Examples of the extremes can be found among the Introit tropes for Easter. The Introit itself, *Resurrexi,* is somewhat more ornate than the average Introit. Yet its tropes range in style from very simple to extremely elaborate. *En ego verus sol* (#54) is largely syllabic, and only three neumes contain more than three notes. The first line is especially close to the simple syllabic style of the Office antiphons. The opening phrase, "En ego verus sol," with six single notes forming a melodic line, is strikingly unlike the Introits, where six successive syllables would rarely be set to single notes, and where, when short syllabic sections do occur, the single notes would usually occur on the same pitch.[1]

At the other extreme we find a trope like *Factus homo de matre* (#56), which is characterized by the large number of extended melismas that it contains. There are four melismas of seven notes, one of eight, two of twelve, one of sixteen, and one of thirty-two. Unlike Introit melismas, these are not limited to the final cadences.

Occasionally one finds tropes which, although basically neumatic, contain an odd mixture of passages in syllabic and melismatic style. This type of writing is found, for example, in the third line of the Introit trope *Ecce veri luminis* (#62) for Easter Monday. The words "psallat unita cohors redemptus" have a setting which consists of a syllabic passage eight notes long, as well as a melisma on "-demp-" of eighteen notes.

These examples, then, indicate something of the variety found in the melodic writing of the tropes. However, the basic style of

---

[1] Cf. Apel, *Gregorian Chant,* p. 258.

the tropes remains neumatic and, in the vast majority of pieces, closely resembles that of the Introits. In other words, we find in the tropes a melodic style very similar to the style of those Gregorian chants which were intended to accompany an action and to serve as processional music.

This basic style is to be found not only in the Introit tropes but also in the tropes connected with other types of chant. Thus, for example, the Epiphany trope *O dux Magorum* (#39) for the purely melismatic sequentia is written in the normal neumatic style of the Introit tropes, resembling quite closely in this respect the Introit trope *Hodie Stephanus* mentioned earlier. So, too, the elaborate Christmas Offertory *Tui sunt caeli* is adorned with the very simple trope *Qui es sine principio* (#8).

The melodic writing of the Communion is very similar to that of the Introit, and it is thus not surprising to find that the Communion tropes are also written in the basic melodic style of the Introit tropes. The Epiphany Communion trope *Stella praevia reges* (#41) furnishes a good example of this relationship.

The Ordinary tropes, too, are largely neumatic, whether connected with a melismatic Agnus Dei, as in the case of the trope *Pro cunctis deductus* (#59), or with a simpler Gloria in excelsis, as in the case of the Gloria trope *Decus aeterni patris*.[2]

We have mentioned above that certain tropes are noteworthy for the simplicity of their melodic style, often coming close in this respect to the simple idiom of the Office antiphons. There is reason to believe that this type of piece represents the earliest style of trope composition, and that as the form evolved the trope melodies became more and more elaborate. Once again, Paris 1240 does not offer unequivocal evidence on this point, since more or less elaborate pieces can already be found side by side with the simplest in this troper.

Nevertheless, certain tropes of one or two lines in Paris 1240 are found again in later St. Martial tropers in an expanded form with additional lines. In these cases, it is possible to detect a stylistic evolution by comparing the melody of the original lines

---

[2] See below, p. 258.

with that of the lines which were added at a later time. Thus, for example, the Easter Introit trope *En ego verus sol* (#54), already mentioned, consists of only two lines in Paris 1240, namely, line 1, "En ego verus sol," and line 4, "Exurge gloria mea." These two lines are extremely simple in style. Lines 2 and 3, on the other hand, are found only in the later St. Martial tropers, and although they are still relatively simple, they are more elaborate than the original two lines, containing melismas on "-to-" in line 2 and on "est" in line 3.

An even more striking example is furnished by another Easter Introit trope, *Ego autem constitutus* (#53). Lines 2 through 4 of this trope occur in Paris 1240 as the continuation of the introductory trope *Quem queritis in sepulchro*. They are very simple; only two of their neumes have as many as four notes. In Paris 1121, and other later St. Martial manuscripts, these three lines are combined with a new introductory trope line which does not occur in Paris 1240, namely, "Ego autem constitutus." The style of this line is much more ornate than that of the subsequent three lines, containing very few single neumes and having, among the larger groups, one melisma of ten notes.

It thus seems probable that increasing ornateness was a characteristic of the developing trope style. We may rule out the possibility that the degree of elaboration was determined by the solemnity of a given feast, since the examples cited were written for use on Easter, the greatest feast of the Christian year. In fact, it is on the greatest feasts, that is, precisely those feasts which because of their importance were undoubtedly the first to be adorned with tropes, that the simple melodic style is apt to be found. Thus, it is difficult to avoid the conclusion that the degree of melodic ornateness was determined more by chronology than by the relative solemnity of the feast.

It should be noted parenthetically that the simplicity of the early trope style in no way supports the hypothesis that the tropes arose through a process of adding texts to preexisting melismas.[3]

---

[3] See, for example, Handschin, "Trope, Sequence, and Conductus," p. 128.

In the first example cited above, *En ego verus sol*, the first line as well as the fourth is written in syllabic style. It would be impossible to argue that melodic interpolations were made to *precede* the Introit itself, and that these then served as the basis for textual additions. Gratifying as it may be to the musician to see the birth of the trope as first of all a musical phenomenon, there is in reality no justification for the view.

Modal Character of the Tropes

The mode of the tropes is, of course, determined by the mode of the chants that they embellish. Since each trope line is attached directly to a chant in a specific mode, the music of the trope will necessarily be set within certain melodic limits. But in a more general way, too, the tropes reflect the modal characteristics of the chant.

The tropes for the Proper of the Mass in Paris 1121 may be divided as follows in terms of the mode of the chants to which they are attached:[4]

	Mode	Introit Tropes	Offertory Tropes	Communion Tropes	Total	
D	1	62	3	2	67	105
	2	32	4	2	38	
E	3	16	1	4	21	39
	4	12	5	1	18	
F	5	0	1	1	2	23
	6	14	4	3	21	
G	7	17	0	2	19	38
	8	10	7	2	19	
		163	25	17	205	

[4] This table includes the four Introit tropes for St. Andrew, which are missing in Paris 1121 and have been supplied from Paris 909. One Communion trope, *Sumitur en corpus*, is omitted because its mode is unknown.

These figures agree with the modal distribution of the Mass chants in only the most general way, being closest to that of the Introits, as we should expect. Dom Ferretti gives the following figures for the modes of the Mass chants in the early eleventh-century Gradual Einsiedeln 121, and these may serve as a basis for comparison:[5]

Mode		Introits		Offertories	Communions	
D	1	29	47	27	25	43
	2	18			18	
E	3	26	46	27	9	27
	4	20			18	
F	5	10	22	17	14	35
	6	12			21	
G	7	19	32	30	15	40
	8	13			25	
		147		101	145	

The reason for the lack of agreement between these two sets of figures is obvious. The chants used for troping are not just a representative selection of chants taken from the Gradual. They are, basically, the chants of the most solemn feasts of the church year. Furthermore, the figure is affected by the larger or smaller number of tropes composed for any given chant. Thus, for example, nearly half of the tropes in the second mode—namely, eighteen—are connected with the single Introit *Terribilis* for the feast of the Dedication of a Church.

Nevertheless, certain striking characteristics stand out concerning the modes of the tropes. The D mode is far and away the most important mode for trope composition. Of the total 205 tropes,

---

[5] Ferretti, *Esthétique Grégorienne*, Vol. I: p. 276 for the Introits and Communions, p. 195 for the Offertories.

105 or over half are in the first and second modes. At the same time, the F mode, particularly its authentic form, is relatively rare. The reasons for this, as we have seen, are purely fortuitous. Yet the dominance of the D mode is bound, to a certain extent, to influence the trope writer.

The Easter Offertory trope *Ab increpatione* (#58) offers an example of how this influence may work. The Offertory *Terra tremuit* is in the fourth mode, although the frequent cadences on d and a give a strong suggestion of the first.[6] This suggestion, however, is so readily accepted by the trope writer that his composition, removed from the framework of the chant, is indistinguishable from a regular first-mode trope. Thus, for example, the fifth leap d–a, which is characteristic of many tropes in the first mode, is used to open three of the four lines. A typical first-mode trope cadence is used to end lines 2 and 4. Compare, for example, the cadence on "Sanctorum surrexerunt" in line 2 with the cadence on "Apostolum dedit" in the first line of *Martialem per secla* (#139) for the first-mode Introit *Statuit ei*. The shape of the opening of line 3, "Quando venit iudicare" —a g f e g-a d—is frequently found in first-mode tropes: for example, at the opening of *Clamat hians caelis* (#14), or, without the final d, at the beginning of the second line, "Honestavit verbum," of *Quem prophetae cecinere* (#123). Thus, the melodic characteristics of the popular first mode are seen to extend to tropes adorning chants ending on other finals.[7]

---

[6] It should be noted that two melodic variants in the eleventh-century Aquitainian Gradual Paris 903 somewhat weaken the impression of the first mode given by the version in the modern Gradual (see *Paléographie Musicale*, XIII, 153): the final note on the opening word "Terra" is e, not f, and the "in" of "in iudicio" is set to f-a instead of to the d-a fifth leap of the modern version. Such variants are particularly significant for this study, since a manuscript like Paris 903 naturally lies closer to the chant tradition of St. Martial than does the modern Gradual.

[7] Bruno Stäblein, "Der 'alt-römische' Choral in Oberitalien und im deutschen Süden," *Musikforschung*, XIX (1966), 3–9, cites certain cases of incorrect modal relationship between trope and chant in various tropers from St. Gall and from northern Italy as possible evidence of the survival of Old Roman chant melodies in those areas.

This reference to the transference of modal patterns from one mode to another does, of course, imply that the tropes in a given mode normally do display characteristics of that mode. And this is indeed the case. A few examples should make this clear.

The Introits do not make an entirely satisfactory basis for comparison here, since they are characterized by strikingly few modal formulas. However, those formulas that do occur are found again with considerable frequency in the tropes of the modes concerned. Thus, for example, the familiar first-mode opening formula of a fifth leap d-a, found in such Introits as *Suscepimus, Gaudeamus omnes,* and *Statuit ei,* occurs again and again in the tropes of the first mode. A few examples will suffice: *Clamat hians caelis* (#14), *O nova res* (#42), *Martialis Dominum* (#145). The extended form d-a-b-a is found, for example, on the second "adest" in the first line of *Adest alma Virgo* (#45).

The common second-mode figure d-c-A-c-d, which is found, for example, at the opening of the Introit *Terribilis est* and, in the shortened form A-c-d, at the beginning of the Introit *Ecce advenit,* also occurs frequently in tropes of the second mode. Among the numerous examples are the opening of line 2 of *Filii carissimi* (#28), each of the three lines of *Descendens ab aetherei* (#37), and the end of the first and third lines of *Culmen apostolicum* (#214). The occurrence of this typical second-mode figure in *Filii carissimi* and other Introit tropes for the feast of the Holy Innocents is particularly interesting, since the Introit for that feast, *Ex ore infantium,* does not itself contain the figure. We may thus conclude that the modal characteristics of the tropes are not necessarily derived from the specific chant to which they are attached, but that there was a common melodic style for each of the various modes upon which the trope writer could draw regardless of the specific chant that he was embellishing.

We can learn something about this general melodic character of the modes from the Greek and Latin modal formulas found in the tonaria which often accompany the St. Martial tropers.[8] A com-

---

[8] See the transcription of the formulas from the tonarium of Paris 1121 on pp. 271-273 below.

parison of these with the trope melodies demonstrates even more
strikingly than did the Introits the strong modal characteristics of
the tropes.

Examples of the fifth leap which opens the Latin formula for
the first mode—Autentus Protus—have already been cited above.
In a more general way, the characteristic melodic descent through
the fifth a-d which is found in both the Greek and Latin formulas
occurs at the beginning of many first-mode trope lines. See, for
example, the opening of *Cantemus omnes* (#171).

The formulas of the second mode—Plaga Proti—show a less
striking outline than those of the first.[9] Yet even here, the formulas are often reflected in the melodic writing of second-mode
tropes. Thus, the "noeagis" formula and the setting of "similem
huic," with its resemblance to the second-mode psalm tone, form
important elements in the melodic line of many tropes. The Dedication Introit trope *Typica visione* (#83), for example, opens with
an elaboration of the "noeagis," and the melody of the second line
suggests the second-mode psalm tone. So, too, in the Introit trope
for St. Andrew, *Sanctorum collegia* (#211), the "noeagis" occurs
at the opening of line 2 on the word "Trinitatis," and the setting
of "climata" in the same line is similar to that of "similem huic"
in the modal formula.

The Greek formula of the third mode—Autentus Deuterus—
suggests the characteristic intonation of the Introit psalm tone of
that mode: g a-c′ c′. And it is from this psalm tone that the third-
mode tropes also derive their most striking modal characteristics.
We may cite, as one example among many, the opening of the
trope for St. Peter, *Divina beatus Petrus* (#131). The word
"Divina" is set to the intonation of the third-mode tone, "beatus
Petrus" corresponds to the standard differentia of the mode, and
"ereptus" brings the melodic line down to the low d of the modal

---

[9] It is interesting to note that the characteristic A—c—d of the second-
mode Introits discussed above does not occur in the modal formulas of
Paris 1121. However, its important modal significance was in time recognized, and we find that, in the tonarium of the twelfth-century troper of
Nevers, Paris n.a. 1235, the opening of the second-mode Latin formula has
become d-A for the first syllable instead of lone d as in Paris 1121.

formulas. The characteristic melodic movement e-d g, which connects the "noioeane" syllables to the following melisma, and which, combined with the psalmodic intonation g a-c' c', forms the striking opening formula of a third-mode Introit like *Confessio,* also occurs frequently in the tropes of this mode. As an example, we may cite the opening of another Introit trope for St. Peter, *Apostolorum principem* (#130).

The modal formulas of the fourth mode—Plaga Deuteri—do not show the striking characteristics of those of the preceding modes, and this melodic neutrality of the mode may help to account for those fourth-mode tropes, such as the *Ab increpatione* cited above,[10] which have the melodic character of other modes. Only occasionally, as in the openings of *Ego autem constitutus* (#53) and *Factus homo tua iussa* (#51), does one find a reminiscence of the "noeais" formula.

Only two tropes in Paris 1121 are in the fifth mode—Autentus Tritus—but even here we can see a strong connection with the modal formulas as well as with the intonation f a c' of the Introit psalm tone. The Epiphany Offertory trope *Regi Xpisto iam* (#40) is, in particular, closely related to the Latin formula of the tonarium. Thus, "Regi Xpisto," "quem adorant," and "cum propheta dicentes" are set to the melody of "Quinque prudentes" in the Latin formula. The descending leap c' g of the Greek formula is found in the trope at "psallite omnes."

The tropes of the sixth mode—Plaga Triti—also have a strong melodic relationship with the modal formulas. Thus, the "noeagis" formula occurs at the opening of *Ecce omnes redempti* (#70),[11] in an elaborated form in *Omnia concludens verbi* (#24), and in a simplified version in *In iubilo vocis* (#159). The simpler opening of the Latin formula is found, for example, at the beginning of *Cantica nunc reboent* (#162) and of *Sacro fonte pectoris* (#23).

---

[10] See p. 80.

[11] The opening of *Ecce omnes* on f reflects the version of the "noeagis" formula found in Paris 1240 and Paris 1084, which begins f–f–d–c–f on the syllable "no–."

In the seventh mode—Autentus Tetrardus—it is unusual to find
tropes opening with the modal formulas of the tonarium, since the
latter begin on the high d′, while tropes in all the modes begin as a
general rule on the finalis of the mode. However, in at least one
case in Paris 1121, *Ecce adest verbum* (#3), the opening phrase of
the trope reflects more or less faithfully the whole melodic line of
the Latin modal formula up to the melisma. Two other melodic
characteristics of the modal formulas are frequently found in the
seventh-mode tropes. These are: the fifth leap g-d′, both descending, as in the Latin modal formula at "spiritus," and ascending, as
in the opening of the Christmas Introit *Puer natus est;* and the
movement through the f triad just before the final cadence of the
melismas in the modal formulas. We find both of these, for example, in the Christmas trope *Deus pater filium* (#4), which opens
with the fifth leap g-d′ and moves through f a c at the word
"gratulanter." The g-d′ leap also occurs frequently in the elaborated form of the seventh-mode Introit psalm tone:
g-c′-b c′-d′ d′. Examples are found in such tropes as *Haec legio*
(#186), where the figure occurs at "duce" and "sponte subiit" in
the first line and at "A patre" in the opening of the second line;
and in the famous Christmas Introit trope *Quem queritis in presepe*
(#1), at "pastores" in the first phrase and at "infantem" in the
second.

The typical modal figures of the tropes of the eighth mode—
Plaga Tetrardi—seem to be derived from a number of sources. The
short "noeagis" formula, although its literal statement is rare in the
tropes, is found, for example, at the opening of the third line of
Mystica paracliti (#110) on the word "Distribuens." With the addition of an initial g, which thus makes it equivalent to the intonation of the eighth-mode tone of the antiphonal psalmody of the
Office, it occurs, for example, in the opening of the second line of
the same trope at the words "Almi certe patris verbi." The opening of the Latin modal formula "Octo sunt" is expanded to form
the melody of the words "de quo sacrosancta ita" in the opening
line of *Inclita refulget dies* (#108), and, in a shortened form, it
opens the trope *Promissionis suae memor* (#63). We thus find that

this characteristic turn to the f triad is as typical of the plagal as of the authentic form of the G mode.

But perhaps the most characteristic melodic figure of the eighth-mode tropes is the movement into the lower part of the modal range g-f-d-f-g. There are numerous examples of it in the tropes, such as the opening of *Paraclitus sanctus* (#109) and of *Inclita refulget dies* (#108). It will readily be seen that this figure, like the other characteristic figures of the G mode, is a literal transposition to the upper fourth of a melodic pattern which we have already met in the D mode.

Perhaps the closest parallel to this characteristic eighth-mode formula is to be found in one of the typical opening patterns of the Office antiphons in the eighth mode, recognized by Gevaert.[12] In fact, another excellent way of demonstrating the modal characteristics of the tropes is by comparing the openings of the trope lines with Gevaert's typical opening patterns for each mode. Once again, it becomes apparent that the melodies of the tropes conform quite closely to the requirements of each mode, and that characteristic modal patterns are found in the tropes whether or not those specific patterns are present in the chants which are being embellished.

We may continue to use the eighth mode to illustrate this point, taking as an example the Introit tropes for the feast of Pentecost. The openings of all but one of these tropes correspond to certain of the modal patterns given for the eighth mode by Gevaert. *Inclita refulget dies* (#108), *Paraclitus sanctus* (#109), *Sanctus en veniens* (#112), and *Psallite candidati* (#113) are all related to the opening pattern already mentioned, that is, to Gevaert's Type No. 15, *Rex pacificus*—g f-d f f-a a.[13] *Mystica paracliti* (#110) is related to Gevaert's Type No. 13, *Magnus Dominus*—f-g g a g g-f.[14] Only the opening of *Discipulis flammas* (#111) is apparently de-

---

[12] F. A. Gevaert, *La Mélopée antique dans le chant de l'Église latine,* Ghent, 1895, pp. 227ff. See, in particular, Gevaert's Type No. 15, p. 277.

[13] *Ibid.,* p. 277.

[14] *Ibid.,* p. 271. Cf. esp. the opening of *Domine iste* on p. 272.

rived directly from the Introit *Spiritus Dominus* itself and not from one of the opening patterns.

The same patterns also occur in tropes connected with other eighth-mode chants. Gevaert's No. 15, for example, is found again in *Integra cum pareres* (#47), a verse trope for the Offertory *Diffusa est;* in *Iam celebranda dies* (#64), for the Introit *Introduxit vos;* and in *Et ecce terre* (#65), for the Offertory *Angelus Domini.*

The preceding discussion of the modal characteristics of the trope melodies is indeed not exhaustive. It is to be hoped, however, that the comparisons made between the tropes on the one hand, and the modal formulas of the tonarium, the Introit antiphons, the psalm tones, and the opening patterns of the Office antiphons on the other, will have demonstrated clearly enough that the tropes display the modal characteristics of each of the modes in much the same way as do the official chants to which they are joined. In other words, from a modal point of view, the same general melodic style characterizes both the chant and the tropes, and it is this general modal style, rather than quotations from the specific chant with which a given trope is connected, that normally controls the melodic writing of the individual tropes.

This is not to say that direct quotation of the chant never occurs. It certainly does, and some striking examples of this borrowing will be discussed below. Nor should one assume that the melodic idiom of one mode never exerts an influence on another mode. We have already seen a trope typical of the D mode attached to a chant in the E mode.[15] Furthermore, specific melodic patterns of the authentic form of a mode often find their way into pieces in the plagal form, and vice versa. Transpositions of this sort are particularly common in the D mode. See, for example, the first-mode trope *Martialem per secla* (#139), which opens with the characteristic second-mode descent into the plagal range: d-c-A-c-d. But even this sort of transference is not unknown in the Introit antiphons themselves. Compare, for example, the

---

[15] See p. 80.

first-mode Introit *De ventre matris,* where, on the word "quasi" in the final phrase, a similar use of the plagal range occurs. In other words, even the modal aberrations of the trope melodies find some precedent in the chant.

It is, of course, quite likely that a greater degree of modal license was tolerated in the music of the tropes than in the official chant. Yet it is difficult to determine the precise extent of this. Take, for example, the question of range. The trope *Martialem per secla* cited above combines the range of the authentic and plagal D modes, and consequently there results a melody which extends from A to e', or a twelfth. There are many similar examples in Paris 1121. Such an extended range is, of course, quite unusual for the Introits themselves—the Introit which is troped by this example, *Statuit ei* for the feast of St. Martial, has a range of only one octave. However, the range is not excessive when we compare it with that of some of the Offertories and their verses.[16] Nevertheless, there is an important distinction even here. Whereas the large range of the Offertories results from combining the varying ranges of the Offertory and its verses, in the tropes this extended ambitus can often be found in a single line. In the Offertory trope *Martialem Dominus roborat* (#155), for example, the range of the third line alone is an eleventh, extending from A to d'.

It is perhaps reasonable to conclude that the modal characteristics of the tropes, like their melodic style, have as their norm the antiphonal psalmody of the Mass, primarily the Introit. However, in both cases, the music of the tropes displays a greater degree of freedom than is found in the official chant. This may be due to the cross-influence of other forms of chant—for example, the Offertory, which is also elaborated by tropes. Or, more probably, the freer style represents a later stage in the evolution of chant composition. It is interesting to note, in this connection, that most of the tropes with extended ambitus do not occur in Paris 1240 and may thus be considered as relatively late additions to the trope repertory.

---

[16] See Apel, *Gregorian Chant,* pp. 150–151.

One further aspect of mode should be considered here, namely, the question of modal terminations. In dealing with the music of the tropes, we must constantly keep in mind the fact that the tropes are not complete compositions in themselves. They must always be considered within the framework of the chants to which they are related as introductions and interpolations. Thus, the question of the modal finalis does not directly concern the tropes as such, since the finalis of the total composition of trope plus chant will belong to the chant itself.

Cadences, however, do play an important structural role in the music of the tropes, and these, in general, follow the modal principles of the chant itself. Thus, for example, in the first mode, the trope cadences fall primarily on the first, fifth, and third degrees of the mode—d, a, and f—in that order. There may also be preparatory, or half, cadences on c, e, and g. In this, they follow the general arrangement of chants in the same mode. Thus, the first-mode Introit *Etenim sederunt* has four cadences on d, two on a, and one each on f and g.

Relationship of Trope to Chant

All of the preceding discussion in this chapter has, in a general way, dealt with the basic problem of the relationship of the music of the tropes to that of the chant. We have concluded that, in terms of the melodic style and the modal characteristics of the tropes, their music follows the same general compositional principles as those which govern the chant itself. We must now look more closely at the specific relationships and connections which tie the lines of an individual trope to the chant upon which it is based.

Although the trope and the chant are composed in the same general melodic idiom, the two stand apart to a certain extent as separate entities. A trope consists of one or more individual lines which serve as introduction to or interpolation within a given chant, but which still in the majority of cases retain their identity as self-contained musical phrases. The text of the individual trope line frequently contains a complete, if parenthetical, idea, and this is set to a musical phrase which has a distinctive opening and a proper cadence at its close.[17]   In general, these trope phrases are placed between two comparable phrases of the chant, that is, at a logical break in the chant rather than somewhere in the middle of a given chant line. In other words, we may think of a trope as consisting of a group of trope lines intercalated between the phrases of an official chant, rather than as an organic internal extension or amplification of the text and music of the chant. And indeed, the contrast between these alternating lines of trope and chant would have been underlined in the performance itself, where the tropes were probably performed by soloists, the chant itself by the choir.[18]

This principle of alternation can be seen clearly in an example like the Easter Introit trope *Factus homo tua iussa* (#51). The Introit *Resurrexi* divides itself into three phrases of more or less equal length, each ending with the word "alleluia." These phrases begin at the words "Resurrexi," "posuisti," and "mirabilis," respectively. The trope *Factus homo tua iussa* contains three lines which are approximately the same length as the phrases of the Introit. Each of these lines ends with a cadence on e, the finalis of the mode. In the finished compositon, these two groups of self-sufficient musical phrases are combined, with a line of trope preceding each phrase of the chant.

Once we have observed this relative structural independence of trope and chant, however, it must be stated again that the individual trope lines were never intended to stand by themselves. They were conceived as additions to the chant, and thus as parts of a larger whole, and it is within this framework that we must study them.

---

[17] There are, of course, certain exceptions to this generalization. See, for example, the fourth line of the Christmas Offertory trope *Qui es sine principio* (#8), in which the text consists of the single word "Praeparatio" and thus anticipates the first word of the following chant. Even here, however, the interpolation occurs at a logical break between two phrases of the chant.

[18] See above, p. 32.

In what way, then, are the alternating phrases of trope and chant joined together, and to what extent is the melody of the individual trope line adjusted to make a smooth connection with the phrases of chant which precede and follow it? There are various techniques for making this connection.

In some cases, indeed, very little adjustment is made, and the relative independence of the trope lines which we have just been discussing is enhanced rather than minimized. Thus, in the trope just cited, *Factus homo tua iussa* (#51), each line is brought to a cadence on the finalis e, even though the phrases of the chant begin respectively on d, f, and c. In the case of the second chant phrase, beginning at "posuisti," the f opening is, in fact, prepared within the chant itself by the final e of the preceding "alleluia." Trope line 2, then, with its cadence on e, is in accord with this melodic connection of the chant. But the c of the third phrase of the chant, beginning at "mirabilis," is approached from f in the chant, while trope line 3, which introduces this phrase, still comes to a cadence on e. Furthermore, the first phrase of the chant, beginning on d, is prepared by a psalm tone differentia ending on f when it is repeated after the psalm verses, according to the tonarium of Paris 1121 (f. 204),[19] but once again the introductory trope line ends with a cadence on e.[20]

It will be seen that this technique of bringing a line of trope to a cadence on the finalis of the mode, regardless of the immediate melodic demands of the chant, gives a certain degree of autonomy to the melodic components of the trope. And this, in turn, may help to account for the occasional occurrence of a trope line which is displaced from its normal position within a given chant. How-

---

[19] F is also the differentia ending in Paris 1240, although it should be noted that in two manuscripts of the non-St. Martial group—Paris 1118 and Paris 903—the differentia is terminated on e.

[20] The trope *Factus homo tua iussa* is, of course, intended for one of the repetitions of the Introit antiphon.

ever, this apparent disregard for the melodic connection of trope and chant is not common, and even in the cases where it occurs, it is possible that the medieval composer found an adequate preparation for the chant phrase in the finalis-cadence of the trope.

A second technique for joining trope and chant, which is found more frequently than the preceding method, certainly takes into consideration the specific pitches of the chant at the point where the trope interpolations are to be made. Its basic principle is, in fact, to make a unison pitch connection, at the beginning and end of a given trope line, with the portions of the chant which precede and follow it.

This principle is found, for example, in the third line of the trope *Fons et origo* (#21) to the Introit *In medio ecclesiae* for the feast of St. John the Evangelist. This line, "Virginitatis quoque," is inserted in the chant between the second phrase, ending with the word "intellectus," and the third, beginning with the word "stolam." The melodic connection in the chant moves from the final c of the second phrase to the opening f of the third. This connection is reflected in the melody of the interpolated trope line, which begins on c at the unison with the preceding chant phrase, and ends with a cadence on f in a unison anticipation of the following phrase.

Another technique which is often employed makes the closest possible fusion between trope and chant. In this method, the melody of a trope line is brought to a close with a literal quotation of the conclusion of the preceding chant line, so that the melodic connection between the trope and the chant phrase which follows will be identical to that between the two phrases of chant when no trope is present. An example will make this relationship clear.

In the trope *Pangite iam socii* (#116) for the Pentecost Offertory *Confirma hoc,* lines 2 to 4 all end with brief quotations from the chant. Thus, line 2 closes with the word "Spiritus" set to the melody of the word "Deus" at the end of the preceding line

of chant.[21] The melody of the last two syllables of "hominibus"
in line 3 of the trope agrees with that of the conclusion of "Ieru-
salem" in the chant, and the melody of "canendo" in the fourth
trope line equals the last two syllables of "munera" in the chant.[22]

It is quite possible that this principle of direct chant quotation
is a relatively late development in the history of the trope. The
manuscripts give a few hints that this is the case. Thus, for example, a comparison of the Epiphany Introit trope *Adveniente Xpisto*
(#36) as it occurs in Paris 1240 and in Paris 1121 shows that while
the later troper quotes the chant at the end of each trope line, the
earlier one does not. For instance, in Paris 1121 the setting of
"sui" at the end of line 2 agrees with the melody of the last two
syllables of "Dominus" in the Introit *Ecce advenit,* whereas Paris
1240 comes to a simple cadence at this point: d-e-e-d d. Paris
1121 goes even one step further and applies what might almost be
considered an extension of the "quotation" principle to the opening trope line by setting the word "quia" to a slightly varied form

---

[21] The melodic correspondence between trope and chant is even more
marked if, in place of the version in the modern Gradual, we use the version of the Offertory contained in chant manuscripts close to the St. Martial
tradition, such as the St. Yrieix Gradual, *Paléographie Musicale*, XIII, 183,
where the first syllable of "Deus" is set to f instead of e.

[22] Again, slight variations are to be found between the version in Paris
1121 and the modern Gradual. It is interesting to note that in a later Aquitainian troper, Paris n.a. 1871, probably from Moissac, the trope melody
agrees exactly with the Gradual version. This suggests one of two possibili-
ties. Perhaps the trope melody in Paris 1121 reflects a particular local version
of the Offertory melody as preserved at St. Martial. It is also possbile that
originally the trope composer was only interested in achieving a general
similarity to the chant, but that in time this version came to be altered so as
to agree literally with the chant. In either case, the principle of utilizing the
chant cadence in order to make a smooth connection between trope and
chant remains constant.

of the second-mode "noeagis" formula of the tonarium.[23]   Paris 1240 simply uses a melisma with the following probable pitches: a-g-f-e-d-c-e-f-e d.

The version of *Adveniente Xpisto* in Paris 1121 illustrates two other points about the use of the "quotation" principle in connecting trope and chant. In the first place, as we have seen, the principle may be extended to the first line of the trope, in this case by the use of a modal formula appropriate to the opening of the chant. In the second place, the chant quotation may be utilized in one of two ways in the trope: it can either 1. be incorporated directly into the body of the trope line, as at "sui" in line 2 and at "aeternum" in line 3, where the cadence of the chant becomes the cadence of the trope line; or 2. be used as an added connective which stands outside of the basic melodic and textual organization of the trope line, as at "quia" in line 1. Let us consider these points in more detail.

The literal use of a modal formula to conclude the opening line of a trope is quite rare. More characteristic are those examples in which the connection between trope and chant is made by quoting the differentia of the appropriate psalm tone at the end of the first

---

[23] This use of a modal formula would reflect its possible function as an intonation to the singing of a given chant. The comparable use of psalm tone differentiae is discussed below, p. 94.   On the relationship of the Byzantine formulas to the differentiae of the Gregorian psalm tones, see Oliver Strunk, "Intonations and Signatures of the Byzantine Modes," *Musical Quarterly*, XXXI (1945), 339ff., especially pp. 354–355. For a further discussion of the Byzantine formulas and their relationship to the Western ones, see also Professor Strunk's articles "Influsso del canto liturgico orientale su quello della chiesa occidentale," *L'enciclica "Musicae sacrae disciplina." Testo e commento*, Rome, 1957, pp. 343–348, and "The Antiphons of the Oktoechos," *Journal of the American Musicological Society*, XIII (1960), 50–67; and Jørgen Raasted, *Intonation Formulas and Modal Signatures in Byzantine Musical Manuscripts*, Copenhagen, 1966.

trope line. In this way, the organic connection of the chant itself, in which each statement of an Introit antiphon except for the first is preceded by the differentia of its psalm tone, is strikingly maintained. As an example of this type of connection, we may cite the trope *Inclita refulget dies* (#108) for the Pentecost Introit *Spiritus Domini replevit.* The setting of "prophetia" at the close of the first line corresponds in general to the eighth-mode psalm tone conclusion, and the final syllable "-a" uses the striking melody of the last syllable of the differentia, that is, precisely that melody which normally introduces the restatement of the Introit *Spiritus Domini:* g-a-d-f-f-g. By this means, then, the "quotation" principle, which allows for the closest possible connection between trope and chant, can be applied to an introductory trope line as well as to the internal trope lines, where its use would appear far more obvious.

In the example just cited, the melody of the differentia is made an essential part of the trope melody. However, as we have seen above, it is possible to use such a connective in a much less organic way. In *Adveniente Xpisto,* the text and music of the first line come to a full close on "baptizatus est," with a cadence on the finalis d. But instead of moving directly from this cadence to the opening of the Introit, the connective "quia" is added to introduce the Introit text "Ecce advenit...." This grammatical function is reflected in the melody, which, as we have seen, is that of the "noeagis" formula and prepares for the opening of the Introit. Thus, the chant is introduced by a word and a melody which stand outside the basic structure of the trope.

Examples of this type of connection, which might aptly be called the "quia" technique, are not unduly common, but they do occur on occasion, particularly in association with a connective like "quia" or with some other word which does not form an integral part of the trope text. In the Introit trope *Mystica paracliti* (#110) for Pentecost, the ubiquitous and conveniently vague "eia" at the end of the first line fulfills much the same function. The trope melody comes to a proper cadence on "laudes," and its melodic extension at "eia," resembling as it does the eighth-mode differentia, makes a most appropriate introduction for the Introit.

The technique of terminal quotation is not limited to the cadences of the chant. On occasion, these chant quotations may be
more extensive. So, for example, in the Introit trope *Ecce veri
luminis* (#62) for Feria II in Easter week, the melody for "-miter
teneatis" in line 2 is identical to the melody of "et mel alleluia"
in the Introit *Introduxit,* and "quia mundus" in line 3 of the trope
equals "in ore vestro" in the chant.

All of the examples of quotation which we have been considering are concerned with the conclusion of a trope line, not its opening, and this fact is particularly significant in any attempt to
understand the basic creative approach of the trope composers.
For them, the really critical point of juncture between trope and
chant came at the end of a given trope line, and their primary concern was to make a smooth connection between the ending of the
trope line and the succeeding line of chant. In other words, the
law of melodic accommodation enunciated by Peter Wagner, according to which the ending of a chant is adapted to fit the chant
which follows, is as important for the tropes as for the chant
itself.[24] The concern for preparing and introducing a chant, which
one sees, for example, in the differentia principle of the psalm
tones, occurs again in the composition of the tropes, not only in
those cases where the differentia itself is quoted, but also, in a
more general way, wherever a trope line utilizes a fragment of
chant or an adaptation of it to prepare the following chant.

This is not to say that the trope composers never used the principle of chant quotation as a connective at the beginning of a trope
line. In the Easter Introit trope *Factus homo de matre* (#56), for
example, the words "Clara dedit" at the beginning of the third
trope line are set to a melody which reflects, in a general way, the
melodic outline of "Mirabilis" at the opening of the following
phrase of chant. In other words, the trope uses the chant melody
which normally occurs at that point in the chant itself. In this

---

[24] Peter Wagner, *Einführung in die gregorianischen Melodien,* Vol. III,
Gregorianische Formenlehre, Leipzig, 1921, especially pp. 78 and 129ff.

way, the same close, organic connection between trope and chant
which we have observed at the end of trope lines is used to join
the opening of a trope line to the chant it follows. But such examples are not common, and the main emphasis remains on the connection at the end of the trope line. This, after all, should not be
surprising when we recall the original introductory function of the
trope. Since the trope composer probably thought of the individual trope lines as introducing the phrases of chant which followed,
rather than as extensions of the chant phrases which preceded, his
primary concern would necessarily be with connecting the end of
the trope and the beginning of the chant.

This emphasis on the terminal connection of the trope is inten-
sified by an interesting and unusual notational practice found in
Paris 1120. Liquescent neumes, which were used to facilitate the
singing of certain combinations of letters within a word or between
two words, never occur for a final sound. Thus, their occasional
use at the *end* of trope lines in Paris 1120 clearly reveals an inten-
tion to establish an organic connection with the chant which
follows.

One sometimes finds in the tropes a more pervasive use of the
melodic material of the chant than the simple quotation of a chant
fragment at the end of a trope line. However, the one technique is
merely an extension of the other. Thus, for example, in the Pentecost Introit trope *Paraclitus sanctus* (#109) the melody of the second line, "Inmensus et aeternus," suggests the melody of the whole
preceding chant phrase, "Spiritus Domini," a parallel which is even
closer in the version of Paris 1118, where the trope line opens with
d f-g̈ g on the word "Inmensus." In line 3, the setting of "Glori-
am" reflects the f triad of "Replevit" in the chant, and the cadence
on "beatis" in the trope is similar to that on "alleluia" in the chant.
Similarly, in another Introit trope for Pentecost, *Sanctus en
veniens* (#112), the third line, "Pectora confirmat," outlines the
melody of the preceding phrase of chant at the beginning and end,
but with a free development inbetween. Thus, "Pectora" in the
trope suggests the melody of "Et hoc" in the chant, and "clausa
relaxans" that of "omnia."

In another example, the Introit trope *Divina beatus Petrus*
(#131) for the feast of St. Peter, the whole third line is apparently
derived from melodic fragments of the preceding phrase of chant.
Thus, the melody of "de manu" in the Introit occurs again at "Sal-
vator" and "de manu" in the trope, and "cruentis predonis" in the
trope is set to the melody of "eripuit" in the chant.

However, there are few such examples, and the rather vague relationship between trope melody and chant melody often suggests
that both may simply be drawing on a common stock of modal
figures and that they consequently give the impression of direct
quotation almost by accident. On the whole, the melody of the
trope remains independent of that of the chant, except for the
above-mentioned direct use of chant cadences for the purpose of
making a smooth connection between trope and chant.

Most of the chant quotations which we have been discussing
have been more or less literal statements of the chant melody.
However, as we have seen, this need not be the case, and certain
other examples which we have cited have made a smooth connection between trope and chant simply by preserving the broad outline of a chant segment in the melody of the trope. Simplifying
this process still further, we find numerous trope lines which preserve merely the final pitch of the preceding chant without using
its precise cadential figure. This method of connection may also
be used at the opening of a trope line, which must thus begin on
the opening pitch of the following phrase of chant. By this technique, in other words, the precise pitch relationship between two
phrases of chant is maintained by the trope line which is interpolated between them.

A trope for Feria IV after Easter offers an example of this type
of connection in its most consistent form. For the trope *Iam
philomelinis* (#68), the Introit *Venite benedicti* is divided into
four phrases:

1. Venite benedicti patris mei,
2. Percipite regnum, alleluia,
3. Quod vobis paratum est ab origine mundi,
4. Alleluia, alleluia, alleluia.

The opening and closing pitches of each phrase, together with the pitch relationship of each successive phrase, may be indicated schematically as follows:

1st Phrase 2nd Phrase 3rd Phrase   4th Phrase

g---------f/ /a---------g/   /g--------d'/   /d'--------g

The precise pitch relationship between the first two phrases of the chant, that is, the melodic movement from f to a, is maintained at both ends of the trope line "Obsequiis michi," which is inserted between them. This is accomplished by beginning the trope line on a and ending it on f. The following relationship is thus achieved:

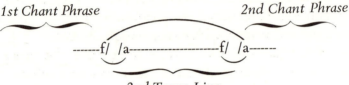

1st Chant Phrase   *2nd Chant Phrase*

------f/ /a---------------------f/ /a------

2nd Trope Line

In a more direct way, the unison pitch connection between chant phrases 2 and 3 is maintained by the third trope line, "Nullius auris," which begins and ends on g. Similarly, chant phrases 3 and 4 are connected by the fourth trope line, "Aethereis retonantes," which begins and ends on d'.

In this way, then, an extremely smooth and natural connection between trope and chant is accomplished by the simplest possible means. By the choice of the pitches which open or close a trope line, it is possible to duplicate the pitch relationships which connect the chant phrases themselves.

One further technique of joining trope and chant may be considered here. It is still possible to make a smooth fusion of the melodic elements of trope and chant even while avoiding literal quotation or exact pitch duplication of the chant, simply by maintaining the general pitch level of the chant in the melody of the trope line. Thus, for example, in the first-mode Introit *Suscepimus* for the feast of the Purification of St. Mary, there is a unison pitch connection on f between "templi tui" and "secundum nomen." In the trope *Adest alma Virgo* (#45), the third line, "In brachiis Sancti

Symeonis," which is interpolated between these two phrases of the chant, does not make use of this f as either an opening or a final pitch, nor is its cadence on the modal finalis d. Instead, it maintains the general pitch level of this section of the chant by moving around f, although it actually opens on g and makes a cadence on e.

This emphasis on a specific range in a chant can also be utilized, in a more general way, along with the various specific techniques of connection which we have already discussed. The Introit tropes for the feast of St. Stephen give a good example of this. The first-mode Introit *Etenim sederunt* remains basically in the lower fifth of its range, d-a, with its primary cadences on the finalis d, until the words "Deus meus," at which point the melody leaps to the high c' with a cadence on a. From "quia servus" on, the melody once again descends gradually through the lower range to the final cadence on d. This melodic shape is invariably represented in the tropes which embellish this Introit. Thus, the opening trope lines move in the lower part of the range, as does the chant itself. But in the final trope line, which comes between "Deus meus" and "quia servus," the melodic high point of the chant is reflected in all but one of the tropes by a movement through the upper part of the range to the high c', even when, as in *Qui primus meruit* (#15), the final trope line itself opens on a low d. In at least one case, *Salus martyrum* (#13), the high pitch level is maintained throughout the final line, which begins and closes on a and moves primarily in the upper fourth of the first-mode range. In another case, *Eia conlevitae* (#12), the cadence of the chant at "meus" is quoted literally in the final line of the trope at "meum." In *Clamat hians caelis* (#14) alone, the final line does not reach the high c'. In this case, however, a tight connection is still maintained with the chant by opening on a and closing on f, that is, by leaving and approaching the chant at the unison.

It has been convenient to discuss each of the various techniques for joining trope to chant as separate, isolated procedures. However, in actual practice, as the Stephen tropes just cited amply demonstrate, any given method is rarely employed consistently throughout the length of any individual trope. Only in the case of

direct quotation of chant cadences at the end of trope lines is one
apt to find a single principle used in each line of a trope, although
even here many individual examples do not use this technique in
every line. Otherwise, the usual method is to employ a combination of various techniques which are suitable for a given trope, or
even, on occasion, to use none at all. In mentioning the latter
case, I do not intend to imply that the composer was oblivious to
the need to make a smooth connection between his trope and the
chant. Rather, he was probably working according to some general
principle of modal propriety which would be difficult for us to
catalogue with precision. What we doubtless see in these cases,
once again, is Wagner's law of melodic accommodation at work.
We have here a situation somewhat like that in the psalm tones,
where a specific antiphon opening is prepared by an appropriate
differentia, even though the connection may not appear logical
to us. In the tropes, too, a given pitch may have been considered
as an adequate preparation for the opening of a chant phrase, even
when this preparation does not utilize one of the more easily recognized techniques of connection.

In order to illustrate this, and to show more clearly the manner
in which the various connective techniques are applied in practice,
it might be helpful to examine a relatively homogeneous group of
tropes and study the actual principles at work in the joining of
trope to chant. For this purpose, the Introit tropes in the sixth
mode will be useful, since they are unified by their modal assign-
ment and form a group small enough to be treated conveniently.
This group includes the Introit tropes for the feasts of St. John
the Evangelist, St. Benedict, and the Octave of Easter, a total of
fourteen tropes.

The tropes of the Introit *In medio Ecclesiae* for the feast of St.
John the Evangelist present a rather consistent picture. There are
five tropes (#20 to #24), all but one consisting of three lines which
precede, in each case, the chant phrases beginning "In medio," "Et
implevit," and "Stolam." *Omnia concludens verbi* (#24), which in
Paris 1240 is a one-line preface trope, consists in Paris 1121 of two
lines, the second line occurring before "Stolam." Of the total of
fourteen lines, all but one closes with a cadence on the finalis f,

regardless of the following chant pitch. However, other principles
are also at work here besides the general suitability of a cadence
on the modal finalis. Thus, although the chant opens on d at "In
medio," the preparation from f is completely natural, reflecting as
it does the preparation of the Introit by the final f of the psalm
tone differentia. In lines 2 and 3, the chant phrases that follow
the trope lines open on f, and therefore the finalis cadences of the
trope make a simple unison connection with the chant.

In the one case in which a trope line does not end on f, namely,
the third line of *Ecce iam Iohannis* (#20), another principle is at
work. The cadence on d duplicates the final pitch of the preceding
chant line,[25] and thus the chant phrase "Stolam" is approached
from the same pitch as it is in the chant itself.

This careful attention to the appropriate conclusion of a trope
line is typical of the tropes as a whole. On the other hand, the
opening of a trope line is treated in a much freer manner. In the
total of nine first and second lines in the tropes for St. John, seven
begin on the modal finalis. The procedure in these seven cases is
quite understandable. The beginning on f is entirely appropriate
for the opening lines, which thus immediately indicate the mode
of the trope and chant. It is equally suitable for the second lines,
since the connection of the chant itself between "os eius" and "et
implevit" is a unison on f. However, in the other two cases, the
trope line opens on a neighboring tone to the finalis, and thus follows none of the techniques outlined above. The first line of
Omnia concludens verbi (#24) begins on e, although the plagal F
mode is quickly indicated by the melodic descent f-d-c and the
cadence on the finalis at the end of "omnia." It thus follows the
outline of the modal "noeagis" formula. The second line of *Ecce
iam Iohannis* (#20), on the other hand, follows the chant cadence
on f with a beginning on g, the degree above.

The final trope lines show even more variation. Only two of
the five follow a recognizable principle for their opening. Line 3
of *Fons et origo* (#21) opens on d at the unison with the preceding

---

[25] It should be noted that in Paris 903 the cadence of the chant at
"intellectus" is on d and not on c as in the modern Gradual. This version,
naturally enough, is the basis of the St. Martial trope.

chant. Line 2 of *Omnia concludens verbi* (#24) begins on f, which
is the opening pitch of the following chant phrase, and thus maintains the connection of the chant itself. In fact, the setting of
"Quem dilexit amans" in the trope may almost be considered as
an elaborated version of the figure f-d-f occurring on "stolam"
in the chant.[26] But for the remaining lines, there is no such precise connection. The third lines of *Ecce iam Iohannis* (#20) and
Sacro fonte pectoris (#23) open on the low c, and to this extent,
at any rate, maintain the low register of the preceding chant
cadence. Line 3 of *Caelica caelesti decantent* (#22), on the other
hand, does not show even this much of a relationship with the
chant, beginning as it does on the high a. The resulting fifth leap
from the final d of the preceding chant phrase is in no way a typical figure of the sixth mode, and one feels that the trope writer
has momentarily deserted the sixth mode for the first.[27]

In no case in the tropes for St. John—which, as part of the major
Christmas cycle, may be considered as one of the earliest portions
of the trope repertory—is the principle of direct chant quotation
used in making connections between trope and chant.

The seven tropes of the Introit *Os iusti* for the feast of St. Benedict present a different picture. Here, more or less extensive quotation is used in a majority of the tropes. Thus, the third lines of
five of the tropes (#159 through #162 and #165) close with the
cadence of the preceding chant phrase at "iudicium." In *Cantica
nunc reboent* (#162), in particular, the quotation at "legis" is both
extensive and literal. A similarly extended quotation is found on
the final syllable of "tenenda" in *Laudibus o Benedicte* (#161),
although here there is a slight melodic variant. In all five cases,
however, at least the four-note figure on "-um" in the chant—
c-d-e-d—is used for the final cadence of the trope line.

---

[26] It is interesting to see how this line, which, it should be remembered,
is of rather later origin, closely follows and embellishes the melody of the
chant phrase that it introduces. Thus, "Quem dilexit amans" corresponds
to "stolam," "divino pneumate" elaborates the melody of "gloriae," and
"plenum" suggests "induit eum."

[27] Apparently, later generations of trope singers were disturbed by this
opening, since in Paris 887 it has been altered to f—e̋ d c g–g on the word
"Principium."

We even find a certain amount of chant quotation at the beginning of some trope lines. Thus, the second line of three of the tropes (#159, #160, and #165) opens with the melody of "et lingua" in the following chant line. Similarly, the opening of the third line of five tropes (#159 to #163) suggests the melodic outline of "lex Dei" at the beginning of the chant phrase that follows, although in no case is the quotation literal, since the tropes merely preserve the general melodic outline of the chant—c d-f f—in a more or less elaborated version. In the remaining two tropes (#164 and #165), at least the opening pitch of "lex Dei" is preserved, even if the movement to f is not.

This rather consistent use of chant quotation at identical points in the various tropes, and, in general, an agreement as to opening and closing pitches and the manner of connecting trope and chant in the various examples, suggest that a general convention for setting tropes to the Introit *Os iusti* did indeed exist. There are variations of technique, to be sure, but particularly in the first four Benedict tropes the consistency from example to example is striking. This is perhaps another characteristic of later trope compositions, in which the specific techniques of one trope would serve as a model for other compositions fashioned to fit the same Introit.[28]

The two tropes of the Introit *Quasi modo* for the Octave of Easter do not show the same consistency. *Ecce omnes redempti* (#70) has four lines, *O populi sacro* (#71) has only three. Although the final note of each of the first three trope lines agrees in the two tropes, *Ecce omnes* makes use of chant quotation, while *O populi* does not. "Salutem," in line 3 of *Ecce omnes,* is set to the cadential melody of "dolo" in the preceding phrase of the chant, and the cadence at "canite omnes" in the fourth line utilizes the preceding "alleluia" of the chant.[29] The opening pitches of the lines of the two tropes agree in only one of the three cases, namely, the third

---

[28] For a further discussion of the interrelationship of the Benedict tropes, see below, pp. 112ff.

[29] It should be noted that line 2 of *Ecce omnes* is preceded by the same chant cadence that precedes line 4. However, in the former case, the trope line does not quote the chant. Obviously, the consistent application of a given compositional technique was not deemed necessary by the medieval musician.

line. Here, the unison connection on d of the chant is reflected in both tropes by a line beginning and ending on d. In the case of line 1, however, *Ecce omnes* begins on the finalis f, while *O populi* uses g. In line 2, the former begins on a, the latter on e.

Thus we can see that a good deal of variation in the manner of connecting trope and chant was possible. In certain cases, recognizable and recurrent techniques were used, but in others a more general and less precise application of the principle of melodic accommodation adequately served the purposes of the trope writer. The following tabulation of the actual pitch relationships between chant and trope at each point of juncture in the sixth-mode Introit tropes gives some idea of the variety of intervallic preparation which was considered satisfactory in a given mode:

I. Opening Pitch of Trope:

   f (the modal finalis): 10 times
   c: 2
   e: 1
   g: 1

II. A trope line   Can prepare a chant phrase
     ending on: beginning on:

        f   f   (20 times)
                                 d   (5)
                                 c   (2)
                                        ⎯⎯⎯
                                        27

        d   c   (7)
                                 f   (4)
                                 d   (2)
                                        ⎯⎯⎯
                                        13

        a   f   (2)
                                        ⎯⎯⎯
                                        2

III. A chant phrase   Can be followed by a trope
      ending on: line beginning on:

f	f	(8 times)
	a	(3)
	e	(2)
	g	(1)
		14
d	d	(7)
	c	(5)
	f	(1)
	a	(1)
		14

For comparison, we may add the pitch connections of the chants themselves at those points where it was customary to add trope lines:

IV. Chant cadence on: Followed by:

f	f	(3 times)
	d	(1)
d	d	(1)
	c	(1)
	f	(1)

The chants concerned open on f, d, and c respectively.

These tables emphasize several important points. In the first place, the final pitches of the individual trope lines and the manner in which they prepare the following chant phrases are apparently determined to a large extent by the procedure in the chants themselves. Thus, all but two trope cadences fall on f or d, as in the chant. Similarly, the manner in which these cadences lead into the following phrase agrees strikingly in trope and chant. Thus, all but four of the forty-two final trope cadences are followed by pitches for which there is a precedent in the chants.

In the second place, the unison connection, which is doubtless
the simplest and most direct method of joining trope and chant,
is also the one method which is most frequently used, both at the
beginning and at the end of a trope line.

Finally, these tables demonstrate once again that the trope composer considered the individual trope lines as introductions to the
chant that followed, and he was thus primarily concerned with
making a smooth connection between the end of the trope line
and the succeeding chant phrase. The opening of the trope line
was of secondary importance, and this fact is reflected in the greater variety of opening pitches presented in Section III.

Let us try to summarize briefly this rather complicated discussion of the relationship of trope to chant by stressing once again
some of the basic concepts of trope composition which have
emerged from it. The individual lines of a trope are relatively independent, self-contained phrases, in terms of both text and music.
Nevertheless, they are composed in the same basic musical idiom
as the chant itself, so that trope and chant form an organic stylistic
unity. Although the tropes only occasionally make use of direct
quotation or melodic paraphrase of the chant, except in the final
cadences of individual trope lines, they do follow the same general
procedures as the chant itself in melodic style, modal characteristics, and even in the manner of connecting phrase with phrase.

There are various methods for making a suitable and smooth
melodic connection between trope and chant. The most striking
of these is perhaps the direct quotation of the appropriate chant
cadence at the end of a trope line, while the simplest and most frequent method is the use of a straightforward unison pitch connection between trope and chant. These and other specific techniques
may be used at one time or another, but in almost all cases the
trope composer seems to be working according to a basic principle
of adequate melodic preparation and smooth connection of trope
line and chant phrase, a principle exemplified in the differentia
system of the psalm tones.

In general, the trope writer is concerned with bringing his
melody into harmony with that of the chant, rather than with

seeking striking contrasts. However, his primary attention is given to the ending rather than the opening of a given trope line, and to the manner in which it approaches and prepares the following chant. Thus, within the basic stylistic unity, the individual trope lines still function as introductions to the succeeding phrases of the chant.

Formal Organization of the Tropes

In order to understand the overall musical structure of the tropes and to appreciate the distinct advances made in terms of formal organization, it is essential to remember the twofold aspect of the tropes. While in terms of general musical style the tropes agree in their essentials with the music of the official chant itself, the individual trope lines nevertheless retain a certain degree of autonomy as self-contained musical phrases. In particular, with the rise and increasing importance of hexameter trope texts, the individual lines of a trope took on a conciseness and symmetry as well as a certain uniformity of length which reflected the structure of the poetic texts themselves, and which came in time to influence even the prose texts.

Within this external agreement of the trope lines, it was possible to develop a more or less precise melodic organization which could relate line to line within a given trope. Since the melody of the official chant that the trope writer wished to embellish was determined in advance, and since, as we have seen, the trope only occasionally makes use of direct quotation or paraphrasing of the chant, the sense of formal relationship must be realized within the lines of the trope itself. Thus, we are faced with a paradoxical situation in which a trope displays a symmetrical organization that stands outside the framework of the chant it adorns.

We need not assume that this represents a faulty aesthetic judgment on the part of the trope composer, since, as we have seen, there has been no attempt to fuse completely the elements of trope and chant. Moreover, the element of contrast is already explicit in the alternating performance of soloist and choir, and it is precisely this interrelationship of the soloist's lines that can help prevent the disintegration of the total composition of trope and chant into extreme sectionalism.

Among the tropes of Paris 1121, the principle of symmetrical organization is found in varying degrees. Many tropes display no sign of it at all. Others are related only by a recurrent pattern of cadential formulas. Still others make an extensive use of melodic repetition from line to line. Does this variation of practice represent a chronological development? As in all questions of chronology regarding the tropes, it is difficult to present a definitive answer. Nevertheless, it is quite probable that the sense of strict formal organization which characterizes certain tropes did develop gradually through the history of the trope, until in time it came to be a dominating principle which might conflict with the structural idea of the trope itself.

Various techniques of musical organization are employed with varying degrees of consistency in the tropes. Certain of these techniques are exemplified in a striking way in an Introit trope for the feast of St. Benedict, *Iubilent omnes fideles* (#165). The basic principle of melodic organization in this trope is the varied repetition in subsequent lines of the melodic material of the opening line. In effect, the familiar compositional technique of centonization, which is frequently found in the repertory of official chant, is here used within a single trope to relate one line to another.

The first line of the trope is composed of three melodic phrases which are clearly marked by the cadences at the end of each. They are:

A = "Iubilent omnes fideles"
B = "catervatim"
C = "depromant psallentes"

The melodic material of this line, although not derived from the Introit that it embellishes, is fully representative of the mode of that chant. It exploits the full range of the plagal F mode, and, in fact, in its general melodic shape and range it might almost be considered a highly elaborate version of the second half of the sixth-mode Introit psalm tone. Thus, A with its intonation and cadence represents the medial intonation of the tone, f g-a. B is merely an elaboration of the psalm tone's movement to the high c′. And C, in a more general way, represents the descent of the differentia to the low d.

This melodic material is now repeated in a varied form in the subsequent lines of the trope. The opening phrase of line 2, "Socius supernarum virtutum effectus," is an amplification of A. The melody agrees literally with the opening line at the intonation "Socius" and the cadence at "effectus." Between these points is a free amplification of the melodic fragment on "omnes" in the opening line. This phrase is followed by the word "atque" set to a slightly varied form of B. The final phrase of the line, "angelicis choris coniunctus est," again uses the melodic material of A, but here the technique is at once more direct and more complicated. Thus, A is quoted literally on the syllables "-cis choris coniunctus est." But in order to expand this melody for the opening syllables of the phrase, the middle figure of A—"omnes" in the first line—is quoted at the beginning of the phrase. The surprising result of this is to create a new melodic phrase, D, with its repetition at the words "angelicis choris" and "coniunctus est." The form of the second line, therefore, is as follows:

A = "Socius supernarum virtutum effectus"
B = "atque"
A = $\begin{cases} D = \text{"angelicis choris"} \\ D = \text{"coniunctus est."} \end{cases}$

In line 3, the demands of fitting the trope to the melody of the chant take precedence, and consequently the line opens with new melodic material in the lower part of the plagal range which makes a suitable connection with the preceding chant cadence on the low d. The melody of "Xpisti sequens vestigia" thus moves from the low c to a cadence on the finalis f. At this point, however, when the opening range of the trope has been reached once again, the principle of melodic repetition is resumed. Thus, "ipse vero illi" is set to a simplified version of A, and the remainder of the line, "reddens sua promissa ideo," is derived from C. The variants between this last phrase and its model are particularly interesting. The melody of "reddens sua promissa" is simply an elaboration of the descent from a to d at "depromant" in the first line, which is made necessary by the increased number of syllables in line 3. The variant between the cadence at "ideo" in line 3 and its model at "psallentes" in the first line is more significant, however. The third-line cadence is altered to agree with the preceding chant cadence at "iudicium," so that it serves not only as a formal element within the trope itself, but also, by means of direct quotation of the chant, as an important element in connecting trope and chant.[30]

In summary, then, the formal structure of *Iubilent omnes fideles* may be indicated as follows:

Line 1: A B C
Line 2: A B A (= D + D)
Line 3: x A C

This example clearly indicates some of the means of achieving formal unity within a trope, and it also suggests the basic formal problem facing the trope composer.

The basic organizational technique is, of course, the recurrent use of the melodic material of the first line in the subsequent lines of the trope. This material may be quoted literally, as at the second A in line 2, or, as is more frequently the case, it may be paraphrased, elaborated, or simplified in order to meet the requirements of the specific text which must be set. Furthermore, the melodic material may even be subjected to motivic development, if we may call it that, as in the derivation of D from the melodic material of A. In addition, one line may be related to another by the use of the same final cadential pattern for both, that is, by melodic rhyme. We see this principle at work, for example, in lines 1 and 3 of the present trope.

But despite these technical means at the disposal of the composer, one basic problem existed which tended to preclude the

---

[30] See the discussion of chant quotation in the preceding section, pp. 91ff.

achievement of complete formal symmetry in the structure of the trope. The trope, after all, was not created to stand by itself, and consequently the composer, if he were at all concerned with the relationship of this trope to the chant he was adorning, would have to sacrifice his strict formal patterns to the demands of blending trope with chant. We see this clearly in *Iubilent omnes fideles*. Although the material for achieving symmetry is there, no overall formal pattern is evolved which would give a symmetrical structure to the trope as a whole. Nonthematic material must be introduced at the beginning of line 3 in order to accommodate the melody to the low range of the chant at this point. Furthermore, the composer has chosen to make the principle of recurring cadential patterns subservient to the connective principle of chant quotation at the end of line 3. We thus have here a clear illustration of the two aspects of the trope mentioned at the opening of this section. The lines of a trope have a certain degree of autonomy and may develop up to a point according to their own melodic laws. But as a completed composition they must stand within the framework of the chant, and in the final analysis the desire to create a harmonious whole becomes the dominating principle.

Several other aspects of *Iubilent omnes fideles* require some comment. For one thing, there is a general uniformity in the length of the lines, even though the text is in prose and thus does not automatically control the length of the line as is the case with a hexameter trope text. Although these prose trope lines are somewhat longer than the average hexameter line, the regularity of the metrical texts may well have set a precedent for the length of line of the prose texts, as we have noted before. This conciseness and uniformity of the individual lines is in itself an important factor in the formal symmetry of the trope as a whole.

Another point concerns the modality of the trope. As we have said, the melody is a straightforward example of sixth-mode writing. Nevertheless, a melodic figure similar to section B in line 1 is frequently found in tropes of the first mode. The characteristic outline of a to c′ with the descent to g and the leap to b-c′-a is found, for example, on "allisis" in line 2 of *Mortificando sua* (#73) for the first-mode Introit *Exclamaverunt*. There are many similar

examples, and the related form c'-b-g-b-c'-a a is found so frequently in first-mode tropes as to be one of the most characteristic
melodic figures of that mode. This is, then, an indication that the
specific range could be as important as the mode in determining
the melodic figure which was employed at a given place in the
trope. This principle is, of course, found in the chant itself. The
most familiar example is the fifth leap, which can occur in various
modes but which is almost always limited to the pitches d-a and
g-d'. Thus, the leap d-a can be found in the E mode as well as in
the D mode, but we never find the leap e-b.

When we compare *Iubilent omnes fideles* to *Psallite omnes*
(#164), we see how the melodic material of one trope may be
used as the basis of a different trope for the same feast. The
cadential melody of "psallentes" in *Iubilent omnes* appears three
times in *Psallite omnes:* once at the opening of line 1 on the
words "Psallite omnes," again at the conclusion of the same line
at "-ta dicentes" (where, however, the top g is omitted), and finally at the conclusion of line 3 on the word "ideo." In the last
case, it will be noticed that the word "ideo" occurs at the end
of the third line in both tropes, but despite this textual identity,
Iubilent has adapted the melody to agree with the chant cadence,
whereas in *Psallite* it retains its original form.

In addition, certain shorter melodic fragments of *Iubilent* occur
in *Psallite*. Thus, the setting of "concivis" in line 2 of *Psallite* corresponds to that of "atque" in the second line of *Iubilent*. The
melody of "omnes fideles" in the first line of *Iubilent* occurs at
"effectus est" in the second line of *Psallite* and again at the cadence on "legionibus" that ends the line.

But the relationship between the two tropes is not limited to
these examples of direct quotation. The whole of line 3 of *Psallite*
can be considered as a paraphrase of the third line of *Iubilent*.
"Scrutatorem" in the former corresponds literally to "Xpisti
sequens" in the latter. "Omnium" is set to the melody of
"vestigia ipse vero" in a very compressed form, which, however,
preserves faithfully the melodic contour of its model. "Corda"
corresponds to "illi reddens." And "sequens precepta ideo" quotes

literally the melody of "sua promissa ideo" except for the cadential variant mentioned above.[31] In other words, the trope writer here makes use of another compositional principle of the official chant, that is, the use of a model melody which he adapts to a new text.

It would perhaps be difficult to determine exactly which of the two trope melodies was written first, but it is certainly not necessary to do so. The important point is that the melodic material of one trope could be transferred to another trope in the same mode.

The particular tropes under consideration show an unusually close relationship. Nevertheless, the other tropes for St. Benedict, although they do not exhibit such striking resemblances, do show certain general melodic similarities.[32] As we should expect, however, this relationship is strongest among the tropes for a given chant. When we look at the other tropes in the sixth mode, we find no melodic reminiscences of the Benedict tropes.

The tropes for St. Benedict have furnished specific examples of what are perhaps the three basic techniques of melodic organization within a trope. These include: 1. the use of the same or similar cadential patterns to end various lines of the trope; 2. the use of model melodies which are adapted or paraphrased to fit the new context of another trope line; and 3. the recurrent use of melodic fragments or figures from line to line or from trope to trope according to the principle of centonization. In other words, the tropes make use of certain techniques of the chant itself, but now, at least in the last two cases, these techniques are used to achieve a formal unity within a single trope, and independent of the chant that it embellishes.

We have considered the technique of using recurrent figures in some detail in connection with the Benedict tropes. But the other two techniques, although also present in those tropes, perhaps require some further comment.

---

[31] The whole end of line 3 in *Psallite* thus corresponds to section C in *Iubilent*. This same phrase also concludes the first line of *Psallite* at the words "cum psalmista dicentes."

[32] See above, pp. 102ff.

The simplest and most straightforward of these methods of relating the music of the various lines of a trope is, of course, the
use of a formal pattern of cadences. We see this method in its
most obvious and rudimentary form in a trope like *Innixum scalis*
(#87), for the Dedication of a Church. Each of the three trope
lines ends with the same simple cadence, c-d d. The accentual
pattern of the text of each line determines the precise form of
the cadence. Thus, in lines 1 and 3, the text accent ∪/∪ of
"-le sonos," and "-ra sui" is set to c-d d d, whereas the two final
unstressed syllables of "perpetua" in line 2 require only c-d d.
Although this use of musical rhyme may seem so elementary as
to appear almost accidental, a more extended relationship between lines 1 and 3 suggests that the composer was in fact con-
sciously attempting to achieve an overall structural pattern.
Thus, the whole cadential melody of "hos dedit ille sonos" in
the first line recurs at "-gere probra sui" in line 3. The simple
cadential relationship of the three lines may be indicated as
A A′ A.[33]

A far more extensive musical rhyme occurs in another Dedication trope, *Agmina perhenniter* (#89), although it affects only
three of the four lines. The melodic repetition is exact at "redeunt
ad patriam" in line 3 and at "haec dicentes carmina" in line 4. In
the opening line, this cadential pattern begins only at the second
syllable of "sacrum" and thus affects the syllables "-crum
dicentia." In line 2, however, the cadence differs completely from
the others, although there is no apparent justification in the chant
for this variation. One can only assume that the trope composer,
while he was prepared to use various devices to give a sense of form

---

[33] It is indeed likely that the cadential passage "praemia perpetuae" of
line 2 is more closely related to the cadences of the other lines than has
been suggested here. In fact, it may be considered an elaboration of them,
with the grouping on "prae—" and the added melisma on "—pe—" determined by the word accents of the text. Although the text of this trope is
in elegiacs, it is interesting to note that the musical setting of each final
half-line is determined by the stress accent and not quantity. The complete melodic agreement of the last four syllables of lines 1 and 3 doubtless results from the identical pattern of stress accent.

to his composition, felt under no compulsion to apply these devices in a consistent manner. There are numerous examples in the trope repertory to support this assumption. The desire for a completely logical formal organization must have evolved only gradually.

In the case of the Dedication trope *Typica visione* (#83), there is perhaps a reason for the incompleteness of the musical rhyme. The opening line of the trope is in prose, while lines 2 and 3 are hexameters. Although there is no external evidence to show that the three lines were not written at the same time, this discrepancy in the text suggests that lines 2 and 3 were possibly a later addition. However this may be, lines 2 and 3 are certainly related by a striking melodic figure which does not occur in line 1. This is the cadential melody on the syllables "-mine celsi" in line 2 and "-tima semper" in line 3. As in other cases we have mentioned, the melodic identity reflects an identical accentual pattern in the text. Here this pattern is the unvarying rhythmic cadence of the hexameter, $|- \cup \cup | - \cup$. In this particular trope, as in so many medieval hexameters, the pattern can be interpreted in terms both of quantity and of accent. It is certainly quite possible that, with the increasing use of hexameters for trope texts and the growing dominance of accent even in quantitative verse, this rhythmic "rhyme" of the hexameter line may have served as the inspiration for the melodic rhyme of recurrent cadential formulas in the music of the tropes.

An even more striking example of the correspondence of musical rhyme and hexameter text is found in an Introit trope for the feast of SS. Philip and James, *Mortificando sua* (#73). The final five syllables of each line, "corpora sancti," "principe victo," and "-nendo per evum," agree exactly in their melodic setting. This setting, moreover, reflects clearly the metrical pattern of the text, with groups of notes on the long syllable of each foot, and with only one or two notes on the short, or unaccented, syllables. This melodic formula could thus theoretically be used at the end of any hexameter trope line in the same mode, and it is indeed interesting to find it used again almost literally at the end of the second line of another trope for SS. Philip and James, *Alme tuum semper* (#74), for the text "noxia sother."

The third basic compositional technique that we noted in connection with the tropes for St. Benedict is the adaptation of the melody of an entire trope line to the text of a different trope line. This is, of course, the familiar principle of melody types or model melodies which we find in the chant itself. In the tropes, however, due to their sectional nature, the technique is limited to individual lines, and as far as I know there is no trope melody modeled entirely, line by line, on the melody of another trope. In this process of adaptation the composer can make use of expansion or compression, paraphrase or literal quotation, according to the demands of the new text which he is setting.

This melodic adaptation or paraphrase occurs in the tropes in two distinct forms. In the case of the Benedict tropes cited above, the melody of a given line in one trope is adapted to a different text at a comparable place in another trope. This method resembles most closely the technique of the official chant, although, as we have noted, it affects only individual lines rather than compositions as a whole.

In other cases, however, the melody of one line of a trope occurs as the setting for other lines of the same trope. In this way, a general technique of chant composition is utilized for specific formal ends, since it gives a very close structural unity to various lines of a given trope composition.

We may cite as an example of this technique the Introit trope *Dulciter agnicolae* (#61) for Feria II in Easter week. The text of this trope is in hexameters, the introductory trope consisting of two hexameter lines while the remaining interpolations are single hexameters. The melodies of each of the opening hexameter lines serve as models for the subsequent trope lines. Particularly close is the relationship between the melody of the second hexameter of the introductory trope, beginning "Iam quia Iordanis," and trope lines 3 and 4. Here, the model melody is taken over quite literally in the subsequent lines, and when changes occur, these can usually be accounted for in terms either of different accentual patterns in the text or of the need to adapt the cadence melody to the subsequent chant line. Thus, for example, in line 1b the melody of the word "Iordanis," with its long syllables and its stress accent on the second syllable, must be simplified and redistributed in order to fit the accentual pattern of "hoc Moyses" and "-mus pariter" in lines 3 and 4 respectively. So, too, the final cadence of line 1b on the word "renasci," which adapts the psalm tone differentia in order to make a smooth connection with the opening of the Introit, is not needed in the subsequent lines and is replaced by the simple cadential formula f g-a a.

The opening hexameter of line 1, "Dulciter agnicolae," serves as the model for line 2, but here the relationship is much freer. Thus, although the melody of the first half of line 2 agrees quite closely with that of its model, the remainder of line 2 ("manantem manna decoris") is a very free paraphrase indeed of the melody of "festivum ducite pascha" in the opening line. The basic melodic outlines of the model are carefully maintained, but they are treated to a considerable degree of elaboration.

Nonetheless, the music of this trope is very tightly organized by means of this process of adapting the melodies of the opening line to the text of the subsequent lines, however flexible the adaptation may be at one point or another. Thus, the lines of the trope are related by the following symmetrical pattern:

A ⎫
B ⎭ = line 1
A   = line 2
B   = line 3
B   = line 4

The Introit trope *Dicite nunc pueri* (#27) for the feast of the Holy Innocents furnishes an example of an even simpler and more direct organization of a trope through melodic paraphrase. Here, both hexameter lines are based on the same melodic model. As frequently happens with hexameter lines of this sort, the first half of the line is treated quite strictly, while the second half presents a much freer paraphrase. Thus, in line 2, "fudere nomini tuo" is set syllabically, with a neume-group occurring only on the syllable "tu-." The second half of line 1, however, is a very melismatic elaboration of this simple melody, and one wonders to what extent the composer was attempting to make his setting reflect the text "psallentes carmina Xpisto."

We have seen here some examples of the various techniques used by the trope composer to give formal organization and a sense of overall unity to his compositions. This interest in formal symmetry seems to have developed gradually in the history of the trope and is seen most strongly perhaps in later compositions with metrical texts. In fact, it is quite probable that poetic texts as such contributed a good deal to this development, since they furnished concise lines, more or less uniform in length and general accentual pattern, which could serve admirably as the framework for melodic symmetry and formal organization.

In most ways, the music of the trope represents an application and extension of the compositional principles of the official chant that it adorned. But it was precisely in the area of form where advances could be made by a new application of certain of the techniques of the chant itself. The conciseness of phrase structure in the tropes and the formal structures which this encouraged were bound to exert an influence on the development of the musical language of the Middle Ages.

In many of the examples we have cited, however, we have seen how various formal schemes had to be adapted to the demands of fitting trope to chant. Obviously, as the interest in formal symmetry became more and more pronounced, the composer was bound to find the structure of the trope, by its very nature as an embellishment of a preexistent composition, far too restrictive to allow the full development of his musical ideas. Thus it is perhaps not surprising that in time the trope fell abruptly out of favor and that the composer turned to other forms. And consequently, it is perhaps not necessary to look for external causes in accounting for the disappearance of the trope in the course of the eleventh century.

Transcriptions

INTRODUCTION

The reasons for selecting Paris 1121 as the basis for transcription have already been discussed at some length, so that here it will perhaps be sufficient to mention briefly the principles of transcription involved and the manner in which the pieces have been presented.

The notation of Paris 1121 is extremely clear and accurate. Although no dry-point line is used for orientation of the neumes, they are heightened with such accuracy that transcription usually presents no problem once the opening pitch has been determined. Furthermore, custodes are used at the ends of lines—either an "e" for "equaliter," to indicate that the following line begins on a unison pitch, or a simple dash at the proper pitch level, to indicate the precise opening pitch of the next line. By this means, it is possible to reconstruct the proper pitch throughout a given trope composition.

A problem which does sometimes arise with the tropes of Paris 1121, however, is that of determining the starting pitch level of a given composition, since, of course, there is no clef sign or letter to indicate pitch at any given point. Fortunately, from the point of view of transcription, the tropes have a unique advantage, since they were sung in connection with a chant of the official repertory whose pitch and mode can, in most cases, be readily determined.

In some manuscripts, the chant cues are furnished with musical notation, so that the trope singer—and the transcriber—can determine with accuracy the pitch connection of trope and chant. Consequently, the pitch level of the trope and chant as a whole can be established, since the pitch of the chant is known. Even in those tropers where the chant cues are not notated—and this unfortunately is the case with Paris 1121—at least the mode of the chant, and thus of the trope, can be determined.

There were, then, various ways to determine the pitch of the tropes of Paris 1121. The most satisfactory method was to compare the Paris 1121 version of a trope with the version contained in tropers like Paris 1119 and Paris 909, which are very closely related to Paris 1121 in their repertory and which, in addition, contain notated chant cues. If this method of pitch determination (which is, of course, the most certain) was not applicable in a given instance, it was still possible in most cases to determine the actual pitch of the tropes, since the mode of the chant was known. Thus, certain melodic characteristics of the trope would indicate its pitch, even without the external help of the notated chant cues. These characteristics include such things as the frequency with which a trope line begins and ends on the finalis of its mode, the frequent use of unison connections between trope and chant, and the reliance on modal formulas and characteristic cadences in trope compositions. By these means, it was possible to determine the pitch of specific tropes with a fair degree of certainty. Once the pitch level was known at any point in the trope, of course, it was then usually possible to transcribe the whole piece, thanks to the diastematic notation and the use of the custos.

In some cases, however, it was not possible to determine the pitch by any of these methods. This was particularly true of compositions like the Fraction Antiphons, which are not tropes and thus are not connected with specific chants of the official repertory. It was also true of those tropes, most frequently for the Ordinary of the Mass, whose chants are no longer to be found in later chant books and whose pitch is therefore no longer ascertainable. In such cases, one has to rely on what one hopes is a sufficiently well-informed guess based on the apparent modal characteristics of the piece in question. These instances are indicated in the footnotes to the transcription.

As indicated earlier, Paris 1121 is on the whole an accurately copied manuscript, and the following transcription is basically an attempt to present the contents of this troper in a straightforward way. Nevertheless, it has been my policy to compare transcriptions with one or another of the closely related St. Martial manuscripts. In particular, these manuscripts have been used for correcting obvious errors in the text or music of Paris 1121. Footnotes are included in the transcription to indicate where such

emendations of the text of Paris 1121 occur, and the original reading is supplied there. However, no effort has been made to indicate
all variant readings, based on a collation of all the St. Martial
tropers, although particularly interesting variations are mentioned
from time to time.

As far as the texts of the tropes are concerned, no attempt has
been made to standardize the Latin spelling, since I believe no useful purpose would be served by removing the orthographical incon-
sistencies of the original. Thus, for example, we find that ae, e,
and ę are used interchangeably throughout the manuscript.
Furthermore, the consistent use of the Greek x and p in the spelling of *Christus* (= Xpistus) in the manuscript has been retained.
Punctuation and all capitals except for initials have been supplied
by the editor, and abbreviations have been expanded throughout.

The musical notation of the transcription calls for relatively
little comment. The only special notational signs used are the
following:

=   (quilisma)

=   (oriscus; two unison notes without the tie would indicate two
puncta in the manuscript)

=   any liquescent neume

Paris 1121, like other of the St. Martial tropers, contains certain
"rhythmic" indications in the occasional use of dashlike puncta,
either alone or in composite neumes. Without wishing to enter
into the vexed question of Gregorian "rhythm" at this time, I will
only say that the precise use of these signs varies so much from
manuscript to manuscript—and, indeed, the difference between a
point and a dash is sometimes so difficult to determine—that the
attempt to reproduce them in the transcription would serve no
purpose.

As far as the general presentation of the manuscript is concerned, the following comments may prove useful. The transcription follows the trope section of the manuscript folio by folio, and the order of the tropes in the transcription is exactly that of the manuscript, except as indicated in the footnotes. The rubrics of the troper are given, in capitals, exactly as they occur in the manuscript, although abbreviations are expanded without comment. Any further editorial additions, however, are indicated in parentheses. These additions include, among other things, indication of the specific Gregorian chant which is being troped and indication of the specific feast where this information has been omitted.

In the transcription, each trope is identified by its number in the total sequence of the manuscript, by its title, and by the number of the folio on which it occurs. This information is supplied at the beginning of each trope, and is not given in parentheses.

The chant cues are given exactly as they occur in the manuscript. Musical notation is supplied only where this is found in Paris 1121, and except for the spelling out of abbreviations no attempt is made to expand either the text or the music of the cues. The text of the official chant is underlined.

The treatment of the Ordinary tropes requires special mention. As indicated earlier, there are some gaps in the contents of Paris 1121, and these primarily affect the tropes to the Ordinary of the Mass. Thus, of the original section set aside for Ordinary tropes, we have only ff. 42-57v, containing Gloria tropes and Regnum prosulae. There are no Sanctus or Agnus tropes at all, except for those few contained in the main sequence of Proper tropes.[1]

Nevertheless, for purposes of illustration, I have included after the Proper tropes a selection of transcriptions exemplifying each of the main categories of Ordinary tropes (pp. 253ff.). Where necessary, the transcriptions have been made from St. Martial sources other than Paris 1121. They include examples of tropes to each of the principal Gloria chants used in the St. Martial reper-

---

[8] For a full list of Ordinary tropes contained in Paris 1121, see the Index of Tropes on pp. 275ff., below.

tory, as well as tropes to the Sanctus and Agnus Dei. The source of each trope, and the chant used, is indicated before each transcription.

The section of transcriptions is concluded by a group of examples illustrating the various types of prosulae found in St. Martial manuscripts (pp. 263ff.) and by a transcription of the modal formulas contained in the tonarium of Paris 1121 (pp. 271ff.).

The transcriptions are followed by an index of the tropes of Paris 1121 arranged alphabetically by first lines under the following categories: Introit Tropes; Tropes to the Introit Psalm; Tropes to the Introit Doxology; Melodic Additions to the Introit; Gloria in Excelsis Tropes; Tropes Ad Sequentiam: Offertory Tropes; Tropes to the Offertory Verses; Agnus Dei Tropes; Communion Tropes; Varia; and Regnum Prosulae. Folio numbers are given for each trope, and this index may thus serve as an index to the transcriptions.

PROPER TROPES
OF PARIS 1121

(IN NATIVITATE DOMINI)

(INTROIT: Puer natus est)

#1. Quem queritis in presepe--f.2

Quem que-ri-tis in pre-se-pe,   pas-to-res, di-ci-te?

Sal-va-to-rem Xpis-tum Do-   mi-num, in- fan-tem pan-nis in-vo-

lu-tum se-cun-dum ser-mo- nem an-ge-li-cum.

Ad-est hic par-   vu-lus cum Ma-ri- a ma-   tre su-a, de qua du-dum

va-ti-ci- nan-do I-sa-i-as di- xe-rat pro-phe-ta: 'Ec-ce vir-go

con-ci-pi-et et pa- ri-et fi- li-um.' Et nunc e- un-tes di-ci-te

qui-a   na-tus est.

AL-LE-LU-IA, al- le-lu-ia. Iam ve-re sci- mus Xpis-tum na- tum

in ter-ris, de quo ca-ni-te om-nes cum pro-phe-ta di- cen-tes:

Puer natus est

ALIOS   #2. <u>Gaudeamus hodie quia Deus</u>--f.2v

1) Gau-de-a- mus ho-   di-e qui-a De- us des-cen- dit de   cae-

lis, et prop-   ter nos in ter-   ris   <u>Puer natus</u>

2) Quem pro-phe-   tae di-u va- ti- ci-na- ti sunt,   <u>Et filius</u>

3) Hunc a pa-tre iam no-vi-mus ad-ve-nis-se in mun-   dum, <u>Cuius</u>

4) Po-tes-tas et reg-num in ma-   nu e-   ius, <u>Et vocabitur</u>

5) Ad-mi- ra-bi-lis con-si-li- a- ri-us, De- us for-tis, prin-ceps

pa-cis,   <u>Magni consilii</u>   <u>Ps</u>. <u>Can-ta-te Domino -ii</u>

ITEM ALIOS   #3. <u>Ecce adest verbum</u>--f.3

1) Ec-ce ad-   est   ver-   bum de quo pro-phe-tae cae-ci- ne- runt

di- cen-tes: <u>Puer</u>

2) Quem vir-   go Ma-ri-a ge-   nu- it,   <u>Et filius</u>

1--MS notated tone lower from here to end of line.

3) No-men e- ius Em- ma-nu-hel vo-ca- bi-tur, **Cuius**

4) Et reg-ni e- ius non e- rit fi- nis, **Et voc.**

5) Pa-ter fu- tu-ri se-cu-li et **Magni**

ALIOS   **#4. Deus pater filium--f.3**

1) De-us pa-ter fi-li-um su- um ho-di-e mi-sit in mun-dum, de quo

gra-tu-lan-ter di-ca- mus cum pro-phe-ta: **Puer**

2) Qui se-de- bit su- per thro-num Da- vid et in ae-ter-

num im-pe-ra- bit, **Cuius**

3) Ec- ce ve- nit De-us et ho-mo de do-mo Da-vid se-de-re in

thro-no, **Et vocabitur**

4) E- o quod fu-tu-ra an- nun-ci-a- bit, **Magni**

1--"Sedere" is marginal in Paris 1121.

132

ALIOS   #5. Quem nasci mundo--f.3v

1) Quem nas-   ci mun- do do-cu-e- re ex or-   di-ne va- tes, Puer

2) Vis-ce- ri-bus sa- cris quem ges-sit ma- ter o- pi-ma,   Cuius

3) Et   di-a- de-ma clu-ens ca-pi-tis in ver-   ti-ce can- det,

Et vocabitur

4) Em- ma- nu-hel, for-tis De- us, rex   om- ni-po-tens, at-que

Magni

ALIOS   #6. Ad aeternae salutis--f.3v

1) Ad ae-ter-   nae sa-lu- tis gau-di-a et nos   sal-van- di

gra-ti-a,   Puer

2) Rex,   lu- men de lu-mi-ne reg-nat   in ius- ti-ti-a,Cuius

3) Qui cae- les-ti-a si- mul et ter-res-tri-a fun-da-   vit pa- tris

sa-pi-en- ti- a,   Et vocabitur

4) Al-tis-si-mi   fi-li-us et   Magni

ALIOS   #7. Hodie orta est--f.3v

1) Ho-di-e or-ta est stel-la ex Ia-cob et ex-sur-re-xit ho-mo de

Is-ra-hel qui-a   Puer

2) Prin-ceps pa-   cis, pa-ter fu- tu-ri se-cu-li,   Cuius

3) Do-mi-na- bi-tur a   ma-ri us- que ad ma-   re et a flu- mi-ne

us- que ad ter- mi-nos or- bis ter- rę,   Et vocabitur

AD OFFERENDAM
(OFF. Tui sunt caeli)

#8. Qui es sine principio--f.4

1) Qui es   si-ne prin-ci-pi-o cum pa- tre et spi-ri-tu sanc-to,

1--MS = futuris. "Futuri" is found in Paris 909, 1119, etc.

fi- li De- i, **Tui sunt**

2) No-bis ho-di-e na-tus de vir-gi-ne De- us ho- mo, **Orbem**

3) Ab i- ni-ti-o et nunc et in se-cu-lum **Iustitia**

4) Prae-pa-ra-ti-o **Praeparatio**

ANTIPHON: **Emitte spiritum sanctum--f.4**

ANTE COMMUNIONEM

ANTIPHONA: E-mit-te spi-ri-tum sanc-tum tu-um, Do- mi- ne, et dig-

na- re sanc-ti-fi-can-do mun-da-re cor-da et cor-po-ra nos-tra

ad per-ci-pi-en- dum cor-pus et san-gui-nem tu-um.

DIACONUS: Nos fran-gi-mus, Do-mi-ne, tu dig-na-re tri-bu-e- re ut

in-ma-cu-la-tis ma-ni-bus il- lud trac-te-mus.

CHORUS: O quam be-a-tum pec-tus il-lud quod Xpis-ti cor-pus me-ru-

e- rit dig- ne per-ci-pe-re.

AD ALTARE: O quam pre-ti-o-sa hu-ius es-cae① co-mes-ti-o quae e-su-

ri-en- tem sa-ti-at② a-ni-mam.

CHORUS: O quam be-a-ti vi-ri il-li qui Xpis-tum me-ru-e-rint sus-ti-

ne-re, cu-i an-ge- li et ar-chan-ge-li mu-ne-ra of-fe-runt im-mor-

ta-li et ae-ter-no re-gi, al-le- lu-ia.

AD AGNUS DEI (= GR II)

#9. Redemptor mundi qui nasci--f.4v

1) Re-demp-tor mun-di qui nas-ci dig-na-tus es ho-di-e pro sa-lu-te

mun-di, mi-se-re-re no-bis e- ia e- ia.

1--MS = aescae
2--MS = satia

136

Ag- nus De- i qui tol- lis pec-ca-ta mun- di, mi-se-

re- re no- bis.

2) Qui se-des ad dex-te-ram pa-tris, so-lus in-vi-si- bi-lis

rex, Mi-se-re- re nobis.

3) Rex re- gum, gau-di-um an-ge-lo- rum, Xpis-te Mi-se-rere

AD COMMUNIONEM

(COM. Viderunt omnes)

#10. Desinat esse dolor--f.5

1) De-si-nat es-se do-lor pro an-ti-qua le- ge qui- a ec-ce, Viderunt

2) Cer-ne-re quod ver-bum Do-mi-ni me-ru-e- re ca-na- mus

Salutare

IN NATALE SANCTI STEPHANI

(INTROIT: Etenim sederunt)

TROPHOS   #11. Hodie Stephanus martyr--f.5

1) Ho- di-e Ste-pha-nus mar- tyr cae-los a-scen-dit, quem pro-phe-ta

du-dum in-tu-ens e- ius vo-ce di-ce-bat: Etenim

2) In-sur-re-xe- runt con-tra me   Iu-dae-o-   rum po-pu- li

i- ni-que, ②   Et iniqui

3) In-vi- di- o- se la-pi- di- bus op-pres-se- runt me, Adiuva

4) Sus-ci-pe me- um in pa-ce   spi- ri- tum,   Quia servus

ITEM ALIOS   #12. Eia conlevitae--f.5v

1) E- ia, con-le-vi-tae in pro-to-mar-ty-ris Ste-pha-ni na-ta-li-ci-o

ex per-so-na ip-si-us cum psal-mis-ta ② o-   van-ter con-cla-ma-te:

Etenim

1--MS = iniquae
2--MS = salmista

138

[musical notation]

2) Pro-ce-res sy-na-go- ge dis-pu-tan-tes con-tra me, Et iniqui

[musical notation]

3) Gra- vi tur-bi-ne la- pi-dum cru- de-li- ter ob- ru-en-tes, Adiuva

[musical notation]

4) Cum tri-um-pho mar-ty-ri-i sus-ci- pi- es spi-ri-tum me- um,

Quia

ALIOS   #13. Salus martyrum--f.5v

[musical notation]

1) Sa-lus mar-ty-rum ho- di-e Ste-pha-num ad cae-los ve-xit co-ro-

[musical notation]

nan-dum di- cen-tem: Etenim

[musical notation]

2) Ro-ga- bat mu-ni-ri di-vi-ni-tus, quod ti-me- bat fo-re fra-gi-

[musical notation]

li-us: Adiuva

[musical notation]

3) Qui Iu- dae-os te Xpis-tum ne-gan-tes con-clu-sis-ti pro-phe-ti-cis

[musical notation]

o- ra-cu-lis, Quia

1--Neum not divided in MS.
2--MS = dicententem

ALIOS   #14. <u>Clamat hians caelis</u>--f.5v

1)   Cla-mat hi-ans cae-lis Ste-pha-nus quos vi-   dit a-   per-tos,<u>Etenim</u>

2)   Sa- xe-a su-   men-tes vi-bran-   ti-bus ar-   ma la- cer-tis,

<u>Et iniqui</u>

3)   Re-spi-ci-ens Hie-   sum de-vo- to   cor-   de pre-ca-tur,

<u>Adiuva</u>

4)   Dum tu-us in   tan-to qua- ti-or dis-cri- mi-ne tes-tis,   <u>Quia</u>

ALIOS   #15. <u>Qui primus meruit</u>--f.6

1)   Qui pri-mus me-ru-it   post Xpis-tum oc- cur-re-re mar-tyr

     Iu-re   su-os ta- li tes-ta- tur vo- ce la-bo- res   <u>Etenim</u>

2)   Non ul-lum no-cu-it   nec le-gum   iu-ra   re- sol-vi, <u>Et iniqui</u>

3)   Xpis-te tu-us fu-e-ram tan-tum qui-a ri- te mi- ni-ster,   <u>Adiuva</u>

140

4) Ne tu-us in-du-bi-o fran-gar cer-ta- mi-ne mi-les,   <u>Quia</u>

ALIOS   #16. <u>Confligunt proceres Ihesu</u>--f.6

1) Con-fli-gunt pro-ce-res Ihe- sus dis-cer-pe-re tes-tem,   <u>Etenim</u>

2) In-se-qui-tur-que pi-um fren-dens in-sa- ni-a fu-rum,   <u>Et iniqui</u>

3) Ex-   er-ce- re tu-is li-bu-it qui-a le- gi-bus al- mis, <u>In tuis</u>

AD OFFERENDAM
(OFF. <u>Posuisti</u>)

#17. <u>Martyrii viam vim</u>--f.6v

Mar-ty-ri-i vi-am vim ca-ri-ta- tis pan-dens Ste-pha-nus tes-tan-do

te mun-do la-pi-da-tur id- e- o iu-re: <u>Posuisti</u>

AD VERSUM (<u>Magna est</u>)   #18. <u>Munere namque tuo</u>--f.6v

Mu-ne-re   nam-que tu-o Ste-pha-num mag-ni-fi-cas-ti,

qui-a: <u>Magna</u>

-13-

AD COMMUNIONEM
(COM. <u>Video</u> <u>caelos</u>)

#19. <u>Intuitus</u> <u>caelum</u>--f.6v

In-tu-i- tus cae- lum be-a- tus Ste-pha-nus a- it: <u>Video</u>

IN NATALE SANCTI IOHANNIS EVANGELISTE

(INTROIT: <u>In medio</u>)

#20. <u>Ecce iam Iohannis</u>--f.6v

1) Ec-ce iam Io-han-nis ad-est ve-ne-ran-da glo-ri-a

Cu-i Xpis-tus am-pli-o-ra do-na cre-dens mis-ti-ca,   <u>In medio</u>

2) Quem vir- gi-ne-o flo-re sa-cra-vit,   <u>Et implevit</u>

3) Pas-to-rem no-bis tri-bu-ens,   <u>Stolam</u>

ITEM ALIOS   #21. <u>Fons</u> <u>et</u> <u>origo</u>--f.6v

1) Fons et o- ri- go sa- pi-en- ti-ae ad pro-pa-lan-da su-ae di-vi-

142

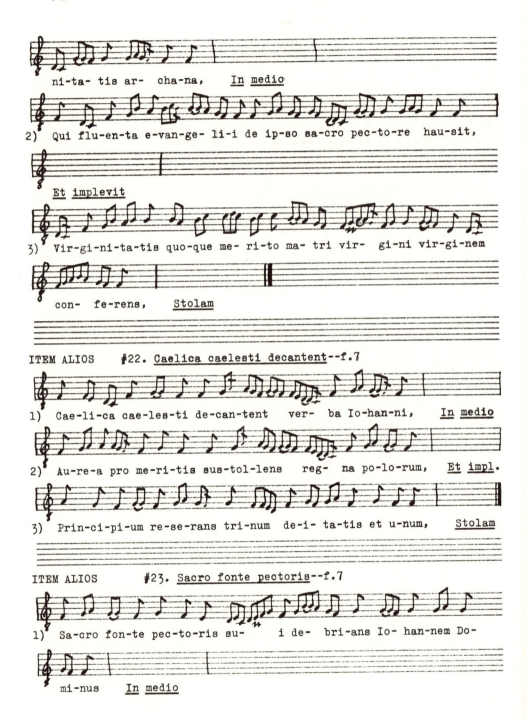

ni- ta- tis ar- cha- na,   In medio

2) Qui flu-en-ta e-van-ge- li-i de ip-so sa-cro pec-to-re hau-sit,

Et implevit

3) Vir-gi-ni-ta-tis quo-que me- ri-to ma- tri vir- gi-ni vir-gi-nem

con- fe-rens,   Stolam

ITEM ALIOS   #22. Caelica caelesti decantent--f.7

1) Cae-li-ca cae-les-ti de-can-tent   ver- ba Io-han-ni,   In medio

2) Au-re-a pro me-ri-tis sus-tol-lens   reg- na po-lo-rum,   Et impl.

3) Prin-ci-pi-um re-se-rans tri-num de-i- ta-tis et u-num,   Stolam

ITEM ALIOS   #23. Sacro fonte pectoris--f.7

1) Sa-cro fon-te pec-to-ris su-   i de- bri-ans Io- han-nem Do-

mi-nus   In medio

2) Re-ve-lans e- i al- ti-us sa-cra-men- ta cae-les-ti-a,   Et impl.

3) Di-li-gen-do au- tem fa-mi-li-a- ri-us u- num,   Stolam

ITEM ALIOS   #24. Omnia concludens verbi--f.7

1) Om-   ni-a con-clu-dens   ver-bi   di-vi-ni   cre-a- ta

In medio

2) Quem di-le-xit a- mans   di-vi- no pneu-ma-te ple- num,   Stolam

AD OFFERENDAM
(OFF. Iustus ut palma)

#25. Psallite dilecto meruit--f.7v

Psal-li-te di- lec-to me-   ru-it qui lau-dem Io-han-ni;

Gra-tu-le-tur om-nis ca-ro di-lec-to Do-mi-ni,   pan-gat om-nis

tur-ba me-los, et in ex-cel-sis cor-da ex-tol-la-mus e- ia: Iustus

1--MS = Pallite

AD COMMUNIONEM
(COM. Exiit sermo)

#26. Corda fratrum--f.7v

Cor-da fra-trum fa-mam vol-vunt in-cli-tam, quod san-ctus car-ne

vi-ve-ret in se-cu-la, cu-i om-nes lau-des per-to-ne-mus e- ia:

Exiit

IN NATALE INNOCENTIUM
(INTROIT: Ex ore infantium)

#27. Dicite nunc pueri--f.7v

1) Di-ci-te nunc pu-e-ri psal-len-tes   car-mi-na   Xpis-to: Ex ore

2) San-gui-nem nam-que su-um fu-de-re no-mi-ni tu- o,   Propter

ITEM ALIOS   #28. Filii carissimi--f.7v

1) Fi-li- i ca-ris-si-mi, Do-mi- no   me-los pan-gi- te u- na

vo-ce cla-man- tes: <u>Ex</u> <u>ore</u>

2) Fe-cis-ti lau-da-re no-men tu- um, <u>Et</u> <u>lactentium</u>

3) Tri-um-phan-tes de hos-te vi-pe-re-o flo-rem ae-ter-nae vir-gi-ni-

ta-tis e-os in cae-les-ti glo-ri-a sus-ce-pis-ti, <u>Propter</u>

ITEM ALIOS   #29. <u>Munera</u> <u>prima</u> <u>patri</u>--f.8

1) Mu-ne-ra pri-ma pa-tri pu-e-ros pu-er ho-di-e mit-tens, <u>Ex</u> <u>ore</u>

2) Pul-chri-us in te-ne- ris cen-ses si-bi sub-de-re for-tes, <u>Propter</u>

ITEM ALIOS   #30. <u>Pangite</u> <u>iam</u> <u>pueri</u>--f.8

1) Pan-gi-te iam, pu-e-ri, lau-des et pro-mi-te Xpis- to, <u>Ex</u> <u>ore</u>

2) Na- te De-i cle- mens par-vu-lo- rum sus- ci-pe lau-des,

<u>Et</u> <u>lactentium</u>

3) Qui ti-bi iam na-to cer- ta-   runt san- gui-ne fu-so, Propter

AD OFFERENDAM
(OFF. Anima nostra)

#31. Erepti secum fantur--f.8

E- rep-ti se-cum fan-tur de mor-   te be-a-   ti: Anima

AD COMMUNIONEM
(COM. Vox in Rama)

#32. Sancta Hieremiae--f.8

San- cta Hie-re-mi-ae re-ci-nunt haec dic-ta pro-phe-tae

Ec-cle-si-ae sig-no cum do- let ec-ce Ra-chel: Vox in Rama

IN EPIPHANIA DOMINI

(INTROIT: Ecce advenit)

#33. Haec est praeclara--f.8v

1) Haec est prae-cla-ra di-es tri-bus sa-cra-ta mi-ra- cu-lis, in

qua cum pro-phe-ta ca-na- mus, di-cen-tes: Ecce advenit

2) Cu-i Ma- gi ho-di-e mu- ne-ra of-fe-runt et ut re- gem su-

per-num a-do-rant qui est u- bi- que, Dominator

3) In Ior-da-ne a Io-han-ne bap-ti-za-tus pa-ter-na vo- ce fi-li-

us est pro-tes-ta-tus cu- ius ho- nor Et regnum

4) Na-tu-ras lim-phe-as ho-di-e mu- ta-vit in sa-po-ri-fe-ros

haus-tus per po-tes-ta-tem Et imperium.

ITEM ALIOS   #34. Ecclesiae sponsus--f.9

1) Ec- cle-si-ae spon-sus, in-lu-mi-na- tor gen-ti-um, bap-tis-ma-tis

1--MS = haustum. "Haustus" is found in Paris 1119, etc.

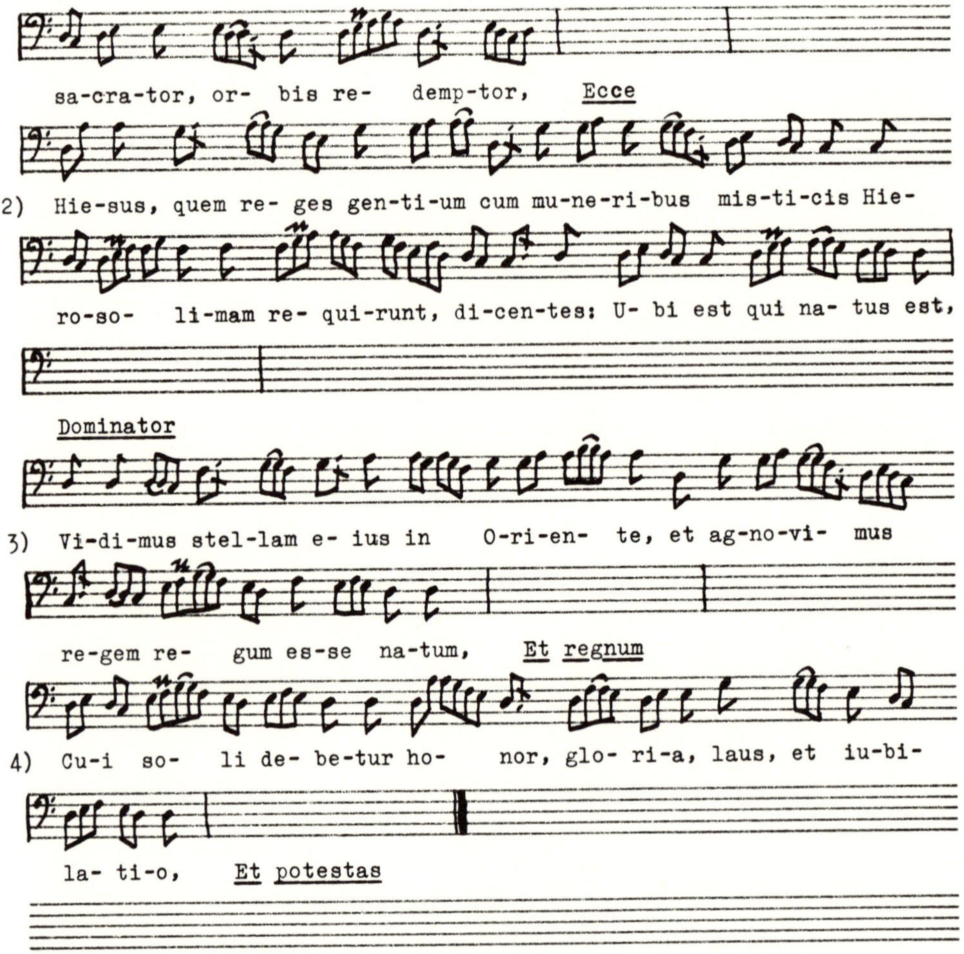

148

sa-cra-tor, or- bis re- demp-tor,   Ecce

2) Hie-sus, quem re- ges gen-ti-um cum mu-ne-ri-bus mis-ti-cis Hie-

ro-so- li-mam re- qui-runt, di-cen-tes: U- bi est qui na- tus est,

Dominator

3) Vi-di-mus stel-lam e- ius in   O-ri-en- te, et ag-no-vi- mus

re-gem re- gum es-se na-tum,   Et regnum

4) Cu-i so- li de-be-tur ho-   nor, glo-ri-a, laus, et iu-bi-

la- ti-o,   Et potestas

ALIOS   #35. Eia Sion gaude--f.9

1) E-   ia Si-on gau-de et lae-ta-re as-pec-tu De-i   tu-i: Ecce

2) Cu-i ma- the-ri- ae cae-li et   ter-rae   fa-   mu-lan-tur, Et regnum

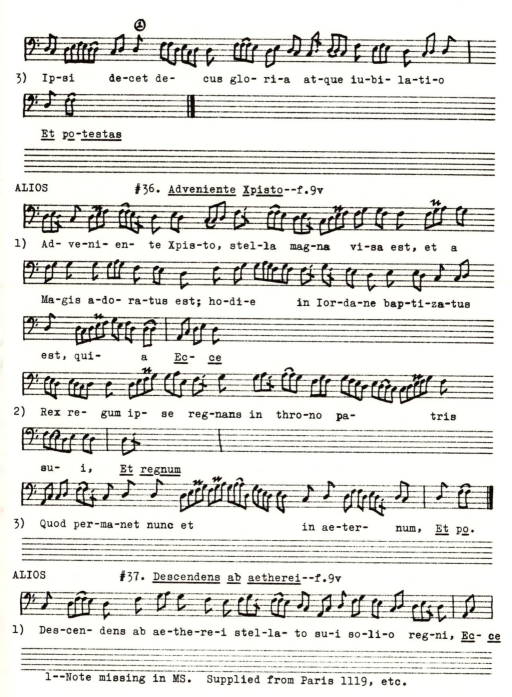

3) Ip-si de-cet de- cus glo- ri-a at-que iu-bi- la-ti-o

Et po-testas

ALIOS #36. Adveniente Xpisto--f.9v

1) Ad- ve-ni- en- te Xpis-to, stel-la mag-na vi-sa est, et a

Ma-gis a-do- ra-tus est; ho-di-e in Ior-da-ne bap-ti-za-tus

est, qui- a Ec- ce

2) Rex re- gum ip- se reg-nans in thro-no pa- tris

su- i, Et regnum

3) Quod per-ma-net nunc et in ae-ter- num, Et po.

ALIOS #37. Descendens ab aetherei--f.9v

1) Des-cen- dens ab ae-the-re-i stel-la- to su-i so-li-o reg-ni, Ec- ce

1--Note missing in MS. Supplied from Paris 1119, etc.

2) Om- nes ut po- pu-los so- ci-et si- bi foe- de-re

fir-mo, Et regnum

3) Quod da- bit ip-se su-is il-lic-que e- rit hic et in ae-vum,

Et po-testas

#38. Ut sedeat in throno--f.9v

1) Ut se- de-at in thro-no Da-vid pa-tris su-i in ae- ter- num,

Ecce

2) A pa- tre cun-cta da-ta Xpis-to sunt se- cu-la nam-que Et potestas

AD SEQUENTIAM
(SEQ. Epiphaniam Domino)

#39. O dux Magorum--f.9v

O dux Ma-go-rum, ti-bi sit laus, glo-ri- a, io-cun-di-tas sem-

1--Note missing in MS.
2--This is the reading of most St. Martial MSS. Paris 1121 = illi-.

pi-ter-na; nos quo-que om- nes di-ca-mus, e- ia:

Al-le-lu-ia

AD OFFERENDAM
(OFF. Reges Tarsis)

#40. Regi Xpisto iam--f.10

Re- gi Xpis-to iam ter-ris ma-ni-fes-ta-to, quem ad-o- rant ho-

di-e Ma- gi, psal-li-te om- nes cum pro-phe-ta di-cen-tes: Reges

AD COMMUNIONEM
(COM. Vidimus stellam)

#41. Stella praevia reges--f.10

Stel-la prae-vi-a re-ges ab O-ri-en-te ve-ni-unt re-gem re- gum

na- tum in-qui-ren-tes di-cen-tes- que: Vi- dimus

152

IN PURIFICATIONE SANCTAE MARIAE

(INTROIT: Suscepimus)

#42. O nova res--f.10

1) O no-va res, en vir-go ve- nit, par-tum ge- rit, et nos

Suscepimus

2) Quod non vi- su- ri pa-tres cu-pi-e- re vi-de- mus, In medio

3) Rex pi-e Xpis-te, tu- um sit no- men sem- per ho-

nes-tum, Secundum

ALIOS #43. Pectore laudifluo--f.10v

1) Pec-to-re lau- di-flu-o de-can- tet mis- ti-cus or- do: Suscepi.

2) Cum te per-fer- ret Si- me- on se-ni- li-bus ul- nis,

In medio

3) Vir-go te gre- mi-o por- tat quem mun-dus a- do-rat, Secundum

4) Nam si-cut est ti-bi vir-tus, ho-nor, ae- ter- na po- tes-tas, Ita

5) Om-ni-a quae con-stant tu-a sunt, do- mi-na- tor, et in- de Iustitia

Glo-ri-a se-cu- lo-rum a- men.

ALIOS   #44. Caelorum rex--f.10v

1) Cae- lo- rum rex, ad-ve- ni-sti ut   nos re- di-me-res,

Suscepimus

2) Quem Si-me-on se-nex pla-ci-de sus-ce-pit in ul-nis,   In medio

3) Te lau-dant om- nes pa-ri-ter cum vo-ce re-sul-tant,   Secundum

4) Tu to-tus dex-ter iu-stus iu-dex-que ven-tu-rus,   Ita

ALIOS   #45. Adest alma Virgo--f.11

1) Ad-est al- ma Vir-go Ma- ri-a, ad- est ver-bum ca- ro   fac-tum,

quem a-do-ran-tes om- nes   Suscepimus

2) Lu-men ae- ter-num, Xpis-tum Do-mi-num,   In medio

3) In bra-chi-is san-cti Sy-me-o-nis,   Secundum

4) Glo-ri-a, sa-lus, et ho-nor   In fines

5) In ple-ni-tu-di-ne gra-ti-ae,   Iustitia

AD OFFERENDAM
(OFF. Diffusa est)

#46. Aurea Davitico--f.11

1) Au-re-a Da-vi-ti-co pro-dis-ti ger-   mi-ne vir-go,   Diffusa est

2) In se- cu-lo-rum se-cu-la   Et in seculum

AD VERSUM (Specie tua)
#47. Integra cum pareres--f.11

In-te-gra cum pa-re-res sed et in- te-gra cum pe-pe-ris-ses, Specie

AD COMMUNIONEM
(COM. Responsum)

#48. Felix qui meruit--f.11

Fe- lix qui me- ru-it pro-mis-sum cer- ne-re Xpis-tum,

Responsum

(IN RESURRECTIONE DOMINI)
(INTROIT: Resurrexi)

#49. Quem queritis in sepulchro--f.11v

Quem que-ri- tis in se-pul- chro, o Cris-ti-co- le?

Hie-sum Na-za-re-num cru-ci-fi-xum, o Cae-li-co-lae.

Non est hic, sur-re-xit, sic-ut prae-di-xe- rat; i- te nun-ti-a-te

qui-a sur-re-xit.   Al-le-lu-ia.

Ad se-pul-chrum re-si-dens an-ge-lus nun-ti-at re-sur-re-xis-se

Xpis-tum.

En ec- ce com-ple-tum est il-lud quod o- lim ip- se per pro-

phe-tam di-xe-rat ad pa-trem, ta-li-ter in-qui-ens: <u>Resurrexi</u>①

ALIOS   #50. <u>Ecce pater cunctis</u>--f.12

1) Ec- ce, pa- ter, cunc-tis ut ius-se-   rat or-   do

per-ac-tis: <u>Resurrexi</u>

2) Vic-tor ut ad cae-los cal-ca- ta mor-te re-di-rem,   <u>Posuisti</u>

3) Quo ge-nus hu-ma-num pul-sis er-ro-ri- bus al- tum/

scan-de-   ret ad cae-lum,   <u>Mirabilis</u>

ITEM ALIOS   #51. <u>Factus homo tua iussa</u>--f.12

1) Fac- tus ho- mo tu-a ius-sa pa- ter mo-ri-en- do per-e-   gi,

<u>R</u>esurrexi

1--This cue is never given in full in the MS. Thus, it is impossible
   to say if it preserves the reading "Resurrexit" of Paris 1120 and
   certain other St. Martial tropers. (Cf. also the Rheinau
   Antiphoner in Hesbert <u>Sextuplex</u>, no. 80.)

2) Ab-tu-le-ras① mi-se-ra-te ma- nes mi-chi red-di-ta lux est,

Posuisti

3) Plebs cae-ca- ta me- um no- men non no- vit a-man- dum,

Mirabilis

ALIOS   #52. Aurea lux remeat--f.12

1) Au- re-a lux re- me-at Ihe-sus iam mor-te per-emp-ta

Sic cru-ci-fer pa- tri Da- vi- dis af-fa- tur, en e- go

Resurrexi

2) Quo com-pos ho- mi- nis cae-los iam vic- tor ad-i-rem,

Posuisti

3) Om- ne quod est, fu-e-rat, su-per-est tu vi- des

1--MS originally read "abtulerat"; corrected to "abtuleras."

u- bi-que,   Mirabilis

4) Te mun-dus cae-   lum pa-ri-ter lau-dan-do pro-cla-mant Alleluia

ALIOS   #53. Ego autem constitutus--f.12v

1) E-   go au-tem con-sti-tu- tus sum rex,   prae-di-cans pre-cep-tum

tu-um, et   mor-te de-vic-ta   Resurrexi

2) Dor-mi- vi, pa-ter, et sur-gam di-lu-cu-lo, et som-nus me- us dul-

cis est mi-chi, Po- suisti

3) I-ta, pa- ter, sic pla-cu-it an-te te, ut mo-ri-en-do mor-tis mors

fu-is- sem, mor-sus in-fer-ni, et mun-do vi-ta,   Mirabilis

4) Qui ab-scon-dis-ti haec sa-pi-en-ti-bus, et re-ve-las-ti par-vu-lis,

al-le-lu-ia,   Alleluia

ALII   #54. <u>En ego verus sol</u>--f.12v

1) En e-go ve-rus sol, oc-ca-sum me-um no- vi, et su-per e-　um so-

lus as-cen-dens   <u>Resurrexi</u>

2) De-struc-to   mor-tis im-pe-ri-o,   <u>Po- suisti</u>

3) Quo-ni-am mors me-a fac-ta est   mun-di vi-ta,   <u>Mirabilis</u>

4) Ex-ur-ge glo-ri-a   me-a, fi-li; ex-ur-gam di-lu- cu-lo, pa-ter,

<u>Alleluia</u>

ALIOS②   #55. <u>Iam tua iussa</u>--f.13

1) Iam tu-a ius-sa, pa-ter, mor-   tem su-pe-ran-do per-e-

gi,   <u>Re-sur-rexi</u>

2) Vin-ce-re quo   mun-dum mor-tem za-bu-lo- que va-le-re,

<u>Posuisti</u>

1--MS originally read "Alia."

3) Mis-ti-ca per- do-cu-i ge-mi-na   sa-cra-men-ta so- phi-

ae,   **Mi -ra- bilis**

.4) Om-ne quod nunc spi-rat, pa-   ter,   te lau-dat ca-nen-

do: **Alleluia**

ITEM ALIOS   #56. **Factus homo de matre**--f.13

1) Fac-   tus ho-mo de ma-tre, pa-ter, tu-a ius-sa se-cu-   tus,

In qua cru- cis lig-no   mor-   tis auc-to-   re

per-emp-to,   **Resurrexi**

2) Ne mi-chi tunc cae-ca-ta co-hors ob- sis-te-re pos- set

No-mi-nis at-que me-i lu-   men fus-ca-   re se-re-num,

Posuisti

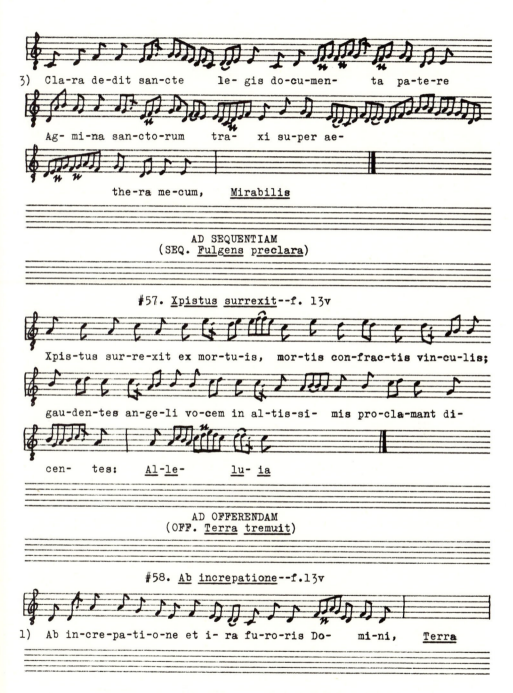

3) Cla-ra de-dit san-cte   le- gis do-cu-men-   ta pa-te-re

Ag- mi-na san-cto-rum   tra- xi su-per ae-

the-ra me-cum,   Mirabilis

AD SEQUENTIAM
(SEQ. Fulgens preclara)

#57. Xpistus surrexit--f. 13v

Xpis-tus sur-re-xit ex mor-tu-is, mor-tis con-frac-tis vin-cu-lis;

gau-den-tes an-ge-li vo-cem in al-tis-si- mis pro-cla-mant di-

cen- tes: Al-le-   lu- ia

AD OFFERENDAM
(OFF. Terra tremuit)

#58. Ab increpatione--f.13v

1) Ab in-cre-pa-ti-o-ne et i- ra fu-ro-ris Do-   mi-ni,   Terra

2) Mo-nu-men-ta a-per-ta sunt, et mul-ta cor-po-ra sanc-to-rum sur-

re- xe-runt, Dum

3) Quan-do ve-nit iu-di-ca-re vi-vos ac mor-tu-os In iudicio

4) Xpis-to sur-gen-te a mor-tu-is, ve-ni-te a-do-re-mus e- um om- nes

u-na vo-ce pro-cla-man-tes: Al- leluia.

ANTIPHON: Venite populi--f.14 ④

Ve- ni-te po-pu-li ad sa-crum et im-mor-ta-le

mis-te-ri-um et li-ba-men a-gen- dum; Cum ti-mo-re et fi-de

ac-ce-da- mus, ma-ni-bus mun-di poe-ni-ten-ti-ae mu-nus

com-mu-ni-ce- mus; Quo-ni-am ag-nus De-i prop-ter nos pa-tris

1--In MS, this and the next item (#59) actually follow #60. Correct
position is indicated by rubric.

sa-cri-fi-ci-um pro-po-si-tum est; Ipsum so-lum ad-o- re-mus,

Ip-sum glo-ri-fi-ce- mus cum an-ge- lis, cla-man- tes:

al- le- lu- ia.

TROPHI AD AGNUS DEI

#59. Pro cunctis deductus--f.14v

1) Pro cun-ctis de-duc-tus ad im-mo- lan-dum fu-is- ti ut ag-nus;

Re- demp-ta ple-be cap-ti-va te lae-ti de-po-sci-mus vo-ce

prae-cel- sa:

Ag- nus De- i, qui tol- lis pec- ca- ta mun-di,

Mi-se- re- re no- bis.

2) An- ti-quus plas- tor et ae- ter-nae vi-tae dis-po-si-tor,

Miserere

3) Nos-tro-rum   cri- mi-num ab- lu-ae sor-des, o   Ihe-su

Xpis-te,   Miserere

4) Pri- o- rum spes an-ti-   qua nos-tro-rum sus-ci-pi-at tu-a

vo- ces cle-men- ti-a,   Miserere

5) De- cus an- ge-lo- rum et rex se-   cu-lo- rum,   Miserere

AD COMMUNIONEM
(COM. Pascha nostrum)

#60. Laus honor virtus--f.14

1) Laus, ho-nor, vir-tus De-o nos-tro, de-cus et im-pe-ri-um re-gi

mag-no,   qui pre-ti-um re-demp-ti-o- nis nos-trae,   Pascha

2) Pec-ca-ta nos-tra ip-se por-ta- vit, et prop-ter sce-le-ra nos-tra

ob-la-tus est   Xpis-tus

3) Le-o for-tis de tri-bu Iu-da ho-di-e sur-re-xit a mor-tu-is, al-le-

lu-ia, in cu-ius lau-de cel-sa vo-ce per-to-na-te: Al-le-   lu-ia

FERIA II
(INTROIT: Introduxit vos)

#61. Dulciter agnicolae--f.14v

1) Dul-ci-ter ag- ni-co-lae fes-ti-vum du-ci-te pas-cha

Iam qui-a Ior-da- nis me-ru-is-tis fon-te re-nas-ci: Introduxit

2) Ci-vi-bus ae- the-re-is ma- nan-   tem man-   na de-co- ris,

Et ut lex

3) Di-xe-rat hoc Mo-y-ses quon-dam, Xpis-tus iu-bet at nunc   In ore

1--"Voce" added, apparently in hand of notator.
2--Paris 1118 gives the cues as follows: Introduxit, In terram,
   Et ut lex, Alleluia.

166

4) Ae-ter hu-mus pa-ri-ter pe-la-gus u- ni-ta vo- ce de-can-tant,①

Alleluia

ALII   #62. <u>Ecce</u> <u>veri</u> <u>luminis</u>--f.15

1) Ec-   ce ve- ri lu-mi- nis ce-le-bran- da nem-pe

cho-rus-cat/ Pas-   chae di-es qua fon-te per-hen-ni iam

re-no-va-   tos: <u>Introduxit</u>

2) Qui de- de-rat pri-o-ra pre-cep-ta le-gis mo-do iu-bet/

Quo mis-ti-ca do-cu- men- ta pa- trum fir-mi-ter te- ne- a- tis:

<u>Et ut lex</u>

3) Lau-di-bus ae-the-re-is re-ci-nen- do pas-chae tri-um- phis/

Psal-lat u-ni-ta co-hors re-demp-   tus est qui-a

1--MS originally read "decantent," corrected as above.

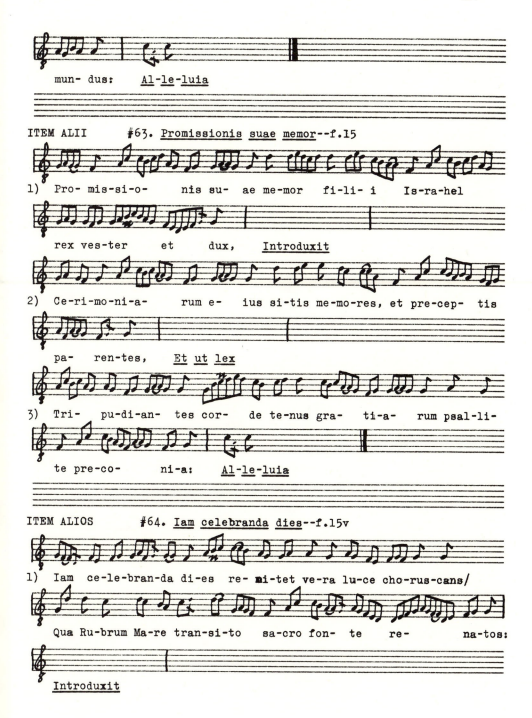

mun- dus: Al-le-luia

ITEM ALII   #63. Promissionis suae memor--f.15

1) Pro- mis-si-o- nis su- ae me-mor fi-li- i   Is-ra-hel

rex ves-ter   et   dux,   Introduxit

2) Ce-ri-mo-ni-a- rum e- ius si-tis me-mo-res, et pre-cep- tis

pa- ren-tes,   Et ut lex

3) Tri- pu-di-an- tes cor- de te-nus gra- ti-a- rum psal-li-

te pre-co- ni-a: Al-le-luia

ITEM ALIOS   #64. Iam celebranda dies--f.15v

1) Iam ce-le-bran-da di-es re- mi-tet ve-ra lu-ce cho-rus-cans/

Qua Ru-brum Ma-re tran-si-to sa-cro fon- te re- na-tos:

Introduxit

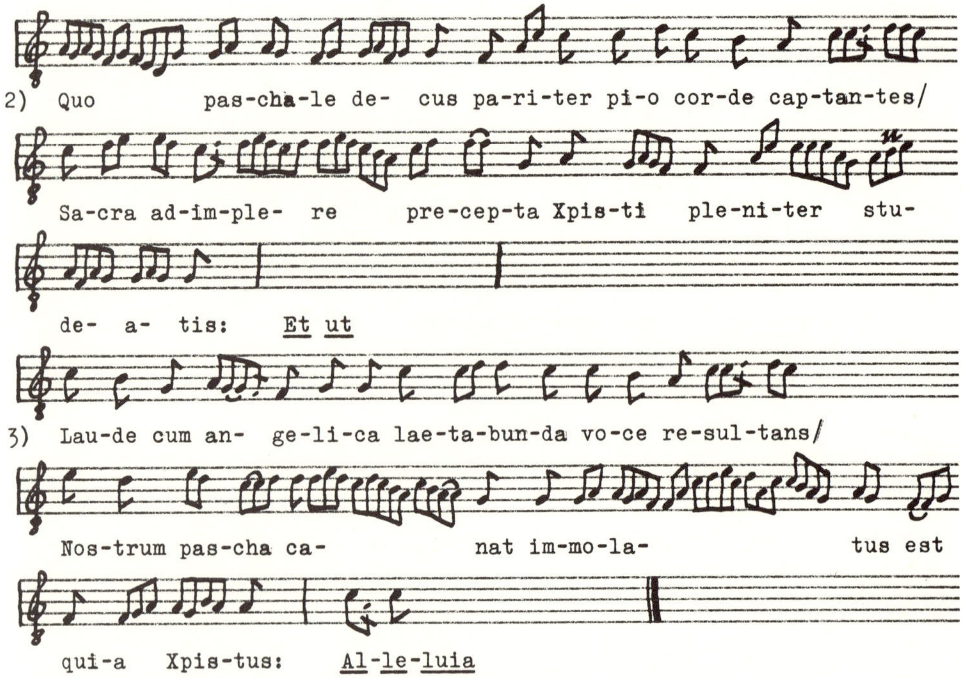

168

2) Quo   pas-cha-le de- cus pa-ri-ter pi-o cor-de cap-tan-tes/

Sa-cra ad-im-ple- re   pre-cep-ta Xpis-ti   ple-ni-ter stu-

de- a- tis: Et ut

3) Lau-de cum an- ge-li-ca lae-ta-bun-da vo-ce re-sul-tans/

Nos-trum pas-cha ca-   nat im-mo-la-   tus est

qui-a Xpis-tus: Al-le-lu-ia

AD OFFERENDAM TROPHI
(OFF. Angelus Domini)

#65. Et ecce terrę--f.15v

1) Et ec- ce ter-rę   mo-tus fac- tus est mag-nus,   Angelus

2) Et ac- ce-   dens re-vol-   vit la-   pi-dem se-dit-que

su-per e-   um,   Et di- xit

3) Non   est hic,   Surrexit

FERIA III

(INTROIT: Aqua sapientiae)

#66. Expurgans populos--f.16

1) Ex-pur-   gans po- pu-los Do-mi-nus bap-   tis-ma-te

tinc-   tos   Aqua

2) Quos-que su-ae sor-tis so- ci-os si-bi ces-se-rit es-   se,

Firmabitur

3) Ac sta-tu-et cel- sa se-   cum re-si-de-   re ca-the-dra,

Et exaltabit

4) Psal-len-tes pla-ci-dum cla- ris cum   vo-ci-bus hym-num:

1--MS = epurgans
2--MS = cesseris
3--Note not in MS; but cf. Paris 909, 1119, etc.

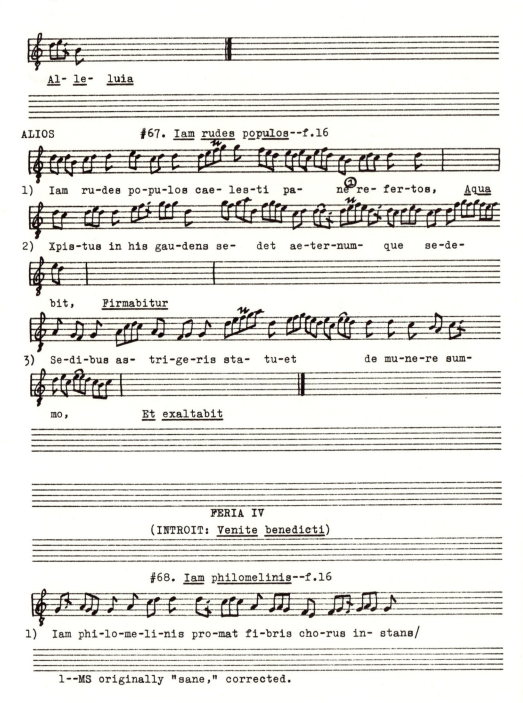

Al- le- luia

ALIOS   #67. Iam rudes populos--f.16

1) Iam ru-des po-pu-los cae- les-ti pa-   ne re- fer-tos,   Aqua

2) Xpis-tus in his gau-dens se- det ae-ter-num- que se-de-

bit,   Firmabitur

3) Se-di-bus as- tri-ge-ris sta- tu-et   de mu-ne-re sum-

mo,   Et exaltabit

FERIA IV
(INTROIT: Venite benedicti)

#68. Iam philomelinis--f.16

1) Iam phi-lo-me-li-nis pro-mat fi-bris cho-rus in- stans/

1--MS originally "sane," corrected.

Ar-bi-ter ae-thre mi-cans po-pu-lis quod fa-bi-tur al- mis,

Venite

2) Ob-se-qui-is mi- chi qui va- ri-is ser-vis-tis in ar- vis, Percipite

3) Nul-li-us au-ris aut cor lu- men cer-ne-re no- vit, Quod vobis

4) Ae-the-re-is re-to-nan-tes clan-gi-te vo-ci-bus o- das: Al-le-luia

ALIOS   #69. Vos quia certastis--f.16v

1) Vos qui-a cer- tas-tis be-ne iam post fu-ne-ra car- nis, Venite

2) Sci-li-cet op- ta- tum a   vi-do quo-que cor- de cu-pi- tum,

Quod vobis

3) Un-de po-lo ter-ra-que pi-um re-so-ne-tur o-   van-ter, Alleluia

OCTAVAS PASCHE
(INTROIT: Quasi modo)

#70. Ecce omnes redempti--f.16v

1) Ec-ce om- nes re-demp-ti, ge-nus e-lec- tum, re- ga- le sa-

cer-do-ti-um, gens sanc- ta, po-pu-lusad-qui-si-ti-o- nis,

de-po- nen-tes om- nem ma- li-ti-am, Quasi

2) Si gus-tas-tis quo-ni-am dul-cis est Do-mi-nus, Rationabile

3) Ut in e- o cres-ca-tis in sa- lu-tem, Lac

4) Ac-ce- den-tes ad la- pi-dem vi-vum ca- ni-te om- nes:

Al-le-lu- ia

ITEM ALIOS   #71. O populi sacro--f.16v

1) O po-pu-li sa- cro Do- mi-ni bap-tis-ma-te na-ti, Quasi

2) Sen- si- bus ef-fec- ti pu- e-ri- que se-ni-li-bus ac-tis, Ratio.

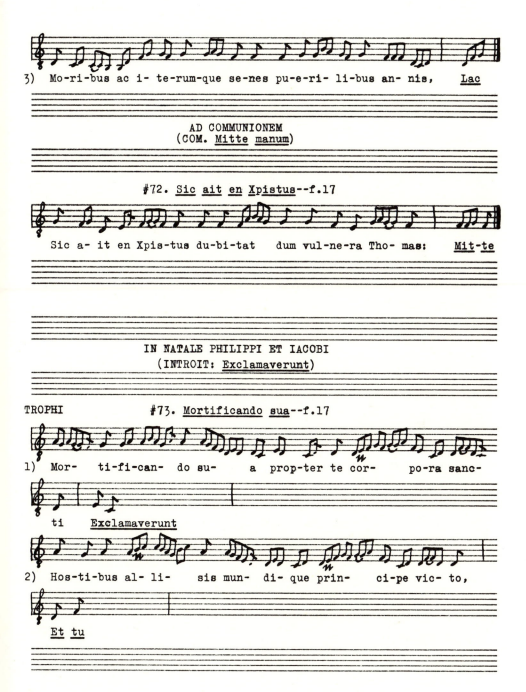

3) Mo-ri-bus ac i- te-rum-que se-nes pu-e-ri- li-bus an- nis,   Lac

AD COMMUNIONEM
(COM. Mitte manum)

#72. Sic ait en Xpistus--f.17

Sic a- it en Xpis-tus du-bi-tat   dum vul-ne-ra Tho- mas: Mit-te

IN NATALE PHILIPPI ET IACOBI
(INTROIT: Exclamaverunt)

TROPHI   #73. Mortificando sua--f.17

1) Mor-   ti-fi-can- do su-   a prop-ter te cor-   po-ra sanc-

ti   Exclamaverunt

2) Hos-ti-bus al- li-   sis mun- di- que prin-   ci-pe vic- to,

Et tu

174

3) Ut ti- bi dul- ci-flu-ę psal- lant re-ci-nen- do per e- vum:

Alleluia

ALIOS   #74. Alme tuum semper--f.17

1) Al- me   tu-um sem-   per cer- nen-tes iu-re re-gi-   men,

Exclamaverunt

2) Nos-tra be- nig-ne li-bens de- ter-gis no-   xi-a so-   ther,

Et tu

3) Un-de fi- de-lis o-   vans pro- cla-met tur-   ba per e- on: All.

ALIOS   #75. Aspera portantes--f.17

As-   pe-ra por- tan- tes prop- ter te cor-   po-ra sanc- ti

Exclamaverunt

IN DEDICATIONE
(INTROIT: Terribilis est)

#76. Celebremus ovanter festa--f.17v

1) Ce-le-bre-mus o- van-ter fes-ta ec- cle-si-ae, nec-ne ca- na-mus

om- nes: Terribilis

2) Qui-a ab al- tis-si-mo fun-da-ta est,   Hic domus

3) In ip-sa e-nim Xpis-tus ha- bi-tat, et hic sca-la an-ge- lo-rum est,

Et porta

4) Per quam cre-den-tes ve-ni-am in e-a pri-us a-dep-tam ad ae-the-ra

me-ren-tur con-scen-de-re,   Et vocabitur

ITEM ALIOS   #77. Divinus succendat amor--f.17v

1) Di-vi- nus suc-cen-dat a- mor fer-ven-ti-a cor-da/

Sanc-to-rum me-ri- tis ut pi-a dig-na ca- nat: Terribilis

176

2) In quo cae-li ter-rae-que com-pos a-do- ra-tur a cunc- tis, Hic do.

3) Ni-si-bus ar-ta De-i po-pu-lo- rum no-   xi-a vi-tans,

Et porta

4) In-trat mox per quam ius-to-   rum gau- di-a vi-tae, Et voca.

ITEM ALIOS   #78. Hic trina sonat--f.18

1) Hic   tri-na so- nat de- i- tas u- na-que po- tes-

tas,   Terribilis

2) Nec-ta-re dul- ce-di-nis di-vo-   rum nu- mi-ne ple-nus, Hic do.

3) Lu-mi-ne lus-tra-ta   pi-o-   rum ste- ma-tis al- ti, Et porta

4) Per quam Xpis-ti-co-lę   tri-um- phan- tes su- pe-ra

scan- dunt,   Et vocabitur

ALIOS   #79. **Est quia terribilis**--f.18

1) Est qui-a ter-ri-bi-lis do-mus is-ta di-ca- ta to- nan-ti,   **Terribil.**

2) Quam De-us in-vi- sit cho- rus an-ge-li-cus-que fre-quen-tat, **Hic domus**

3) Per quam ius-to- rum trans-cen-dunt si-de-ra   vo-   ces, Et **voca.**

ALIOS   #80. **Haec meruit sponsum**--f.18

1) Haec me-ru-it spon-sum ci-vi-tas am-plec-te-re Xpis-tum/

Ma-net e- nim fe- lix et   pa-   ri-ens id- e- o,   **Terribilis**

2) Di-vi-nis ful-gens re-   bus de   mu-ne- re spon-si,   **Hic domus**

3) An-ge-li-cis con-fer-ta bo- nis u-bi sanc-ta di-   can-tur,

Et porta

4) Per quam plebs ho-no-ra- ta De-i   sa-cra li- mi-na   lus-trat,

Et vocabitur

178

ITEM ALIOS   #81. Concinat en plectrum--f.18v

1) Con-ci-nat en plec-trum fe-li- cis pos-tu-lo lin-   guae, Terribilis

2) So-the-ris et dex-tra per-sis-tat nunc   be-ne-dic-ta, Hic domus

3) Qua cri-mi-num mi-nu-at hic fas per se-   cu-la cle-mens,

Et vocabitur

ALIOS   #82. Haec est etenim aula--f.18v

1) Haec est et-e-nim au- la De-i de qua dic-tum est: Terribilis

2) Sub-plan-tans   vi-   ti-a   ple-bis pro-   cla-mat o- van-

ter,   Hic domus

3) Per-vi-a pul-san-ti re-se-ran-tur li- mi-na cor-dis,   Et porta

4) A Xpis-to gra-tis pos-cen-ti-bus or-   ri-da ter-

gi,   Et vocabitur

1--The bracketed neums, supplied here from Paris 909, were erased
    in Paris 1121.

ALIOS   #83. <u>Typica visione</u>--f.18v

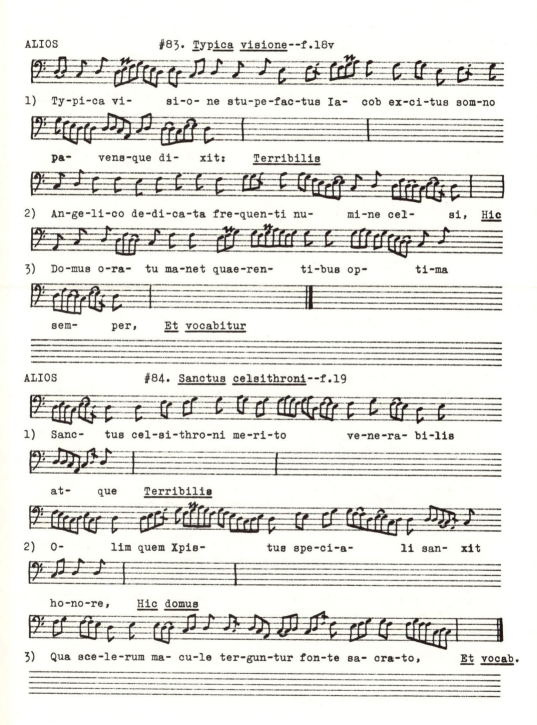

1)   Ty-pi-ca vi-   si-o- ne stu-pe-fac-tus Ia-   cob ex-ci-tus som-no

pa-   vens-que di-   xit: <u>Terribilis</u>

2)   An-ge-li-co de-di-ca-ta fre-quen-ti nu-   mi-ne cel-   si,   <u>Hic</u>

3)   Do-mus o-ra-   tu ma-net quae-ren-   ti-bus op-   ti-ma

sem-   per,   <u>Et vocabitur</u>

ALIOS   #84. <u>Sanctus celsithroni</u>--f.19

1)   Sanc-   tus cel-si-thro-ni me-ri-to   ve-ne-ra- bi-lis

at-   que   <u>Terribilis</u>

2)   O-   lim quem Xpis-   tus spe-ci-a-   li san-   xit

ho-no-re,   <u>Hic domus</u>

3)   Qua sce-le-rum ma- cu-le ter-gun-tur fon-te sa- cra-to,   <u>Et vocab.</u>

180

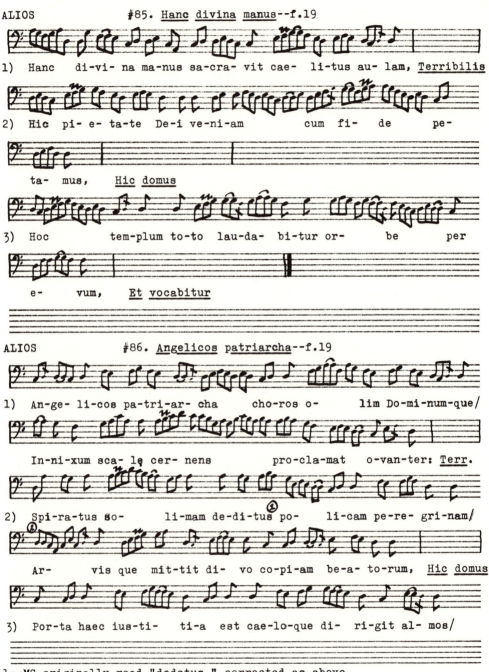

ALIOS   #85. Hanc divina manus--f.19

1) Hanc di-vi- na ma-nus sa-cra- vit cae- li-tus au- lam, Terribilis

2) Hic pi- e- ta-te De-i ve-ni- am cum fi- de pe-

ta- mus,   Hic domus

3) Hoc tem-plum to-to lau-da- bi-tur or- be per

e- vum,   Et vocabitur

ALIOS   #86. Angelicos patriarcha--f.19

1) An-ge- li-cos pa-tri-ar- cha cho-ros o- lim Do-mi-num-que/

In-ni-xum sca- le cer- nens pro-cla-mat o-van-ter: Terr.

2) Spi-ra-tus so- li-mam de-di-tus po- li-cam pe-re- gri-nam/

Ar- vis que mit-tit di- vo co-pi-am be-a- to-rum, Hic domus

3) Por-ta haec ius-ti- ti-a est cae-lo-que di- ri-git al- mos/

1--MS originally read "dedetus," corrected as above.
2--MS reads a fifth higher from this point on.

Ac ius-ti pe-ne-trant pa-ra-dy-sum sem- per o- van-ter, Et porta

4) Spe-que fi-de Do-   mi-num re-   ti-nent prae-cor-di-

a   sa- cra/ Quae tem-plum Do-mi-ni cor-pus quo-que

iu- rae fa- ten-tur,   Et vocabitur

ALIOS   #87. Innixum scalis--f.19v

1) In-ni-xum sca-lis Do-mi-num ut vi- dit Ia-cob/

An-ge- li-cos-que glo-bos hos de-dit il- le so-nos: Terribilis

2) Om- ni-a il- la bo-nis con-fer-ta   per om- ni-a ius-tis/

Qui spe-rant vi-tae prae-mi-a per-pe-   tu-ae,   Hic domus

3) Haec do-   mus est con-la-ta pi- is si-ne no-mi-ne cunc-tis/

Qua va-le-ant sce-le-ris   ter- ge-re pro-bra su-i, Et vocabitur

182

ITEM ALIOS   #88. <u>Sanctus evigilans</u>--f.19v

1) Sanc-tus e-vi-gi- lans Ia-cob a som-no pa- vens-que ce-ci-nit

di- cens: <u>Terribilis</u>

2) Ve-   re Do-mi- nus est in lo-co   is- to,   <u>Hic domus</u>

3) Quae Xpis-ti-co-lis su- per-na   ag-mi-na pan-   dit, <u>Et vocabitur</u>

ITEM ALIOS   #89. <u>Agmina perhenniter</u>--f.20

1) Ag-mi-na per-hen-ni-ter iu-bi- lant an- ge-li-ca hunc lo-cum pro-

tes-ta-tur sa-   crum di- cen-ti-a,   <u>Terribilis</u>

2) Hanc do-mum De-   o as- sig-nant pro-se-quen-do fi-de-li-um prae-

cor-di- a,   <u>Hic domus</u>

3) Ad-est por-ta per quam ius-ti pro-pe-ran-tes re-de- unt ad pa-

tri-am,   <u>Et porta</u>

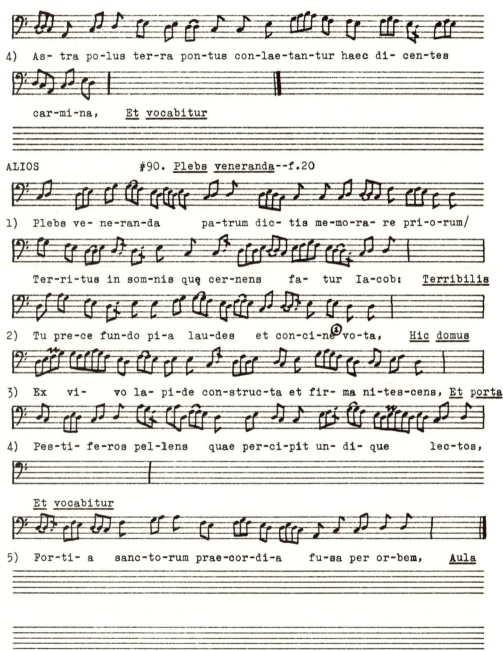

4) As- tra po-lus ter-ra pon-tus con-lae-tan-tur haec di- cen-tes

car-mi-na,   Et vocabitur

ALIOS   #90. Plebs veneranda--f.20

1) Plebs ve- ne-ran-da   pa-trum dic- tis me-mo-ra- re pri-o-rum/

Ter-ri-tus in som-nis quę cer-nens   fa- tur Ia-cob: Terribilis

2) Tu pre-ce fun-do pi-a lau-des   et con-ci-ne vo-ta,   Hic domus

3) Ex vi-   vo la- pi-de con-struc-ta et fir- ma ni-tes-cens, Et porta

4) Pes-ti- fe-ros pel-lens   quae per-ci-pit un- di- que   lec-tos,

Et vocabitur

5) For-ti- a   sanc-to-rum prae-cor-di-a   fu-sa per or-bem,   Aula

1--MS corrected from "concione."

184

#91. Festa templi--f.20v

1) Fes- ta tem-pli re-vol-ven- tes sal-va-to- ris dex-te-ra me-re-

a- mur be-ne- di-ci ut fe-cun-di psal-le-re pos-

si- mus di-cen-tes: Terribilis

2) Mul-to-que hor-ren-dum est hic a- li-quid in- de-cens co-gi-ta-

re qui-a Hic domus

3) Con- ce-de hoc no-bis sanc-te De- us ut do- mus tu-

a si- mus, Et porta

4) Te e- nim Xpis-te di-li-gens ha-bi-ta- to-rem pro-me- re-tur,

Et vocabitur

AD PSALMUM (Dominus regnavit)
#92. Tripudiantes reboemus--f.20v

Tri-pu-di-an-tes re-bo-e- mus o- das mag-ni-fi-ci De-i:

Do-mi-nus regnavit

AD GLORIA
#93. In hoc templo--f.20v

In hoc tem-plo tri-ni-ta-tis laus per-se-ve-ret que il-li sem-per

fo-re gra-ta ag-nos-ca- tur,   Glo-ri-a   se-cu-lo-rum a- men.

AD SEQUENTIAM
(SEQ. Ad templi huius)

#94. Regi inmortali laudes--f.20v

Re- gi in- mor-ta-li lau-   des nunc di-ci-te   cel-sas/

Al-le- lu- ia ca-nens nos-tra ca-ter-va   so-net:

Al-le- lu- ia

AD OFFERENDAM
(OFF. Domine Deus)

#95. Concrepet ecclesia--f.21

1) Con-cre-pet ec-cle-si-a lau- des vo-   ce Sa-lo-mo-nis, nos-tra

ca-ter-va si- mul de-can-tet Do-   mi-no di-cens: Do-mi-ne Deus

1--MS reads a tone lower from this point on. Transcription follows
   Paris 909 and 1119.

2) Tan-tam sol-lemp-ni-ta-tem ce-le-bran-ti-um pro-pi-ci-a- re dig-

ne-tur pec-ca- tis, De-us Is- rahel

ALIOS   #96. Depromit haec templi--f.21

1) De-pro-mit haec   tem-**pli** struc-tor rex ver- ba to-nan-ti:

Do-mi-ne Deus

2) Be-a- ti e- runt qui te e- di-fi-ca-ve- runt, tu   au-tem in

fi-li-is tu-is lae- ta-be-ris, Deus

AD VERSUS①(1. Maiestas)
#97. Consummata est domus--f.21

Con-sum-ma-ta est do-mus Do-mi-ni De- i e- ia yp-pa- ne:

Ma-iestas

1--MS gives the incorrect rubric "Ad C(ommunionem)."
2--MS = consumata.

ALIOS (V.2. Fecit Salomon)
#98. Rex pacificus Salomon--f.21

Rex pa-ci-fi-cus Sa-lo-mon e-di-fi-ca-vit tem-plum in Hie-ru-sa-lem

Do-mi-no, dic dom-ne e- ia: Fe-cit

AD COMMUNIONEM
(COM. Domus mea)

#99. Domum istam--f.21

1) Do-mum is-tam tu pro-te-ge-re dig-ne-ris, Xpis-te, qui di-xis-ti:

Do-mus

2) Est do- mus haec ius-tis di-ca-ta per om- ni-a vo-tis/

In qua per-ci-pi-et quis-quis pi-a do- na fre-quen-ter, In ea

IN DIE ASCENSIONIS
(INTROIT: Viri Galilei)

#100. Quem creditis super astra--f.21v

Quem cre- di-tis su-per as-tra as-cen-dis-se, o Xpis-ti-co-le?

Xpis-tum qui sur-re-xit de se-pul-chro, o Cae-li-co-lae.

Iam as-cen-dit ut prae-di-xe-rat: 'As-cen-do ad pa-trem me-um et

pa-trem ves-trum, De-um me-um et De- um ves-trum.' AL-LE- LU-IA.

Reg-na ter-rae, gen-tes, lin-gue, de-can-ta- te Do- mi-no/

Quem a- do- rant cae-li ci-ves in pa-ter-no so- li-o:

Vi-ri Ga- lilei①

ITEM ALIOS   #101. Hodie redemptor mundi--f.21v

1) Ho-di-e re- demp-tor mun-di as-cen- dit cae- los mi-ran-ti-bus

a- pos-to-lis; an-ge-li au- tem e- is lo-cu-ti sunt di-cen-

1--MS = galileae.

tes: <u>Viri</u>

2) Hoc sci-to-te qui-a ven-tu-rus est iu-di-ca-re vi-vos ac

mor-tu-os, <u>Quemadmodum</u>

3) Red-di-tu-rus e- nim u- ni-cu-i- que iux-ta su-a o-

pe-ra, tunc <u>Ita</u>

ITEM ALIOS #102. <u>Cum patris dextram</u>--f.22

1) Cum pa- tris dex-tram vic-tor cons-cen-de-ret ag- nus,/

Ec- ce vi-ri cla-ri du-o al- mis fan-tur a- lum- nis: <u>Viri</u>

2) Iu-dex ad-ve-ni-et gen- tes ut iu- di-cet om- nes, <u>Quemadmodum</u>

3) Cor-pus hoc re-fe-rens cae-les-ti se-de re-ful-gens, <u>I-ta ve- ni-et</u>

ITEM ALIOS   #103. <u>Terrigenis summis</u>--f.22

1) Ter-ri- ge-nis sum-mis af-fa- tur cae- li-cus or- do, <u>Viri</u>

2) Hic De- us et Do-mi- nus cae-lo- rum com-pos et or- bis, <u>Quem.</u>

3) Ut red-dat cunc-tis ges-to-rum do- na su-o- rum,   <u>Ita</u>

ITEM ALIOS   #104. <u>Montis Oliviferi</u>--f.22

1) Mon-tis O- li-vi-fe-ri Xpis-tus de ver- ti-ce scan-dens,/

Ec- ce du-o vi- ri cla-ra vo-ce cla-ma- runt di- cen-tes: <u>Viri</u>

2) Ad pa-trem per-git fi- li-us ser-vans ves-ti- gi-a pa-cis

Quemadmodum

3) Ad di- em mag- num quo iu- di-ca- tu-rus est or-

bem,   <u>I-ta veniet</u>

1--Syllable "-gi-" added, perhaps by notator.

AD OFFERENDAM
(OFF. Viri Galilei)

#105. Elevatus est rex--f.22v

1) E-le- va-tus est rex for-tis in nu-bi-bus ho-di-e; cer-nen-ti-bus a- pos-to-lis, an- ge- li tes-ti-mo-ni-um pro-fe-ren-tes di-xe- runt: Vi- ri

2) Stig-ma-ta vi- vi-fi-cae se- cum cru-cis ar- ma re-por- tans, In caelum

3) Ut iu- di-cet mun- dum in ae-qui-ta-te, Sic

AD VERSUM (Cumque intuerentur)
#106. Ab intuentium oculis--f.22v

Ab in-tu-en-ti-um o- cu-lis e-vec-tus est ad ae- the- re-a reg- na, Cum- que

1--Chant cue as in Paris 1120. Paris 1121 reads d-a.

192

AD COMMUNIONEM
(COM. Psallite Domino)

#107. Corpus quod nunc--f.22v

Cor-pus quod nunc in ter-ra su-mi-mus, iam se- det ad dex-te-ram

pa-tris in cae-lum, et id-e- o con-so-na vo-ce Psal-li-te Dno.

IN PENTECOSTEN
(INTROIT: Spiritus Domini)

TROPHI   #108. Inclita refulget dies--f.23

1) In- cli-ta   re-ful-get di-es, val-de cun- ctis ve-ne-ran-

da, Spi-ri-tus San-cti ad- ve-ni-en-ti gra-ti-a con-se-cra-ta,

de quo sa-cro-san-cta i- ta an-te pre-ci-nu-it pro-phe-ti-a:

Spiritus

2) Cun-cta re-git, cun-cta-que re-plet, cun-cta-que re-for-mat, Et hoc

ALIOS   #109. Paraclitus sanctus--f.23

1) Pa-ra- cli-tus san-ctus pos-tu-lans pro no- bis ge-   mi-ti-bus

in-e- nar-ra-bi-   li-bus ho-   di-e   Spiritus

2) In-men-sus et ae-ter-   nus,   Re-plevit

3) Glo-ri-am su-a dans pre-sen-ti-a be-a- tis,   Et hoc

4) Ter-res-tri-a at-que su-per-na,   Scientiam

5) San-cto-rum ka-ris-ma-ta   Ha-bet

6) Pre-stans lin-gua-rum no-ti-ti-am: Alleluia

ALIOS   #110. Mystica paracliti--f.23v

1) Mys-ti-ca pa-ra-cli-ti vir-tu-tum flam- ma cho-rus-cans/

Ec-ce di-em de-co-rat ce-le-brem cu-i psal-li-te lau-des,/

E- ia,   Spiritus

194

(musical notation)

2) Al- mi cer-te pa-tris ver- bi quo-que spi-ri-tus i- dem, Replevit

(musical notation)

3) Dis- tri-bu-ens lin-guas Xpis-ti iu-ni-o- ri-bus om- nes, Et hoc

(musical notation)

4) In-fe-ra dig-ni-ter et su-pe-ra fac-ta cun-cta per-hor-nans, Scien.

(musical notation)

5) An-ge- li-cis mo-du-lis pro-ma- mus vo-ce ca-no- ra: Al-le- luia

ITEM ALIOS   #111. Discipulis flammas--f.23v

(musical notation)

1) Dis-ci- pu-lis flam-mas   in-fun- dens cae- li-tus al-mas, Spiritus

(musical notation)

2) Om- ni-ge-nis lin-guis re-se-rans mag-na- li-a Xpis-ti, Et hoc

(musical notation)

3) Ip-si per- spi-cu-as di-ca- mus vo- ci-bus o-das:

(musical notation)

Al-le- luia

ITEM   #112. Sanctus en veniens--f.23v

(musical notation)

1) San-ctus en ve- ni-ens san-cto- rum pec- to-ra

lus-trans   Spiritus

2) Et qui-a   ter-ra- rum flam-ma-   vit reg-na ca- na-mus   Et hoc

3) Pec-to-ra con-fir- mat lin-gua-rum   clau-sa re-la-xans   Scientiam

ALIOS   #113. Psallite candidati--f.24

1) Psal-li-te can- di-da-ti spi-ri-tus pa-ra-cli-ti lau-   dem,

di- cen-tes: Spiritus

2) Mis-sus ab ar- ce pa-   tris,   Replevit

3) Ig-ne-is lin-guis,   Et hoc

4) Pe-ne-tra-li- a in-tu-en- do   Om- ni-a

GLORIA GRECA (i.e., Gloria Patri)[1]
#114. Doxa Patri--f.24

Do-xa Pa-tri ke I- o   ke A- gi-o   Pneu-ma-ti   ke e-nim ke

1--MS gives text in Greek characters, with Latin transliteration
   in margin.

a- gis ke is tos   e-o- nas ton e-on. A-min.

AD SEQUENTIAM ①

#115. Hodie replevit--f.24

Ho-di-e re-ple-vit Do- mi- nus cor-da dis-ci-pu-lo-rum ra-   di-an-

ti-a Spi-ri-tu San-cto, Al- le-   lu- ia.

AD OFFERENDAM
(OFF. Confirma hoc)

#116. Pangite iam socii--f.24

1) Pan- gi-te iam, so-ci-i, do- cu-it quos   Spi- ri-tus al-   mus,

Con-firma

2) Do-num San-   cti Spi-ri-tus,   Quod (operatus)

3) Ac-ci-pe do- na in ho-mi-   ni- bus,   Tibi

1--The sequentia is unidentified. Mode 2 has been arbitrarily
   chosen for the transcription.

4) Psal-len- tes et nos of-fe-ri-mus ti- bi vo-ta ca-nen-do: Alle.

SANCTUS IN GRECUM

#117. Agios agios agios①--f.24v

A- gi-os, a- gi-os, a-gi-os, Kir-ri-os o The-os sa-ba-oth,

pli-ris o u-ra-nos ke i gi tis do-xis, O-san-na en tis ip-sis-tis.

Ev-lo-gi-me-nos o er-cho-me-nos en o-no-ma-ti Kir-ri-u , O-san-

na en tis ip-sis-tis.

AD COMMUNIONEM
(COM. Factus est)

#118. Dum essent discipuli--f.24v

Dum es-sent dis-ci- pu-li prop-ter me- tum Iu-   dae-o-rum in

u- num con- gre- ga-ti,   Fac-tus est

1--MS gives text in Greek characters only. Transliteration here used
is that of Paris 1119. Mode 3 has been arbitrarily chosen for the
transcription.

IN NATALE SANCTI IOHANNIS BAPTISTAE
(INTROIT: De ventre matris)

#119. Festus adest almi--f.24v

1) Fes-tus ad-est al- mi Io-han-nis di- es, qui vo-ce pro-phe-ti-ca

de se lo- qui-tur, di-cens: De ventre

2) Quem an-te tem-po-ra se-cu-la-ri-a pre- sci-vit, Et posuit

3) Ven- tu-ra po-pu-lis mit-tens di-xis-se ne-fandis, Posuit

ALIOS   #120. Ad demonstrandum--f.25

1) Ad de-mon-stran-dum prae-cla-ri lu- mi-nis or- tum/

Per-so-nam te- nens He-li-ae vo- ce fi- de-li, De ventre

2) Ca-nat no-vo dig- ne pe-re-ant ut cri- mi-na bel-lo, Sub te.

3) Il- li per-fec-tam quo pos-sem sub-

de-re ple-bem, Posuit

AD PSALMUM (Bonum est)
#121. Turba fidelis--f.25

Tur-ba fi-de-lis o-vans cas-   to de   pec- to-re cla-met:

Bo-num est

ITEM   #122. Prescius olim sermo--f.25

1) Pre-sci-us o-lim ser-mo pro-phe-ta- lis or-tum prae- cur-so-ris

va-ti-ci-nan-do   prae-di- xit: De ventre

2) Post lon-ge- vam ste-ri-li-ta-tem mi-ra-bi-li-ter fe-cun-da- tam,

Vo-ca- vit

3) Quod an-te mun-di con-sti-tu- ti-o- nem prae-sci-vit et prae-

des-ti-na-vit,   Et posuit

4) Ad vi-ti-o- rum ca- pi-ta tri-um-pha- li-ter ab- sci-den-da,

Sub tegumento

5) Ne hos-ti-lis im-ma-ni-tas su-pe-ra-ret me, Protexit

6) Va-len-ti-o- rem fa-ci-em me-am om-ni-um mun-di po-ten-ti-um

red-dens, Posuit

ITEM ALIOS   #123. Quem prophetae cecinere--f.25v

1) Quem pro-phe-tae ce-ci-ne- re ag- ni fo-re prae-cur-so-rem

di-cit: De ven-tre

2) Ho-nes-ta-vit ver-bum su- um o-re me- o, Et posuit

3) Con-sti-tu- ens me su-per gen- tes at-que reg-na, Sub

4) For-mans me ab u-te-ro ser- vum si- bi, Posuit

ITEM ALIOS   #124. Iste puer magnus--f.25v

1) Is-te pu-er mag- nus pro-phe-ta vo-ca-tus ab u-te-ro ma- tris

nam   di-cit ip- se: De ventre

2) Hie-re-mi-ae mo-re quon-dam va-tis ve-ne- ran-di,   Sub

3) Par- ce-re pa- ci-fi-cis et de-bel-la-re su-per-bos,   Posuit

ALIOS   #125. De sterili genetrice--f.25v

1) De ste- ri-li ge-ne-tri-ce sa- tus Bap-tis-ta be-a-tus,/

Vo-ci- bus his po- pu-los af- fa- tur in or- di-ne cun-ctis,

De ventre

2) Con-sti-tu-en- do su-per gen-tes reg-na quo-que cun- cta,/

Ri-te pro-phe-ta- li com- ple-vit pneu-ma-te nec-ne,   Et posuit

3) Hos-ti-le fre-mi-tus va- le-am quo vin-ce-re sem-per/

Ac me-re-ar   cla-ros ex his   re-tu-lis-   se tri-

1--The text setting at the opening of this line follows Paris 1119
    and Paris 1120.
2--The word "regna" a later addition in MS.

202

um- phos,   Sub tegumento

4) At-   que de-dit lux cla-ra su-is ut gen-   ti-bus es- sem,/

Do-nec a- do-ra-tum re-se-ram per om- ni-a Xpis-tum,   Posuit

AD OFFERENDAM
(OFF. Iustus ut palma)

#126. Iohannes est hic--f.26

Io-han-nes est hic Do- mi-ni   pre-cur-sor de   quo ca-ni-te om-

nes   cum Psal-mis-ta   di-cen-tes: Ius- tus

AD COMMUNIONEM
(COM. Tu puer)

#127. Previus hic--f.26

1) Pre-vi-us hic de quo pa-ter   pro-phe-ti-zat ex-cla-mans: Tu puer

2) Pa-ran-do vi-am il- li cu- ius prae-co-ni-o   tu-   tus, Preibis

1--Paris 1120 reads "referam."

3) An- ge-lus ce- ci-nit in al- vo ma- tris pru-den- ter

Io-han- nem, Parare

INCIPIUNT TROPHI NATALE SANCTI PETRI APOSTOLI
(INTROIT: Nunc scio)

#128. Ecce dies adest--f.26v

1) Ec- ce di-es ad- est a- pos-to-lo- rum prin-ci-pis fes-ti-

vi-ta- te val-de sub-li-mis, qua ab an-ge-lo e- rep-tus de

car-ce-re, ad se re-ver-sus, dix- it: Nunc

2) Non tu- lit en Xpis-tus me- met sub car-ce-re ten- tum,

Et eripuit

3) In-fan-di si-mul ac sol-vit for-mi-di-ne cun-cta Plebis

1--In MS, custos would make remainder of line a third lower.
Reading here follows Paris 1119, etc.

204

ITEM ALIOS   #129. Angelico fretus--f.26v

1) An- ge- li-co fre-tus di- xit mu-ni- mi-ne Pe- trus: <u>Nunc scio</u>

2) Cus-to- dem ac de-fen-so- rem vi-   tae me-ae, <u>Et eripuit</u>

3) Con-stan-tis- si-mum no- mi-nis su-i con-fes-so-rem, <u>De manu</u>

4) San- cti col-le-gi-i nos-tri ma- lig-ni per-va-so- ris, <u>Et de</u>

5) Cun- cto-que coe-tu ma- lig-no   <u>Plebis</u>

ALIOS AD PSALMUM (<u>Domine probasti</u>)
#130. <u>Apostolorum principem</u>--f.27

A- pos-to-lo-   rum prin-ci-pem ce- le-bre col- lau-de-mus Pe-trum,

gra-tu-lan-tes-que cum e-   o, psal-la-   mus pro-phe-ti-ca

vo-   ce: <u>Do-mi-ne pro-bas-ti</u>...et re-<u>sur-rec-ti- o- nem</u>

<u>me-am.</u>   <u>Glo-ri-a</u>...<u>se-cu- lo-rum a- men.</u>

ITEM ALIOS   #131. <u>Divina beatus Petrus</u>--f.27

1) Di-vi-na be- a- tus Pe-trus e- rep-tus cle-men-ti-a,   ad se

red- i- ens, di-xit: <u>Nunc   sci-o ve- re   qui-a...</u>

su- um,

2) Lu-cem-que ius-ti-ci-ae su-ae, qua me   il-lu-mi-na- vit, et

de car-ce-re   e- du- xit,   <u>Et eripuit</u>

3) Sal-va-tor me- us de ma-nu cru-en- tis pre-do-nis   He- ro-

dis   <u>et de   om- ni ex-pec-ta-ti-o- ne,</u>

4) Quae me cir-cum-de-de- rat con-ci-li-o i- ni- quo,   <u>Plebis</u>

ALIOS   #132. <u>Angelus Domini</u>--f.27v

1) An-ge-lus Do- mi-ni sus- ci-tans Pe-trum e- du- xit de car-

ce-re, at il-le ad se red-i-ens di- xit: Nunc

2) E- rep-tus de cus-to-di-a   mi- li-tum, et ca-the-na re-so-

lu-tum, lae-tus pro-ce-dens, di-cit: Et eripuit

3) Con-lau-dat-que re- gem Xpis-tum, qui li- be-ra-vit e-um de ob-scu-

ro car-   ce- ris et de ma- nu im-pi-i He-ro-   dis, Et de

ITEM ALIOS   #133. Petrus ad se reversus--f.27v

1) Pe-   trus ad se re-ver-sus di-xit: Nunc

2) Vi-de-o   pla-ne,   Quia

3) Spes me-a, vi-ta ac sa-lus,   Et eripuit

4) Xpis-tus li- be-ra-   vit me   De manu

5) De   fau-ce pes-si-mi le-o-   nis,   Et de omni

1--MS reads e-f f.
2--Capital omitted in MS.

6) Se-vi-en-tis in me   Plebis

AD OFFERENDAM
(OFF. Constitues eos)

#134. Mundum velut stercora--f.27v

Mun-dum vel-ut ster-co-ra cal-ca-runt pe-   de, et   te au- cto-rem

vi-tae se- cu-ti sunt, id-   e- o   Constitues

AD COMMUNIONEM
(COM. Simon Iohannis)

#135. Simonis eia--f.27v

Si-mo-nis e-   ia vi-ro Xpis-   ti pi-a   ver-ba ca-   na-

mus: Simon

208

IN NATALE SANCTI PAULI
(INTROIT: Scio cui credidi)

#136. Qui dilexit--f.28

1) Qui di-le-xit me, et tra-di-dit se-ip- sum pro me, Scio cui

2) Dum se-gre-ga- vit me, et vo-ca-vit per gra-ti-am su- am, Quia potens

3) A-po-ri-or nunc ut per ip-si-ma sed tunc an- ge-los iu-di-ca-bo, In

ALIOS #137. Martyrio magni--f.28

1) Mar-ty-ri-o mag-ni re-co-lens doc-to- ris in or-be,/Ec-cle-si-ae

cle- rus nunc e- ius vo-ce re- sul-tet, Scio cui

2) Cer-ta- men cer-tan-do bo-num cur-sum-que fi-de- le, Quia

3) In so-li-o reg- ni red-dens hoc cen- tu-pli-ca- tum, In illum

#138. Ecce fidem magni--f.28

Ec-ce fi-dem mag-ni...

1--MS begins line a fifth higher.
2--Paris 1121 gives only this, without rubric. Paris 909, etc.,
   indicate trope is to continue as #137, beginning at
   "recolens...."

INCIPIUNT TROPHI DE SANCTO AC BEATISSIMO
DOMNO NOSTRO MARTIALE,
PASTORE ET DUCE AQUITANORUM

(INTROIT: Originally <u>Statuit ei</u>, but through #146 cues have
been replaced by those for <u>Probavit</u>. See   Chapt. 3.)

#139. <u>Martialem per secla</u>--f.28v

1) Mar- ti-a- lem per se-cla   cun- cti- po-   tens le-git,

no-   bis-que a-pos-to-lum de-dit,   <u>Probavit</u> (= <u>Statuit</u>)

2) Qui-a dig-   num fo- re prae-vi- dit, i-de-o-   que il- lum

dig- ne or- na-vit,   <u>Cognovit</u> (= <u>Et principem</u>)

3) Gal-li-am   cun-   ctam tan- to pas-   to- re per-

or- nans,   <u>Deduxit</u> (= <u>Ut sit illi</u>)

4) Quem de-cen-ter ad-   or-   nans po-lo-rum a-dep-tus est   reg-

na u- bi cum De-o reg- nant   <u>Et nimis</u> (=<u>In aeternum</u>)

1--"Apostolum" added over erasure.
2--"Galliam cunctam" added over erasure.
3--From here to end of line MS reads a fifth higher.

210

ALIOS #140. Plebs devota Deo--f.29

1) Plebs de-vo-ta De-o nos-trum nunc sus- ci-pe car-men,/

Nem-pe vi- rum co- li-mus de quo sa-pi-en-ti a fa- tur,

Probavit

2) Ex-tu-lit at-que su-is co-ram al-ta-ri-bus al-mis, (Cognovit)

3) Le-mo-vi-cis fa- mu-lum sta-tu-ens di-ca-re pa-tro-num, (Et nimis)

ITEM ALIOS #141. Martialem duodenus--f.29

1) Mar-ti-a- lem du-o-de- nus a-pex qui-a iu- re

be-a- vit, Probavit

2) Quem pri-mum no- vit tel- lus A-qui-ta- ni-

ca pa-trem, Cognovit

3) Le-mo-vi-cam se-dem tan-to pas-to-re per-or- nans,

Deduxit

1--Cues at end of lines 2 and 3 have been erased, but no
new ones added.

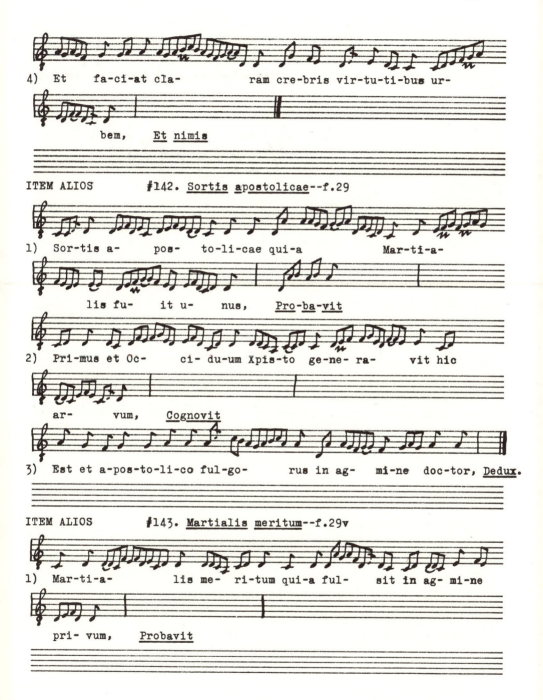

4) Et fa-ci-at cla- ram cre-bris vir-tu-ti-bus ur-

bem, Et nimis

ITEM ALIOS   #142. Sortis apostolicae--f.29

1) Sor-tis a- pos- to-li-cae qui-a Mar-ti-a-

lis fu- it u- nus, Pro-ba-vit

2) Pri-mus et Oc- ci- du-um Xpis-to ge-ne- ra- vit hic

ar- vum, Cognovit

3) Est et a-pos-to-li-co ful-go- rus in ag- mi-ne doc-tor, Dedux.

ITEM ALIOS   #143. Martialis meritum--f.29v

1) Mar-ti-a- lis me- ri-tum qui-a ful- sit in ag- mi-ne

pri- vum, Probavit

212

2) Plebs A-qui-ta- na su- um glis-cens hunc es- se mo-nar-chum,

Cognovit

3) Le-mo-vi-ce ple-bi pri- mus no-va dog-ma-ta spar-sit, Deduxit

4) Qua Xpis-to ge- ni-tos fa- ci- at su- per as-tra be-a- tos

Et nimis

ITEM ALIOS   #144. Sedibus externis--f.29v

1) Se- di-bus ex- ter- nis ad-ve- nit pas-tor hic al- mus/

Sor-tis a-pos-to-li-cae qui-a Mar-ti- a- lis fu- it

u- nus, Probavit

2) Hic pa- ter e- xi-mi-us A-qui-ta- ni-ca ru-ra per- a-

grans, Cognovit

3) Spar-mo- lo-gus po- pu-lis dif-fu-dit se- mi-na ver-bi,

Deduxit

4) Fon-te sa-cra tin-ctos post haec be-ne-di-cit o- van-ter,

Et nimis

ALIOS　　　#145. Martialis Dominum--f.30

1) Mar-ti-a- lis Do- mi-num qui-a ies- sit①

pec- to-re Xpis-tum, Probavit

2) Lu-cis in ar-chae lo- cans ip-sum su-a vo-ta Le-mo-vix, Cogn.

3) Pri-mus in Oc-ci-du-is fi- dem spar-sit tri-ni- ta-tis,

Deduxit

4) Hoc tel-lus A-qui-ta- na ni-tet doc-to-re ma-gis-tro

Et nimis　　　1--Paris 1119 = gessit
2--Paris 1119 = arce

ITEM ALIOS   #146. <u>Inclita refulget</u>--f.30

1) In-cli- ta   re-ful-get   di-es di-ca-ta   Mar-ti-a- lis ho-

no-re, qui Xpis-   tum in car-   ne fe-lix me-ru- it   cer-

ne-re,   <u>Probavit</u>

2) Ae-ter-ne   pa- cis e-   rit ef- fec-tus, no-bis-que   prin-ceps

ad-e- o di-rec- tus,   <u>Cognovit</u>

3) Gal-   li-ae to-ti- us ut pa-tri-ar-   cha sit   sum-mus, <u>Dedux.</u>

4) I-ter pre-bens su-   is qua-li- ter Xpis-to pos-sint nec-ti in

cae-lis   <u>In aeternum</u>①

ALIOS   #147. <u>Inclitus hic rutilo</u>--f.30v

1) In-cli-tus hic   ru- ti-lo ce-le-bra-tur②ste- ma-te   pre-sul,/

Plebs ve-ne- ran-da fra- trum mo-du-lan-do   ca-na- mus in u-   num:

<u>Statuit</u>

1--Original cue unchanged in MS.
2--MS = celebatur.

2) Quem- que sum-mus he- ros di-ta- vit mu- ne-re sum-mo,

Et principem

3) Ec-cle-si-ae pro- pri-ae fir- mans per se-cla pa-tro-num, Ut sit

4) Et de-cus splen-dor o- vans vi-ta re- qui-es-que

be-a- ta, In aeternum

ALIOS   #148. Martialis meritis--f.30v

1) Mar-ti-a- lis me- ri-tis vir-tu- tum ste- ma-te

pol-let, Statuit

2) Car-ce-re qui ne-xus car- nis a-ni-ma- tus ab as-tris,

Et principem

3) Cu-ius pon-ti-fi-ca-lis a- pex fla-ves- cit a- bun-de,

Ut sit

216

4) Moe- ni-bus as- tri-fe-ris pu- ro con- scrip-tus in al- bo,

In aeternum

ALIOS   #149. Ut esset sacerdos--f.30v

1) Ut es-set sa- cer-dos se-cun-dum or- di- nem

Mel- chi-se- dech,   Statuit

2) Ut vi- ge- at sum-mus sto-la ver-nan-te sa- cer-dos,   Et prin.

3) In-ter pri-ma- tes reg-ni cae-les- tis he- ri- lem, Ut sit

4) Grex tu-us Mar-ci- a-lis pe- tit me-mo-ra- re tu- o-rum   In aeter

ITEM ALIOS   #150. Qui placuit Domino--f.31

1) Qui pla-cu-it Do-mi-no mag-nus nunc ec- ce sa-cer- dos: St.

2) Lus-tra- vit sa-cris pec- tus pur-gan-do lu-cer-nis, Et p.

3) Ius-ti-ti-ae ca- put or-nat di-a-de- ma sa-cra- tum, **Ut sit**

4) Al- ma glo-ri-fi-ca-tur o- vans pi-e-ta- te① per as-tra, In aeter.

ITEM ALIOS   #151. <u>Ecce dies magni</u>--f.31

1) Ec-ce di- es mag- ni me-ri-tis ve-ne-ran- da pa- tro-ni/

Qui fu-it in po-pu-lo splen-dor o-vans, i- de-o **Statuit**

2) Rex re-gum cun- ctis pan-den-tem ver-ba sa-lu-tis/

Tu-ta- vit fa-mu-lum an-te mi- nas pro-ce-rum, **Et principem**

3) Con-sti-tu-ens dig-ne mi-nis-tran- tem do- na su-per-na/

Pa-tri in ex-cel-so pon-ti-fi-cem so-li-o, **Ut sit**

4) Qui be-ne cer- ta-vit ter- ris, mo-do reg-nat in as-tris/

Col-lau-dat-que su-um lae-tus in a- xe De-um, **In aeternum**

1--MS = pitate.

ITEM ALIOS   #152. <u>Celsa polorum pontus</u>--f.31v

1) Cel-sa po-lo-rum pon-tus et i-ma pre- su-lem is- tum lau-dent,

ca-nen- tes: <u>Statuit</u>

2) Co-ro-nam sa-cer-do-ci-i,   <u>Testamentum</u>

3) Qui u-ni-ti si-mus fi-   de,   <u>Et principem</u>

4) In se-de sub-li-   mans,   <u>Ut sit</u>

5) Ma-nens in-de-fi-ci-ens   <u>In aeternum</u>

ALIOS   #153. <u>Pangamus omnes</u>--f.31v

1) Pan- ga-mus om-nes pre-co-ni-a fes-ti-vi-ta-tis ho- di-er-ne

Mar-ti-a- lis pre-su-lis ad-iu-ta suf-fra-gi-is qui- a   <u>Statuit</u>

2) In-ter pon-ti-fi-cum ag-mi-na cel- si-o- ris e- mi- cat

gra-ti-a,   <u>Et principem</u>

1--The a on "-tum" lacking in MS.
2--MS gives the incorrect cue "Ut sit."

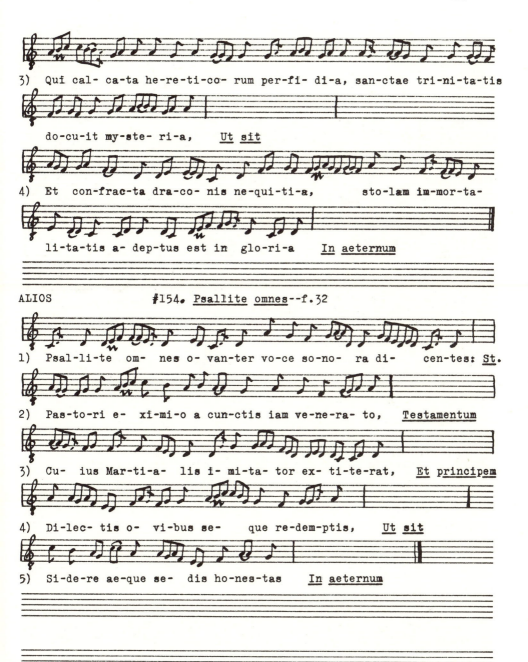

3) Qui cal- ca-ta he-re-ti-co- rum per-fi- di-a, san-ctae tri-ni-ta-tis

do-cu-it my-ste- ri-a,   Ut sit

4) Et con-frac-ta dra-co- nis ne-qui-ti-a,   sto-lam im-mor-ta-

li-ta-tis a- dep-tus est in glo-ri-a   In aeternum

ALIOS   #154. Psallite omnes--f.32

1) Psal-li-te om- nes o- van-ter vo-ce so-no- ra di-   cen-tes: St.

2) Pas-to-ri e- xi-mi-o a cun-ctis iam ve-ne-ra- to,   Testamentum

3) Cu- ius Mar-ti-a- lis i- mi-ta- tor ex- ti-te-rat,   Et principem

4) Di-lec- tis o- vi-bus se-   que re-dem-ptis,   Ut sit

5) Si-de-re ae-que se- dis ho-nes-tas   In aeternum

AD OFFERENDAM
(OFF. <u>Veritas mea</u>①)

#155. <u>Martialem Dominus</u>--f.32

1) Mar- ti-a- lem Do- mi-nus ro- bo- rat pro-phe-

ti-ce pro-mens, (<u>Ve-ri- tas</u>)

2) Pax, be- nig- ni-tas, at- que vic-to-ri-a, (<u>Et misericordia</u>)

3) A- so- ma-tas for- tis su-pe-ra- bit nem-pe

ca- ter-vas, (<u>Et in nomine</u>)

AD VERSUM (<u>Misericordiam</u>)
#156. <u>Martialis meritum ceu</u>--f.32

Mar-ti-a-lis me-ri-tum ceu si-dus lam-pat ut um- quam   <u>Misericordiam</u>

AD COMMUNIONEM
(COM. <u>Beatus servus</u>)

#157. <u>Hic dictis</u>--f.32

Hic dic- tis prae-lu-cens mo- rum pro-bi-ta- te de-co-rus, <u>Beatus</u>

1--The <u>Veritas</u> cues, given here in parentheses, have been erased in
  MS but not replaced by others.
2--MS reads a fifth higher from this point on. But cf. Paris 903.

ALIOS · #158. Ultima venturae--f.32v

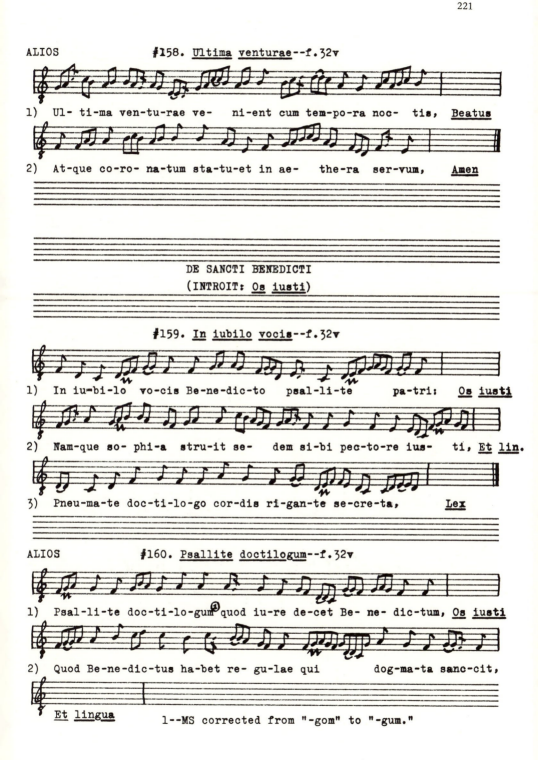

1) Ul- ti-ma ven-tu-rae ve-   ni-ent cum tem-po-ra noc-   tis,   Beatus

2) At-que co-ro- na-tum sta-tu-et in ae-   the-ra ser-vum,   Amen

DE SANCTI BENEDICTI

(INTROIT: Os iusti)

#159. In iubilo vocis--f.32v

1) In iu-bi-lo vo-cis Be-ne-dic-to psal-li-te   pa-tri: Os iusti

2) Nam-que so- phi-a stru-it se-   dem si-bi pec-to-re ius-   ti, Et lin.

3) Pneu-ma-te doc-ti-lo-go cor-dis ri-gan-te se-cre-ta,   Lex

ALIOS · #160. Psallite doctilogum--f.32v

1) Psal-li-te doc-ti-lo-gum quod iu-re de-cet Be- ne- dic-tum, Os iusti

2) Quod Be-ne-dic-tus ha-bet re- gu-lae qui   dog-ma-ta sanc-cit,

Et lingua   1--MS corrected from "-gom" to "-gum."

222

3) Quo ma-gis in-nor-met fra-tres quam de-ni-que dam-pnet, Lex

ALIOS #161. Laudibus o Benedicte--f.32v

1) Lau-di-bus, o Be-ne-dic-te, tu-is cho- rus in- so-net

om-nis: Os

2) Le- gi-bus in-for-mat mo- na-chos de mu-ne-re Xpis-ti, Et lingua

3) Ae- ter-na pre-cep-ta mo-net si-ne fi-ne te-nen-da, Lex

ALIOS #162. Cantica nunc reboent--f.33

1) Can-ti-ca nunc re-bo-ent sa- cri pre- co- ni-a pa-tris, Os

2) San- cta do- cet san- ctos du-ra quo-que dog-ma-ta pra- vos, Et l.

3) Ap-ta-ta re- se-rans sa- crae pe-ne-tra-li-a le- gis, Lex

1--MS = sanctis

224

id- e- o **Lex**

ITEM ALIOS   #165. <u>Iubilent omnes fideles</u>--f.33v

1) Iu-bi-lent om- nes fi-de- les, ca- ter-va-tim de-pro-mant,

psal- len-tes: <u>Os</u>

2) So-ci-us su-per-na-rum vir-tu-tum ef-fec- tus at- que

an-ge-li-cis cho-ris con- iunc-tus est, <u>Et lingua</u>

3) Xpis-ti se-quens ves- ti-gi-a, ip-se ve- ro il-li red-dens su- a

pro-mis-sa, id- e- o **Lex**

SANCTI LAURENTII
(INTROIT: Confessio)

#166. Lauream regni--f.33v

1) Lau-re-am reg- ni te-net le-vi-ta Lau-ren- ti-us ec-ce,

Confessio

2) Cul-ti-bus di-vi- nis ful-get Xpis-ti- co-la De-i,

Sanctitas

3) Tor-ri-da car-ne ni-tet ha-bun-dat pas- si-o ve-

ra, In sanctificatione

ALIOS   #167. Grata Deo nimium--f.33v

1) Gra-ta De-o ni-mi-um sunt is-ta pro-phe-ta fa-te-tur, Confessio

2) Haec ge-mi-na re-tu-lit Do- mi-no Lau-ren- ti-us ac-ta,

In sanctificatione

IN ASSUMPTIONE SANCTAE MARIAE
(INTROIT: Gaudeamus)

#168. Aulam sanctam--f.34

1) Au-lam san-ctam nunc in-gres-si, Xpis-ti-co-le, as- sump-ti-o-

nem Ma-ri-ae   sem-per vir- gi-nis ce-le-bran-tes o- van-

ter,   Gaudeamus

2) Hym-ni- di-cos re-so-nan- do mo-dos vo-ce- que io-cun-dos,   Sub

3) Quae me-ru-it pe-pe-ris-se De-um per se-cu-la nos-trum,   De cuius

ALII   #169. Festiva per orbem--f.34

1) Fes-ti-va per or- bem ad-est nunc di- es, qua al-ma Ma-ri-a con-

scen-dit ad ae- thra; su-pe-re   gau-dent cun-cte vir-tu-tes,

nos-que cum il- lis con- so-na vo- ce   Gaudeamus

2) Sus-ci-pit lae-tum pre-si-dens cel-sus col-lo-cat se-cum se-de

1--MS suggests f. Reading here follows Paris 909, etc.
2--Note missing in MS. Reading follows Paris 1119.

pa-ter-na, De cuius

3) Po-lo-rum ca-ter-vae hym-num an-te se-dem di- cunt, Et collaudant

ALII   #170. Fulget nempe dies--f.34v

1) Ful-get nem-pe di-es cun- ctis ve- ne-ran-da per or- bem,/

Qua Ma-ri- a Vir- go cae-los pe-ne-tra-vit ab ar- vo,/

un- de: Gaudeamus

2) Cu- ius ho-no-re sa-cram do- mi-nam lau- da- mus in au- lam, Diem

3) Per- so- nis tri-nis u- num re- gem re- co-len-tes, Sub ho.

4) Et qui-a ef- fec-ta est, ma-ter sal-va-to- ris mo- do so-

ci-a- ta est an-ge-li-cis cho- ris, De cuius

5) Quem om-nis a- do-rat mor-ta- lis et om-ni-a nu- mi-na sur- sum,

Et collaudant

228

#171. <u>Cantemus omnes</u>--f.34v

1) Can-te-mus om- nes mel-li- flu-um car-men, fi-bra-rum o- re

psal-len-tes: <u>Gaudeamus</u>

2) Qui-a ho-di-e so-la in-nup- ta Vir-go Ma- ri-a cae-los con-scen-

dit, e-xul-te- mus, <u>Diem</u>

3) Quae so-la dig-na in-ven-ta est re-gem cae-li gig-ne-re, et post

par-tum vir-go in-nup-ta ma-ne- re, <u>De cuius</u>

4) Be-ne-dic-tam con-lau-dan-tes do- mi-nam u-ni-ver-sae ma-chi-nae

mun-di be-ne- di-cunt <u>Et collaudant</u>

ALII TROPHI   #172. <u>Pangamus socii</u>--f.35

1) Pan-ga-mus so-ci-i hu-mi-li vo- ce lau- dum ca- no-ra,

et <u>Gaudeamus</u>

2) Qui-a mag-na e- ius mu-ne-ra mag-na ri-te per- to-nant sol-

lemp- ni-a, Sub

3) Ip-sa Xpis-ti ma-ter ho-di-e fe-li-ci-ter a-scen-dit ad ae-the- ra,

De cuius

4) Plau-dent coe-tus ce-li, lae-tam- tur om- nes Xpis-ti-

co- lae, Et collaudant

#173. Quia naturam--f.35

1) Qui-a na- tu-ram nos-trae hu- ma-ni-ta- tis co-pu-la-vit na- tu-

rae su-ae di-vi-ni- ta- tis, Gaudeamus

2) In quo nos be- a- tus gau-de- re mo-net a- pos-to-lus, Diem

3) Quae ho-di-e cae-los a- scen-dit, mor-tis de-vic-to prin-ci-pe,

De cuius   1--Syllable missing in MS.

4) Ad-mi-ran-tes e- am ge-nu-is- se De- um et ho- mi- nem,

Et collaudant

INCIPIUNT DE SANCTI AUGUSTINI
(INTROIT: Statuit)

#174. Sanctus Agustinum--f.35v

1) San-ctus A-gus-ti- num mun-do qui-a ri-te be-a- vit/

Spi-ri-tus e-xi- mi-um con-sti-tu-en- do pa-trem, Statuit

2) Doc-tri-ne ra- di-is per-lus-trans ab-di-ta men-tis/

Cum de-dit hunc or-bis par-mo-lo-gum do- ci-li, Et principem

3) Tu-ri-fi-can-do pre-ces ce- dens re-do-le-re per- hen-nes/

Vo-ta De-um pri-mo sol-vat et al-ti-thro-no, Ut sit

4) Nunc me-mo-ra-re tu- ae pre-sul su-per ae-the-ra tur-me/

Quo va-le-at sum-mo can- ti-ca fer- re De-o, In aeternum

ITEM ALII   #175. Ecclesiae doctor--f.35v

1) Ec- cle-si- ae doc-tor Do- mi-ni quo- que for- tis a- ma-tor,

Mi-tis A- gus-ti-nus quo-ni-am fu- it ac ve-ne-ra-tor,

Statuit

2) Iu- ra sa-cer-do-tis tri-bu-ens quo san-ctæ be-a- ret,

Et principem

3) Pon-ti-fi-cis-que pi- a sta-tu-it re-si-de-re ca-the-dra,

Ut sit

4) Qui po-pu-li pi-a vo-ta tu-lit al- ta- ri-bus al-mis

In aeternum

IN NATIVITATE SANCTA MARIA
(INTROIT: Gaudeamus)

#176. Fulget nempe dies--f.36

1) Ful-get nem-pe di-es cun- ctis ve- ne-ran-da per or- bem,/

Quo ex stir-pe Da- vid vir-go pro-ces-sit Ma- ri-a,   Gaudeamus

2) Cu- ius ho-no-re... Diem   3) Per- so-   nis... Sub honore

4) I- dem Ies-se-a vir-ga o-   lim pro-mis-sa ho-di-e no- bis est

na-ta,   De cuius

5) Mi-ra-bi-li lae-ti-ti- am,   Gaudent

6) Ad-mi-ran-tes ex-or-   tam tan- tae mag-ni-tu-di-nis re-gi-nam,

be-ne-di-cunt, ad-   or-nant,   Et collaudant

7) Con-di-to-rem mun-di,   Filium

1--The cues for lines 2 and 3 refer to #170 above.

ITEM ALII TROPHI #177. Caelitus instructi--f.36v

1) Cae-li-tus in-struc-ti so-phi-ae   spi-ra-   mi-ne

san-   cte,   Gaudeamus

2) Stir-pe Da- vid ful-sit re- gis haec ste-ma-te cel-si, De cuius

3) Spi-ri-tus ae-the-re-i pro qua pi-a can-ti-ca sol-vunt, Et collaudant

ITEM ALII   #178. Aurea post Xpistum--f.36v

1) Au- re-a post Xpis-tum vo-lu-mus sic scan-de-re reg-na, Gaudeamus

2) Dul- ci-flu-is dig- ne re-ci-nen- do can- ti-bus o-   das, Diem

3) Al-ter-ni so-nis mo-du-los pro-   ma-mus o- van- ter,   Sub

4) Ag-mi-ni-bus va-   ri-is Do- mi- num qui lau-de fa-ten- tur,

Et collaudant

234

ALII #179. Pangamus socii--f.36v

1) Pan-ga-mus socii. UT SUPRA. Gaudeamus 2) Qui-a mag-na... Sub

3) Ip-sa Xpis-ti ma-ter ho-di-e ex stir-pe or-ta est Da- vi-ti- ca,

De cuius 4) Plau-dent... Et collaudant

IN EXALTATIONE SANCTAE CRUCIS
(INTROIT: Nos autem)

#180. Glorientur cuncti--f.36v

1) Glo-ri-en-tur cun-cti fi-de- les Xpis-ti in in-ven-ti- o- nis

di-e lig-ni pre- ti-o- si, Nos autem

2) In e-o qui nos pro-pri-o re-de-mit cru-o- re, In cruce

3) Cu-ius com-ple-xu De-us pa-ter re-git un- di-que mun-dum, In quo

4) Per ip-sum in-du-ti sto-lam im-mor-ta-li-ta-tis, Per quem

1--The cues for lines 1, 2, and 4 refer to #172 above.

AD PSALMUM (Deus misereatur)
#181. Se ipsum offerens--f.37

Se ip-sum of-fe-rens hos-ti-am im-ma-cu-la- tam De-o pa-tri pro

no-bis,   Deus misereatur

AD GLORIA
#182. Gloria nostra crucis--f.37

Glo-ri-a nos-tra cru-cis est vic-to- ri-a et pa-ra-dy-si ia-nu-a,

Glo-ri-a patri

ITEM ALII   #183. Caelestem Xpiste--f.37

1) Cae-les-tem, Xpis-te, lar-gi-re be-ne-dic-ti-o-nem, pro no-bis

fun-dens in cru-ce san-gui-nem,   Nos autem

2) Cum caeli pariter plaudentes esse ministris
    Ordinis ac cunctis superis iubilare beati,   In cruce

3) Qui summus pietate polo descendit ab alto
    Vagiit et cunis gestatus virgine matre,   Per quem

1--Lines 2 and 3 not notated in MS.

-108-

AD OFFERENDA (Protege)④
#184. De detrophea ferens--f.37v

De detrophea ferens ad caelos victor averni
Orbis regnator, hominum quoque Xpiste redemptor,   **Protege**

AD COMMUNIONEM (Crux Ihesu)
#185. Sumitur en corpus--f.37v

Sumitur en corpus salutare cruorque sacratus
Vexillo crucis, ergo boans dic turma fidelis: **Crux Ihesu**

SANCTI MAURICII

(INTROIT: Venite benedicti)

#186. Haec legio--f.37v

1) Haec le-gi-o du- ce Mau-ri-ti-o pro no- mi-ne Xpis-ti/

Mor- tem spon-te su-bi-it cum mox e- i Xpis-   tus et

in- quit: **Venite benedicti**

2) Iu- re co-he-res me- i vos   pa-ci-en- do se-qua- ces, **Percipite**

3) A pa- tre spon-te da-   tum sed a-go- ne   co-emp-   tum,

Quod vobis   1--#184 and #185, found only in Paris 1121,
                    are not notated in MS.

4) Vos le- gi-o me- a cum su-pe-ris iam de- can- tan-tes: <u>Al-leluia</u>

INCIPIUNT DE SANCTO MICHAHELE
(INTROIT: <u>Benedicite</u>)

#187. <u>O vos quos</u>--f.37v

1) O vos quos in prin-ci- pi-o cre-a- vit om- ni-po-tens

ad lau-dem et glo- ri-am no- mi-nis su-i, <u>Benedicite</u>

2) De-si-de-ran-tes e- um in-tu-e-ri cu-ius vul-tum cer-ni-tis sem-per

pre-sen-tem, <u>Potentes</u>

3) Ip-sum con-lau-dan-tes per quem ge- ri-tis mi-ra-bi-les res,

<u>Qui facitis</u>①

4) Ad-im-plen-tes ius- sa iu-gi- ter ip- si-us, <u>Ad audiendam</u>

1--MS here and elsewhere reads "Quid facitis."

238

ALII #188. Festivo iam imminente--f.38

Fes- ti- vo iam im-mi- nen- te di-e ves-tro splen-do-re lus-

tra- to u-na vo-bis-cum et Mi-cha-e- le Ar-

chan-ge-lo, Benedicite

ALII #189. Quem cuncta laudant--f.38

1) Quem cun-cta lau-dant si- mul cre-a-ta re- gem ae-ter-num at-

que tre-men-dum, Benedicite

2) Im-pa-ri-bus vos of- fi-ci-i qui ius-sa re-fer- tis, Potentes

3) Sol- ven-tes po-pu-lis di-vi-na dog-ma-ta iu- ris, Ad audiendam

ALII #190. O Michahel--f.38

1) O Mi- cha-hel su- pe- re quae ob nos gau-den-do co-hor-

tes, Benedicite

2) Nos qui sa-net ae-gros vos sta-re fa-cit-que be-a-tos, Potentes

3) Or- di-nat hic le- gem per vos ho- mo fac-tus he- ri-lem,

Ad audiendam

#191. Principis aetherei--f.38v

1) Prin-ci-pis ae- the-re-i Mi- cha-e- lis fes-ta ca- nen-do/

Cae-li-ca tur-ba De-o fes- ti-vo nab-lo ci-e- to, Benedicite

2) Lau-di-bus al-ter-nis ter tri-nis coe-ti- bus al-mis, Potentes

3) Ter-ri-ge-nas in-ter-que De-um ce-le-res vo-li-ta-tis he- ro- es,

Ad audiendam

ITEM ALII   #192. Ecce iam caelicolae--f.38v

1) Ec- ce iam, cae-li-co-lae, in hu- ius prin-ci-pis ves- tri Mi-cha-

1--MS suggests g g-e' e' etc. Transcription follows Paris 1119.

e- lis sol-lemp-ni-ta- te pre-ces nos- tras ves- tris iun-

gen-tes laudi-bus, **Benedicite**

2) Et ex-o- ra-te que-su-mus ip-sum pro no- bis, qui vos ad se lau-

dan-dum cre-a- vit tam dig-nis-si-mos at-que prae-cla-ros, **Potentes**

3) Er- go pe- ti-mus ut ves-tro iu- va- mi-ne sur- sum sub-le-

va-ti me-re- a- mur vo- bis con-iun-gi, **Ad audiendam**

ITEM ALII TROPHI   #193. Angelici nunc--f.39

1) An-ge-li-ci nunc ri-te cho-ri Xpis-ti-que mi- nis-tri, **Bene.**

2) Vos ad-sta-re De-o Da-vid do-cet ec-ce su-per-no, **Potentes**

3) Iu-ra da-tis cun- ctis sa-cre quo-que mis-ti-ca le- gis, **Ad audi.**

ITEM ALII   #194. <u>Hodie regi</u>--f.39④

1) Hodie regi archangelorum laudes promamus cum psalmista: <u>Benedicite</u>
2) Habentes divinam cuius vultum cernitis persepe, <u>Potentes</u>

3) Adimplentes iussa iugiter Domini,⑦ <u>Ad audiendam</u>

AD OFFERENDAM
(OFF. <u>Stetit angelus</u>)

#195. <u>Factum est silentium</u>--f.39

1) Fac-tum est si-len-ti-um in cae-lo qua-si me-di-a ho-ra, et sep-

tem an-ge-li stan-tes e-rant in con-spec-tu De- i, et da-te sunt

il-lis sep-tem tu-bae, et ve-nit a-li-us et   Ste-   tit angelus

2) Ut a-do-le-ret e- a su-per al-ta-re au- re-um quod est an- te

thro-num,   <u>Et ascendit</u>

1--#194 not notated in MS.
2--MS = dominum

AD COMMUNIONEM
(COM. Benedicite)

#196. Auctorem omnium--f.39

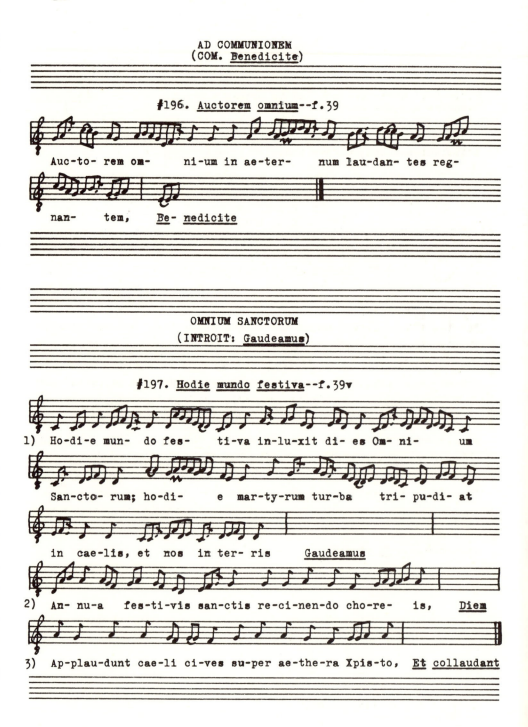

Auc-to- rem om- ni-um in ae-ter- num lau-dan- tes reg-

nan- tem, Be- nedicite

OMNIUM SANCTORUM
(INTROIT: Gaudeamus)

#197. Hodie mundo festiva--f.39v

1) Ho-di-e mun- do fes- ti-va in-lu-xit di- es Om- ni- um

San-cto- rum; ho-di- e mar-ty-rum tur-ba tri- pu-di- at

in cae-lis, et nos in ter- ris Gaudeamus

2) An- nu-a fes-ti-vis san-ctis re-ci-nen-do cho-re- is, Diem

3) Ap-plau-dunt cae-li ci-ves su-per ae-the-ra Xpis-to, Et collaudant

ITEM ALII   #198. Eia plebs devota--f.39v

1) E- ia plebs de-vo-ta De-o   nunc   cor- de se-re-no   Gaudeamus

2) Con-so-net o-   re si-   mul nos-   tro-rum flos   me-ri- to-rum,

Diem festum

3) Ae-   ter-ni so-   ci-i   ful-go-   ris ger-mi-nis al-ti,   Sub

4) Im qua ho-   di-e om-nes san-cti con-dig-   nis lau-di-bus ve-

ne- ran-tur,   Et collaudant

ALII   #199. Sanctorum sancto--f.40

1) San-cto-rum   san-cto cun-cto-   rum lau-   de ca-nen- do,   Gaudeamus

2) His re-ci-nen-do so- nos sup-pli- ci mo-du-la-   mi-ne dul-

ces,   De quorum

3) Qui vi-ce con-ser-ta   si-mul al-ter-nan-do re-sul-tant,   Et collaudant

244

ALII   #200. <u>Secla Deus gratis</u>--f.40

1) Se-cla   De-us gra-tis   quos pre-sci-it an- te fi-de-les/

In con-   val-le li-cet   la-cri-ma-rum cor- de cru-en- tos,

<u>Gaudeamus</u>

2) Glo-ri-a nos- tra   ma-net qui-a nunc lac-ta- mur in ip- so, <u>Diem</u>

3) Cu- ri-am   or-na- tam cae-les-ti plau- dat hi-a- tu, <u>De quoru</u>

4) Pas-to-ris vi-dent   so-ci-a- ta cui vul-ne-re cau- lis, <u>Et coll</u>.

ITEM ALII   #201. <u>Ecce Xpisticole</u>--f.40

1) Ec-   ce Xpis-ti-co-le   psal- len-tes   car-

mi-na lau-dum,   <u>Gaudeamus</u>

2) Cor-   de si-mul o-re lae-ti vis-ce- ri-bus to- tis, <u>Diem</u>

3) Pri-mo-rum   pa-trum pre-sen- ti-um ac   fu-tu-ro- rum,

<u>De quorum</u>

4) Cer-nen- tes gre- gem so-ci- um si-bi nam be-ne- di-

cunt, Et collaudant

ALII   #202. Eia canendo sonos--f.40v

1) E- ia ca-nen-do so- nos sup-pli- ci mo-du-la- mi-ne

dul- ces, Gaudeamus

2) Or-ga-na nunc la- xis re-so-ne-mus in or-di-ne fi-bris,   Diem

3) Qui me-ru- e- re De-o iun- gi su-per as-tra su-per-no,   De quorum

---

ALII   #203. Hodie est fratres--f.40v

1) Ho-di-e est, fra-tres, Om-ni-um San-cto-rum fes-ti-vi-tas, qui

cum Xpis-to reg-nant in ae-ter-num, un- de Gaudeamus

2) Nunc san-ctis iun-cta re-so-ne- mus or- ga-na cun-ctis,   Diem

---

1--MS gives the single neum ♪ for the syllables "-e est," thus
    perhaps implying an elision.
2--Notes missing in MS; reading here follows Paris 1119, etc.
3--MS reads incorrectly "De cuius"; "Diem" found in Paris 1120, etc.

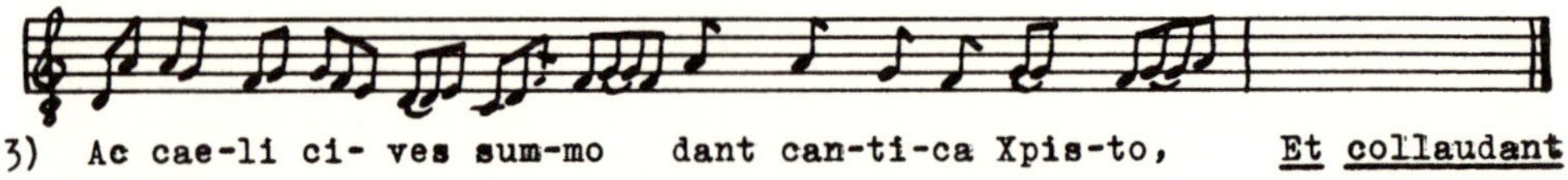

246

3) Ac cae-li ci- ves sum-mo   dant can-ti-ca Xpis-to,   Et collaudant

ITEM ALII TROPHI   **#204. Nos sinus--f.40v**

1) Nos si- nus ec-cle-si-ae ma- tris quos e- ru-dit al-   me,

e-   ia: Gaudeamus

2) Sum-mus ho-   nor qui-bus est   sum-mi pi-a vi- si-o   re-gi,

De quorum

3) Com-ple- ri nu- me-rum cer-nunt qui-a ri-   te su-per-num,

Et col-lau-dant

DE SANCTO MARTINO
(INTROIT: Statuit)

#205. Laetabunda per orbem--f.41

1) Lae-ta-bun-da   per or- bem nunc e-   mi-cat di-es qua pau-

per et mo-di-cus hic pre- sul Mar-ti- nus cae-   lum in-

gre- di-tur di- ves, qui- a   Statuit

2) Pon-ti-fi- ca-le de-dit il-li de-cus auc-tor ho-no-rum, Et principem

3) Pre-bu-it hac a- ris pro ple- be ad-sta-re sa-cra- tis,   Ut sit

4) Vo-ta fe-rat Do-mi-no lau-dis in mu-ne-re sum-mo   In aeternum

ALII   #206. Dicat in aethra--f.41

1) Di- cat in ae-thra De-o lau-des haec con-ci-o sa-cra,/

Mar-ti- ni-que me-los de-can-tent or- ga-na vo-cis: Statuit

2) Quo po-pu-lis pro-pi-na-ret o- vans do-cu-men-ta fi-de-i, Et princi.

248

3) Xpis-tus ut ec- cle-si-ae su-ae sa-cra iu- ra li-ba- ret, **Ut sit**

4) Pal-ma de- co-ris vel-ut lu-cet ae- ther in or- di-ne phe-bi,

In aeternum

ALII   #207. **Eia gaudete Martino**--f.41v

1) E- ia gau-de- te Mar-ti-no   qui-a   pi-um est hunc pa-ra-dy-si-

co-le   ho-di-e ex- ci-pi-unt gau-den-tes, qui- a   **Statuit**

2) Mu- ni-a il-li-us de- vo-   tus im- ple-vit sa-   tis

est quod huc us- que   cer-ta-vit,   **Et principem**

3) O   ve- re be-a- tum in   quo do- lus non fu- it, **Ut sit**

4) Est e- nim il-   le ut est con-ser-   tus a-   pos- to-lis

ac   pro-phe-   tis,   **In aeternum**

AD OFFERENDAM
(OFF. Posuisti)

#208. Celse Deus precibus--f.41v

Cel-se De-us pre-ci-bus Mar-ti-ni ple-bi-bus ad-sis,

qui-a: Posuisti ℣. Desiderium

(AD VERSUM: Magna est)
#209. Munere namque tuo--f.41v

Mu-ne-re nam-que tu-o Mar-ti- num mag-ni-fi-cas-ti,

qui-a: Magna est

AD COMMUNIONEM
(COM. Beatus servus)

#210. Hic dictis--f.41v

Hic dic- tis pre-lu-cens mo- rum pro-bi-ta- te de-cho-rus,

Beatus

NATALE SANCTI ANDREAE APOSTOLI
(INTROIT: <u>Michi</u> <u>autem</u>)

#211. <u>Sanctorum</u> <u>collegia</u>--f.41v and Paris 909, f.60v

1) San-cto- rum col-le-gi-a   a-pos-to-lo-rum o-   vans con-lau-

dat i- ta   pro- phe-ta: <u>Mi-chi</u> <u>au-tem</u>

2) Tri-ni-ta-   tis no-men spar-gen-   tes per mun-di cli- ma-ta

pa- ra-cli-ti re- ple- ti do-   nis per ver-bum pa-tris,

<u>Ho-no-rati</u>

3) Or-   tum de-i- fi-cum a-pos-to- li-ci cul- mi-nis tri-bu-unt,

un- de   <u>Ni-mis</u>

4) Ac- tum a-pos-to-lis ar-va de-dis-ti re-gi- men dum ad ae- the-

re-a lo- ca mag-ni-fi-ca-tus est,   <u>Principatus</u>

1--There is a break in the contents of the MS at this point. The
   remainder of this trope, as well as the following tropes for
   St. Andrew, are transcribed from Paris 909.

AD PSALMUM (Domine probasti)
#212. Laeta cohors--Paris 909, f.61

Lae-   ta co-hors pro-cla-   met o- vans nunc   cor-   de

se-re-   no: Do-mi-ne probasti   Glo-ri-a

#213. Alma dies--Paris 909, f.61

Al- ma di-es cun-ctis ni- mi-um ve-ne-ran-da re- ful-get/

An-dre- ae San- cti fes-ti-vo ho-no-ran-da-que cul-tu;/

Vo-ci-bus al- ti-so-nis cu- ius psal-la-   mus ho-   no-re:

Mi-chi au-tem

#214. Culmen apostolicum--Paris 909, f.61v

1) Cul-men a- pos-to-li-cum An- dre-as su- per as- tra be-a-tus/

In-sig-nis re-   ni-tet, nos in- de ca-na-   mus o-van-ter:

Michi

2) Mi-ro lus-tran-tes va-ri-o- que vi-bra- mi-ne cos-

mum, A-mi- ci

3) Se-di-bus ae- the-re-is ges-tan-tes ser- ta per e- on,

Nimis

EXAMPLES OF ORDINARY TROPES

The following section contains examples of the principal types of Ordinary tropes found in the early St. Martial tropers. The largest group consists of tropes for the Gloria in excelsis. Of these I have chosen three examples to illustrate the three basic Gloria melodies used for troping in the St. Martial manuscripts. The Gloria tropes are followed by representative Sanctus and Agnus tropes, both of which have wide distribution among the St. Martial manuscripts.

1. *Omnipotens altissime:* a Gloria trope for the feast of Christmas. The Gloria melody, indicated in the manuscripts as *Gloria Prima,* serves as the basis of a great majority of the St. Martial Gloria tropes. Since *Gloria Prima* is not found in the modern chant books, I have given a full transcription taken from Paris 1119, with the pitch level and the optional flat signature suggested by the version in staff notation in the twelfth-century Nevers troper, Paris n.a. 1235. This trope also contains the Regnum prosula *Sceptrum cuius nobile.*

2. *Decus aeterni patris:* a trope to the so-called *Gloria Secunda,* which corresponds to Gloria VI in the modern Gradual.

3. *Quod patris ad dextram:* a trope to the *Gloria Minor,* corresponding to the modern Gloria XI.

4. *Sanctus ante secula Deus:* a Sanctus trope transcribed from Paris 1119 and using the melody of Sanctus XV in the modern Gradual.

5. *Omnipotens aeterne:* a trope to the Agnus Dei transcribed from Paris 1119. This particular Agnus melody is not found in the modern books, but the similarity of the second half-line ("miserere nobis") to Agnus Dei II suggests the pitch level used here (see above, #9, p. 135).

**(1) GLORIA PRIMA (Paris 1119, f.90) with trope
Omnipotens altissime and prosula Sceptrum (Paris 1121, f.42)**

Glo-ri-a in ex- cel-sis De- o et in ter-ra pax ho-mi-ni- bus

bo-ne vo-lun-ta- tis.

1) Om-mi- po-tens al-tis- si-me ver-bum pa-tris et ge-ni-

te, Lau-da-mus te.

2) Quem be-ne-di-cit cho-rus cae-les-tis, glo-ri-am pan-gens Do- mi-

no in al-tis-si-mis, Be-ne-di-ci-mus te.

3) Quem con-ven-tus ad- o- rat pas-to- ra-lis an- ge-lo nun-ti-

an- te ve-nis, Ad-o- ra-mus te.

4) Quod ver-bum ca-ro fac-tum ma- ter vir-go pre-se-pe po-su-it

Ma-ri-a, Glo-ri-fi-ca-mus te.

5) Na-ti-vi-ta-tem tu- am, Xpis-te, qui re-co-lunt vi-si-ta,

Gra-ti-as a-gi-mus ti-   bi,

6) O de-co-ra-ta pro-les sub-   li-mis ho-di-e mun-do nas-ci dig-na-

ris ex u- te-ro vir-gi-nis,   Prop-ter mag- nam glo-

ri-am tu-   am, Do-   mi-ne De-us, rex ce- les-

tis, De- us pa-ter om-   ni-po-tens.

7) Prop-ter mum-dum re-di-men-dum et ho-mi-nem dig-na-tus fu-is-ti

de cae-lis in ter-ris de-scen-de-re, Do-   mi-ne fi-li u-

ni-ge-ni-te,

8) Par-vu-lus na- tus in or- be quam mag- nus es in po-li ar-

ce,   Ihe- su Xpis- te.   Do- mi-

ne De-us, ag- nus De-i, fi- li-us pa-tris. Qui tol- lis pec-ca-ta

mun- di, mi-se- re-re no- bis. Qui tol- lis pec-ca-ta

mun- di,

9) Quem ho-di-e na-tum de vir-gi-ne con-fi-te-mur, Sus-ci-

pe de-pre-ca-ti-o-nem nos- tram.

10) Ut ho-mi-nem cae-lo re- du-ce-res ho-di-e in ter-ris ho-mo vi-

sus es, Qui se-des ad dex-te-ram pa- tris, mi-se- re-re

no- bis.

11) O de-cus om-ni-um, Quo-ni-am tu so-lus san-ctus.

12) Pro-lis e ru-ti-lis pa-tri co-e- vus, Tu so-lus Do-mi-nus.

13) He-ros po-li, he-ros sum-ma re-si-dens in ar-che, Tu so-lus

al-tis-si-mus.

14) Te re- gem mag-num no- bis ho-di-e na-tum ad- o- ran-tes hu-

mi-li vo-ce lau-da- mus: Ihe- su Xpis- te.

15) Scep-trum cu-ius no- bi-le Tu-um be-nig-ne do-mi-nan-tem cae-

li ter-rae-que ma-chi-ne, Na-tus ho-di-e ne-

bis ma-tre qui sem-per es de vir-gi-ne, At-

tol-lens ex-ten-de pro-te-ge ab hos-te, Quo nos

te lau-da-re me-re-a-mur ve-re, Cu-ius no-men

per-ma-ne-bit in ae-ter-num, Cum san-cto spi-ri-tu in glo-ri-a

De-i pa- tris. A- men.

258

(2) <u>Decus aeterni patris</u> (Paris 1121, f.53v),
trope for the GLORIA SECUNDA (= GR Gloria VI)

1) De-cus ae-ter- ni pa- tris me-ri-to ti-bi flec-ti-tur er- bis,

<u>Laudamus</u>

2) Pon-tus et i- ma po-lus ti-bi-met be-ne-di- cat nunc De-us,   <u>Bene.</u>

3) Qui tri-nus u-nus i-dem-que es plas- tor an-ti-quus,   <u>Adoramus</u>

4) An-ge-   li-cus coe-tus te po-scit de- vo-te prae-cla-rus,

<u>Glorificamus</u>

5) Qui re-si-des in ar- ce po-li, Do-mi-ne rex ae-ter-ne,   <u>Gratias</u>

6) O qui per-pe-tu-a mun- dum ra-ti-e- ne gu-ber-nas, <u>Domine Deus</u>

7) Tu na-tu-re om-nis De-us in-nu-me-ra- bi-lis u-nus, <u>Domine fili</u>

8) O pi-e cun-cti-po-tens De-us rex mun-di- que re-dem-ptor, <u>Qui tollis</u>

9) Rex De-us in-men-se quo con-stat ma- chi-na mun-di,   <u>Qui sedes</u>

10) U-nus e- nim re-rum pa-ter es u- nus cun- cta mi-nis-trans,

Quoniam tu

11) Tu so- lus, tu mul-tus, i- tem tu pri-mus et i-dem,

Cum Sancto Spiritu

(3) Quod patris ad dextram (Paris 1121, f.56),
trope for the GLORIA MINOR (= GR Gloria XI)

1) Quod pa-tris ad dex- tram col-lau-dant om-ni- a ver-bum, Laudamus

2) Om-ni-a quem san- ctum be-ne-di-cunt con-di-ta re- gem, Benedicimus

3) Tel-lus at-que po- lum ma- re quem ve-ne-ran-ter ad-o- rant,

Adoramus

4) Glo-ri-fi-cant ag-num ci-ves quem digni-ter al- mi, Glorificamus

1--MS = que

5) Gra-ti-a   san-cto-rum splen-der de- cus et di-a- de-ma,   Gratias

6) Cul-pas ges-te- rum sol- vens si-ne cri-mi-ne se-lus, Qui sedes

7) In- sons as- tri po-tens nos-tris tu par-ce ru-i-nis, Qeniam tu

8) Cun-cta te-nens et cun-cta fe-vens et cun-cta per-er- nans, Tu sel.Dem.

9) Nos nos-tras- que pre-ces cae-le de-scri-be   re-dem-pter, Cum sce.

10) De-pel-lat se-vum pas-sim per se- cla le- o-nem,   Amen.

(4) Sanctus trope: Sanctus Ante secula Deus (Paris 1119, f.244v)
(Sanctus melody = GR Sanctus XV)

1) San-ctus An- te se-cu-la De-us pa-ter,

2) San-ctus In prin-ci-pi-o cum pa- tre ma-nens na-tus,

3) San-ctus De-mi-nus Pa-tris na-ti-que spi-ri-tus et ip-se De-us

Sa-ba-oth. Ple-ni sunt cae-li et ter-ra glo-ri-a tu-a. O-

san-na in ex-cel-sis.

4) Nos cer-nu-i tu-i fa-mu-li de tu- o ad-ven-tu gra-tu-lan-tes di-

ci-mus: Be-ne-di-ctus qui ve- nit in no-mi-ne Do-mi-ni. Q- san-

na in ex-cel- sis.

(5) Agnus Dei trope: Omnipotens aeterne (Paris 1119, f. 248v)

A- gnus De- i qui tol- lis pec-ca- ta mun- di,

mi-se- re- re no- bis.

1) Om-ni- po-tens ae-ter-ne De- i sa-pi-en- ti-a Xpis-te, Mi-se-

re- re no-bis.

2) Ve- rum sub-sis- tens ve- ro de lu- mi-ne lu- men, Mi-se- re- re

3) Ob-ti-ma per-pe-tu-ae con-ce- de gau- di-a vi-te, Mi-se-

re- re

EXAMPLES OF PROSULAE

The prosulae are discussed above, on pages 9ff. The examples mentioned there are presented below, with notes on the specific transcriptions:

Example 1: The Alleluia *Mirabilis Dominus* and its two prosulae, *Psallat unus* for the Alleluia itself and *Mirabilis atque laudabilis* for the verse, are here transcribed from Paris 903, f. 88v (= *Paléographie Musicale,* XIII, 176). The pieces occur for the feast of SS. Nereus and Achilleus in this manuscript. The order of the pieces is as follows: *Alleluia* (melismatic), prosula *Psallat unus,* Alleluia verse *Mirabilis Dominus,* and prosula *Mirabilis atque.* In the following transcription, however, the prosulae are given directly beneath the chant in order to facilitate comparison.

Example 2: The prosula *Invocavi te altissime* is one of a group of prosulae written to supply a text for the final melisma of the second verse *Respice in me* of the Offertory *Ad te Domine levavi* for the first Sunday in Advent. Each of these prosulae open with the words "invocavi te," which are, in effect, the closing words of the Offertory verse. The following transcription was made from Paris 903, f. 2 (= *Paléographie Musicale,* XIII, 3). The Offertory and its verses can be found in the same manuscript on ff. 1v-2.

Example 3: The transcription of the Kyrie prosula *Tibi Xpiste supplices* was made from Paris 1119, ff. 84-85. In this troper, each line of the prosula is followed by its Kyrie line without added text, and this arrangement is observed in our transcription. In other manuscripts, one often finds the prosula alone, unaccompanied by its melismatic Kyrie. The Kyrie used in this example is Kyrie Ad Libitum VI of the modern Gradual. Its St. Martial form can be found, among other places, in Paris 1120, ff. 68v-69.

Example 4: The Osanna prosula *Osanna dulcis est* is transcribed from Paris 1119, ff. 249v-250. This supplies a text for the melismatic second "Osanna in excelsis" of a Sanctus which is no longer in the modern chant books. The complete Sanctus can be found in Paris 1119, ff. 246v-247, and the melody of the second Osanna has been supplied below the prosula in our example for ease of comparison.

Example 5: This is the Regnum prosula *Per te Xpiste,* transcribed from Paris 1119, f. 134. A Regnum prosula was a text added to the long central melisma of a specific Gloria trope line beginning "Regnum tuum solidum...." This line, from the Gloria trope *Laus honor Xpiste,* is given with its cues in Example 5a as it occurs in Paris 1084, f. 115v. This is then followed, in Example 5b, by the Regnum prosula. In keeping with the practice in Paris 1119, each line of the prosula is to be followed by a repetition of the melody sung melismatically, although it will be seen that the cues are not complete. It is interesting to note the incipient "double versicle" construction of the prosula, which is thus reminiscent of the structure of the prosa. (Note that another Regnum prosula, *Sceptrum cuius nobile,* will be found on p. 254 in connection with the Gloria trope *Omnipotens altissime.*)

EXAMPLE 1--Alleluia <u>Mirabilis Dominus</u> and prosulae.

Al- le- lu- ia.

PROSULA: Psal- lat u-nus spi-ri-tus et u-na om-ni-um lin-gua vo-ce Xris-

tus ho-no-re pro qui-bus co-ro-nas re-pro-mi-sit se su-is da-tu-rum

VERSE: <u>Mi-ra-bi-lis</u>

sanc-tis. PROSULA: Mi-ra-bi-lis at-que lau-da-bi-lis co-len-dus-que

<u>Do- mi- nus nos- ter in sanc-</u>

ni-mis Do- mi- nus nos- ter in sa-cra-tis-si-mo- rum pre-cep-

<u>tis su-</u>

to-rum sup-pli-cis at-que gra-vi-is tor-men-to-rum ac-ce-pe-runt co-

<u>is.</u>

ro-nas vic-ti sunt se-vis-si-mi per-se-quu-to- res.

EXAMPLE 2--Offertory Verse Prosula <u>Invocavi te altissime</u>.

In-<u>vo</u>-<u>ca</u>-<u>vi</u> <u>te</u> al-tis-si-me ven-tu-rum-que lon-ge ce-ci-ne-re de-

vo-te glo-ri-a laus et ho-nor Xris-te sic di-ci-tur ti-bi rex pi-e

qui ve-nis sal-va-re me et te ve-ra fi-de in te blan-de sus-ce-pit

et de-vo-te te vo-len-te.

EXAMPLE 3--Kyrie Prosula <u>Tibi Xpiste supplices</u>.

1) Ti- bi Xpis-te sup-pli-ces ex-o-ra-mus cunc-ti-po-tens ut nos-tri

dig-ne-ris e-lei-son. <u>Kir- ri-e-</u> <u>lei-son</u>.

2) Te de-cet laus cum tri-pu-di-o iu-gi-ter qua ti-bi pe-ti-mus ca-

nen-tes e-lei-son. <u>Kir- ri-e-</u> <u>lei-son</u>.

3) O bo-ne rex qui su-per as-tra se-des o do-mi-ne qui cunc-ta gu-

ber-nas e-lei-son. <u>Ki</u>.

4) Tu-a de-vo-te plebs im-plo-ret iu-gi-ter ut il-li dig-ne-ris e-

lei-son. Xpis-te e- lei-son.

5) O The-os a-gi-e sal-va vi-vi-fi-ce re-demp-tor nos-ter e-lei-son.

Xpis-te e- lei-son.

6) Qui ca-nunt an-te te pre-ci-bus an-nu-e et tu nobis sem-per e-

lei-son. Xpiste.

7) Cla-mat in-ces-san-ter nunc quo-que con-ti-o et di-cit e-lei-son.

Kir- ri-e- lei- son.

8) Mi-se-re-re nos-tri fi-li Da-vid tu no-bis sem-per e-lei-son.

Kir- ri-e- lei- son.

9) In ex-cel-sis De-o mag-na sit glo-ri-a ae-ter-no pa-tri qui nos re-

de-mit pro-pri-o san-gui-ne ut vi-vi-fi-ca-ret de mor-te di-ca-mus

in-ces-san-ter u-na vo-ce om-nes e-lei-son. Kir- ri-e- lei-

son.

EXAMPLE 4--Osanna prosula _Osanna dulcis est_.

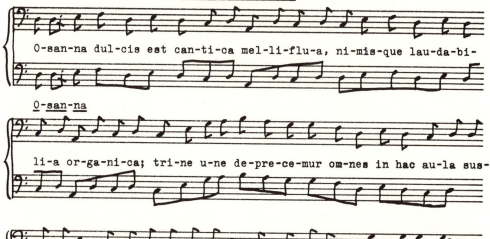

O-san-na dul-cis est can-ti-ca mel-li-flu-a, ni-mis-que lau-da-bi-

O-san-na

li-a or-ga-ni-ca; tri-ne u-ne de-pre-ce-mur om-nes in hac au-la sus-

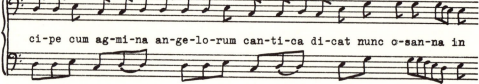

ci-pe cum ag-mi-na an-ge-lo-rum can-ti-ca di-cat nunc o-san-na in

in

ex- cel- sis.

ex- cel- sis.

EXAMPLE 5--(a) Excerpt from Gloria trope <u>Laus honor Xpiste</u>.

<u>Tu solus al</u>. Reg-num tu-um so- li- dum per-

ma-ne-bit in e- ter-num, <u>Cum scō</u>.

(b) Regnum prosula <u>Per te Xpiste</u>.

<u>Reg-num tu-um</u> so- <u>li-dum</u> Per te Xpis-te sis-tit om-ni-po-ten-

tis-si-me, Qui in cru-ce sig-num no-bis de-dis-ti

vi-vi-fi-ce, Te lau-da-mus rex cle-men-tis-si-me,

Ti-bi laus et ho-nor <u>Per-ma-ne-bit in ae</u>-

<u>ter-num</u>, Ihesu. [sic]

THE TONARIUM OF PARIS 1121

The following transcription of the Greek and Latin modal formulas is taken from the tonarium of Paris 1121, ff. 202-206. In the manuscript, the formulas for each mode are followed by the differentiae for Antiphons and Responds, Introits, and Communions. The differentiae, however, have been omitted in our transcription.

It should be noted that the earliest St. Martial tonaria, such as that in Paris 1240, contain only the initial Greek formula. Apparently, the melismatic extension of the Greek formula and the addition of the Latin formula represent later modal developments.

The modal formulas and their relationship to the tropes are discussed above on pages 81ff. and 92f.

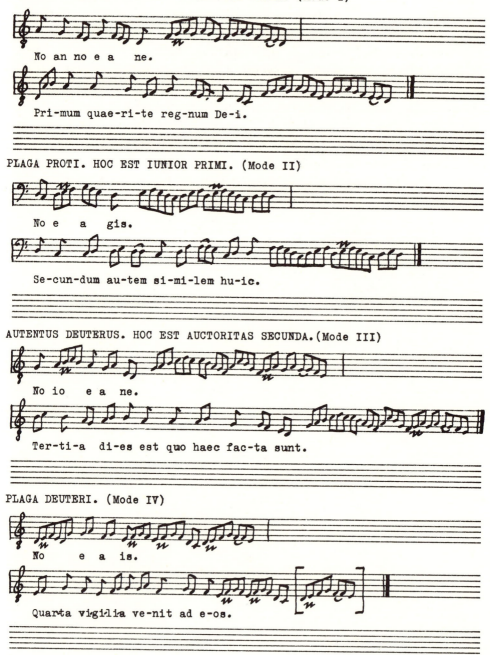

272

AUTENTUS PROTUS. HOC EST AUCTORITAS PRIMA. (Mode I)

No an no e a ne.

Pri-mum quae-ri-te reg-num De-i.

PLAGA PROTI. HOC EST IUNIOR PRIMI. (Mode II)

No e a gis.

Se-cun-dum au-tem si-mi-lem hu-ic.

AUTENTUS DEUTERUS. HOC EST AUCTORITAS SECUNDA.(Mode III)

No io e a ne.

Ter-ti-a di-es est quo haec fac-ta sunt.

PLAGA DEUTERI. (Mode IV)

No e a is.

Quarta vigilia ve-nit ad e-os.

AUTENTUS TRITUS. ID EST AUCTORITAS TERTII. (Mode V)

No io   e a ne.

Quin-que pru-den-tes in-tra-ve-runt ad nup-ti-as.

PLAGA TRITI. (Mode VI)

No   e a gis.

Sex-ta ho- ra se-dit su-per pu-te-um.

AUTENTUS TETRARDUS. HOC EST AUCTORITAS IIII. (Mode VII)

No io e a ne.

Sep-tem sunt spi-ri-tus an-te thro-num De-i.

PLAGA TETRARDI. (Mode VIII)

No e   a gis.

Oc-to sunt be-a- ti-tu-di-nes.

INDEX OF TROPES[1] IN PARIS 1121

INTROIT

		folio
+7	Ad aeternae salutis	3v
1	Ad demonstrandum	25
+1	Adest alma Virgo	11
+2	Adveniente Xpisto	9v
2	Agmina perhenniter	20
1	Alme tuum semper	17
3	Angelici nunc rite	39
+3	Angelico fretus	26v
2	Angelicos patriarcha	19
3	Angelus Domini	27v
1	Aspera portantes	17
+1	Aulam sanctam	34
4	Aurea lux remeat	12
1	Aurea post Xpistum	36v
4	Caelestem Xpiste (*)	37
+6	Caelica caelesti decantent	7
1	Caelitus instructi	36v
1	Caelorum rex	10v
1	Cantemus omnes	34v
6	Cantica nunc reboent	33
+2	Celebremus ovanter festa	17v
+1	Celsa polorum pontus	31v
+1	Clamat hians caelis	5v
2	Concinat en plectrum	18v

---

[1] An asterisk * following a trope title indicates a trope text without musical notation. An asterisk in parentheses (*) indicates a trope with only partial notation. A sign + occurs before the name of a trope when its text appears in Paris 1240. The mode, when known, is indicated by the number appearing before the trope title.

1	Confligunt proceres Ihesu	6
7	Cum patris dextram	22
+1	De sterili genetrice	25v
+2	Descendens ab aetherei	9v
+7	Deus pater filium	3
+1	Dicat in aethra	41
2	Dicite nunc pueri	7v
+8	Discipulis flammas	23v
+3	Divina beatus Petrus	27
2	Divinus succendat amor	17v
8	Dulciter agnicolae	14v
+7	Ecce adest verbum	3
3	Ecce dies adest	26v
1	Ecce dies magni	31
1	Ecce fidem magni	28
3	Ecce iam caelicolae	38v
+6	Ecce iam Iohannis	6v
6	Ecce omnes redempti	16v
+4	Ecce pater cunctis	12
8	Ecce veri luminis	15
1	Ecce Xpisticole	40
1	Ecclesiae doctor	35v
2	Ecclesiae sponsus	9
4	Ego autem constitutus	12v
1	Eia canendo sonos	40v
1	Eia conlevitae	5v
1	Eia gaudete Martino	41v
1	Eia plebs devota	39v
+2	Eia Sion gaude	9
+4	En ego verus sol	12v
2	Est quia terribilis	18
7	Expurgans populos	16
4	Factus homo de matre	13
+4	Factus homo tua iussa	12

3	Principis aetherei	38v
+8	Promissionis suae memor	15
8	Psallite candidati	24
6	Psallite doctilogum	32v
6	Psallite omnes huius sancti	33
1	Psallite omnes ovanter voce	32
7	Quem creditis super astra	21v
3	Quem cuncta laudant	38
+7	Quem nasci mundo	3v
+1	Quem prophetae cecinere	25v
7	Quem queritis in presepe	2
+4	Quem queritis in sepulchro	11v
1	Qui dilexit me	28
1	Qui placuit Domino	31
1	Qui primus meruit	6
1	Quia naturam	35
6	Sacro fonte pectoris	7
+1	Salus martyrum	5v
2	Sanctorum collegia	41v
1	Sanctorum sancto	40
1	Sanctus Augustinum	35v
2	Sanctus celsithroni	19
8	Sanctus en veniens	23v
2	Sanctus evigilans	19v
1	Secla Deus gratis	40
1	Sedibus externis	29v
1	Sortis apostolicae	29
+7	Terrigenis summis	22
2	Typica visione	18v
1	Ut esset sacerdos	30v
2	Ut sedeat in throno	9v
7	Vos quia certastis	16v

INTROIT PSALM

3	Apostolorum principem	27
4	Se ipsum offerens	37
2	Tripudiantes reboemus	20v
1	Turba fidelis	25

INTROIT DOXOLOGY

| 4 | Gloria nostra crucis | 37 |
| 2 | In hoc templo | 20v |

MELODIC ADDITIONS TO THE INTROIT

1,3	Gloria patri + melisma	10v, 27
3	Nunc scio (*S. Petri*)	27v
3	Psalm verse + melisma	27

GLORIA IN EXCELSIS

	Angelica iam pater	55v
	Angelico affatu iungentes	49v
	Ave Deus summa trinitas	55
	Decus aeterni patris	53v
+	Laudat in excelsis	44v
	Laus angelorum salus et vita	54
+	Laus tibi Domine celsa	48v
	Laus tibi summe Deus	50
+	Laus tua Deus resonet	43
+	O gloria sanctorum	44
+	O laudabilis rex Domine Deus	43v
	Omnipotens altissime verbum	42
	Omnipotens piae rex	47
+	Prudentia prudentium	49
	Qua iugi voce affantes	57
	Quem cives caelestes	57v
	Quem glorificant sancti	56v
+	Qui indiges nullius laude	44
	Quod patris ad dextram	56

REGNUM PROSULAE

BIBLIOGRAPHY

Ademarus Cabannensis. *Chronique d'Adhémar de Chabannes.* Edited by J. Chavanon. Collection de textes pour servir à l'étude et l'enseignement de l'histoire, Vol. 20. Paris, 1897.

Amalarius. *Amalarii Episcopi Opera Liturgica Omnia.* Edited by J. M. Hanssens. 3 vols. Vatican City, 1948-1950.

Amann, Émile. *L'Époque Carolingienne.* Histoire de l'église depuis les origines jusqu'à nos jours, edited by Augustin Fliche and Victor Martin, Vol. 6. Paris, 1947.

Apel, Willi. *Gregorian Chant.* Bloomington, Indiana, 1958.

Apt. Basilica. *Catalogue descriptif et illustré des manuscrits liturgiques de l'Église d'Apt.* Compiled by Abbé J. Sautel. Carpentras, 1921.

Ardo. *Vita S. Benedicti Anianensis.* Patrologia Latina, Vol. 103, cols. 351-384.

Bannister, Henry Marriott. "The Earliest French Troper and its Date," *Journal of Theological Studies,* II (1901), 420-429.

——. "Un Tropaire-Prosier de Moissac," *Revue d'Histoire et de Littérature Religieuses,* VIII (1903), 554-581.

Bishop, Edmund. *Liturgica Historica.* Oxford, 1918.

Chailley, Jacques. "Les anciens tropaires et séquentiaires de l'École de Saint-Martial de Limoges (Xe-XIe S.)," *Études Grégoriennes,* II (1957), 163-188.

——. *L'École Musicale de Saint-Martial de Limoges jusqu'à la Fin du XIe Siècle.* Paris, 1960.

Corbin, Solange. *La Notation Musicale Neumatique—Les Quatre Provinces Lyonnaises: Lyon, Rouen, Tours et Sens.* Unpublished thesis for the Doctorat ès Lettres, Université de Paris, Faculté des Lettres, 1957. 3 vols.

Crocker, Richard L. *The Repertoire of Proses at Saint Martial de Limoges (Tenth and Eleventh Centuries).* Unpublished Ph.D. dissertation, Yale University, 1957.

——. "The Repertory of Proses at Saint Martial de Limoges in the 10th Century," *Journal of the American Musicological Society,* XI (1958), 149-164.

——. "The Troping Hypothesis," *The Musical Quarterly,* LII (1966), 183-203.

Delisle, Léopold. *Le Cabinet des Manuscrits de la Bibliothèque Impériale.* 4 vols. Paris, 1868-1881.

——. *Notice sur les Manuscrits Originaux d'Adémar de Chabannes.* Paris, 1896.

——. *Les Manuscrits de Saint-Martial de Limoges, Réimpression Textuelle du Catalogue de 1730.* Limoges, 1895.

Dreves, Guido Maria, Clemens Blume, and H. M. Bannister, eds. *Analecta Hymnica Medii Aevi.* 55 vols. Leipzig, 1886-1922.

Duchesne, Louis. *Christian Worship, its Origin and Evolution. A Study of the Latin Liturgy up to the Time of Charlemagne.* Translated by M. L. McClure. 5th edn.; London, 1919.

Duplès-Agier, H., ed. *Chroniques de Saint-Martial de Limoges.* Paris, 1874.

Evans, Paul. "Northern French Elements in an Early Aquitainian Troper," *Festschrift Heinrich Husmann.* Munich, 1969.

——. "Some Reflections on the Origin of the Trope," *Journal of the American Musicological Society,* XIV (1961), 119-130.

——. "The Tropi ad Sequentiam," *Studies in Music History: Essays for Oliver Strunk.* Edited by Harold Powers. Princeton, 1968.

Ferretti, Paolo. *Esthétique Grégorienne, ou Traité des Formes Musicales du Chant Grégorien,* Vol. 1. Translated by A. Agaësse. Paris, 1938.

Frere, Walter Howard. *The Winchester Troper.* The Henry Bradshaw Society, VIII. London, 1894.

Froger, Jacques. *Les Chants de la Messe aux VIIIe et IXe Siècles.* Paris, 1950.

Gautier, Léon. *Histoire de la Poésie Liturgique au Moyen Age. Les Tropes.* Paris, 1886.

Gerbert, Martin. *De Cantu et Musica Sacra a Prima Ecclesiae Aetate usque ad Praesens Tempus.* 2 vols. St. Blasien, 1774.

Gevaert, F. A. *La Mélopée antique dans le chant de l'Église latine.* Ghent, 1895.

Graduale Romanum. Rome, 1908.

Le Graduel Romain. Édition Critique. Edited by the Monks of Solesmes. Vol. II: *Les Sources.* Solesmes, 1957.

Handschin, Jacques. "Trope, Sequence, and Conductus," *New Oxford History of Music,* II (1954), 128-174.

——. "The Two Winchester Tropers," *Journal of Theological Studies,* XXXVII (1936), 34-49 and 156-172.

Hesbert, René-Jean, ed. *Antiphonale Missarum Sextuplex.* Brussels, 1935.

Hooreman, Paul. "Saint-Martial de Limoges au Temps de l'Abbé Odolric (1025-1040). Essai sur une pièce oubliéé du répertoire limousin," *Revue Belge de Musicologie,* III (1949), 5-36.

Hughes, Anselm. *Anglo-French Sequelae, Edited from the Papers of the Late Dr. Henry Marriott Bannister.* London, 1934.

Hughes, David G. "Further Notes on the Grouping of the Aquitanian Tropers," *Journal of the American Musicological Society,* XIX (1966), 3-12.

Huglo, Michel. "Antifone Antiche per la 'Fractio Panis,'" *Ambrosius* (May-June 1955), 85-95.

Husmann, Heinrich. "Die älteste erreichbare Gestalt des St. Galler Tropariums," *Archiv für Musikwissenschaft,* XIII (1956), 25-41.

——. "Alleluia, Vers und Sequenzen," *Annales Musicologiques,* IV (1956), 19-53.

——. "Die St. Galler Sequenztradition bei Notker und Ekkehard," *Acta Musicologica,* XXVI (1954), 6-18.

——. "Sequenz und Prosa," *Annales Musicologiques,* II (1954), 61-91.

——. "Sinn und Wesen der Tropen, veranschaulicht an den Introitustropen des Weihnachtsfestes," *Archiv für Musikwissenschaft,* XVI (1959), 135-147.

——. *Tropen- und Sequenzenhandschriften.* Répertoire International des Sources Musicales, Vol. B V 1. Munich, 1964.

Kantorowicz, Ernst H. *Laudes Regiae. A Study in Liturgical Acclamations and Mediaeval Ruler Worship.* With a study of the music of the Laudes and musical transcriptions by Manfred F. Bukofzer. Berkeley, California, 1958.

Knowles, David. *The Monastic Order in England.* Cambridge, 1940.

Lasteyrie du Saillant, Charles de. *L'Abbaye de Saint-Martial de Limoges.* Paris, 1901.

Leroquais, Victor. *Les Sacramentaires et les Missels Manuscrits des Bibliothèques Publiques de France.* 3 vols. and 1 vol. of plates. Paris, 1924.

Lesne, Émile. *Histoire de la Propriété Ecclésiastique en France.* Vol. IV. *Les Livres; "Scriptoria" et Bibliothèques, du commencement du VIIIe à la fin du XIe Siècle.* Lille, 1938.

Levy, Kenneth. "The Byzantine Sanctus and its Modal Tradition in East and West," *Annales Musicologiques,* VI (1958-1963), 7-67.

Limoges. Musée Municipal. *L'Art Roman à Saint-Martial de Limoges. Les Manuscrits à Peintures. Historique de l'Abbaye. La Basilique.* Catalogue de l'Exposition, 17 juin-17 septembre 1950. Limoges, 1950.

Mansi, J. D. *Sacrorum Conciliorum Nova et Amplissima Collectio.* 31 vols. Florence and Venice, 1759-1798.

Ott, Karl, ed. *Offertoriale sive Versus Offertoriorum.* Tournai, 1935.

Paléographie Musicale. Les Principaux Manuscrits de Chant Grégorien, Ambrosien, Mozarabe, Gallican, Publiés en Facsimilés Phototypiques. Published under the direction of Dom André Mocquereau. Vol. XIII: *Le Codex 903 de la Bibliothèque Nationale de Paris (XIe Siècle), Graduel de Saint-Yrieix.* Notes historiques et liturgiques, by Gabriel Tissot. Étude sur la notation aquitaine d'après le Graduel de Saint-Yrieix, by P. Ferretti. Tournai, 1925.

Paris. Bibliothèque Nationale. *Catalogue Général des Manuscrits Latins de la Bibliothèque Nationale de Paris,* Vol. I. Paris, 1939.

Raasted, Jørgen. *Intonation Formulas and Modal Signatures in Byzantine Musical Manuscripts.* Copenhagen, 1966.

Raby, F.J.E. *A History of Christian-Latin Poetry from the Beginnings to the Close of the Middle Ages.* 2nd edn.; Oxford, 1953.

Rönnau, Klaus. "Regnum tuum solidum," *Festschrift Bruno Stäblein.* Edited by Martin Ruhnke. Kassel, 1967. Pp. 195-205.

———. *Die Tropen zum Gloria in excelsis Deo.* Wiesbaden, 1967.

Schubiger, Anselm. *Die Sängerschule St. Gallens vom achten bis zwölften Jahrhundert.* Einsiedeln and New York, 1858.

Smits van Waesberghe, Joseph. "Die Imitation der Sequenztechnik in der Hosanna-Prosulen," *Festschrift Karl Gustav Fellerer.* Edited by Heinrich Hüschen. Regensburg, 1962. Pp. 485-490.

Stäblein, Bruno. "Der 'altrömische' Choral in Oberitalien und im deutschen Süden," *Die Musikforschung,* XIX (1966), 3-9.

———. "Saint-Martial," *Die Musik in Geschichte und Gegenwart.* Edited by Friedrich Blume. Kassel, 1949-1968. Vol. XI, cols. 1262-1272.

———. "Tropus," *Die Musik in Geschichte und Gegenwart.* Edited by Friedrich Blume. Kassel, 1949-1968. Vol. XIII, cols. 797-826.

———. "Die Unterlegung von Texten unter Melismen. Tropus, Sequenz und andere Formen," *Report of the Eighth Congress of the International Musicological Society, New York 1961.* Edited by Jan LaRue. Vol. I: *Papers.* Kassel, 1961. Pp. 12-29.

———. "Zum Verständnis des 'klassischen' Tropus," *Acta Musicologica,* XXXV (1963), 84-95.

Steinen, Wolfram von den. *Notker der Dichter und seine geistige Welt.* 2 vols. Berne, 1948.

Strunk, Oliver. "The Antiphons of the Oktoechos," *Journal of the American Musicological Society,* XIII (1960), 50-67.

———. "Influsso del canto liturgico orientale su quello della chiesa occidentale," *L'enciclica "Musicae sacrae disciplina" Sua Santita Pio XII. Testo e commento, a cura dell'Associazione italiana S. Cecilia.* Rome, 1957. Pp. 343-348.

——. "Intonations and Signatures of the Byzantine Modes," *The Musical Quarterly,* XXXI (1945), 339-355.

Suñol, Gregory M. *Introduction à la Paléographie Musicale Grégorienne.* Translated from the Catalan. Tournai, 1935.

Van Doren, Rombaut. *Étude sur l'Influence Musicale de l'Abbaye de Saint-Gall (VIIIe au XIe Siècle).* Brussels, 1925.

Vecchi, Giuseppe, ed. *Troparium Sequentiarum Nonantulanum (Cod. Casanat. 1741). Pars Prior.* Monumenta lyrica medii aevi Italica, Ser. 1 *(Latina),* Vol. 1. Modena, 1955.

Wagner, Peter. *Einführung in die gregorianischen Melodien.* 3 vols. Leipzig, 1911-1921.

Weakland, Rembert. "The Beginnings of Troping," *The Musical Quarterly,* XLIV (1958), 477-488.

——. "Hucbald as Musician and Theorist," *The Musical Quarterly,* XLII (1956), 66-84.

Weiss, Günther. " 'Tropierte Introitustropen' im Repertoire der sudfranzösischen Handschriften," *Die Musikforschung,* XVII (1964), 266-269.

——. "Zum Problem der Gruppierung sudfranzösischer Tropare," *Archiv für Musikwissenschaft,* XXI (1964), 163-171.

——. "Zur Rolle Italiens im frühen Tropenschaffen. Beobachtungen zu den Vertonungen der Introitus-Tropen *Quem nasci mundo* und *Quod prisco vates," Festschrift Bruno Stäblein.* Edited by Martin Ruhnke. Kassel, 1967. Pp. 287-292.

INDEX